IMAGES
of America

BATH AND WEST BATH

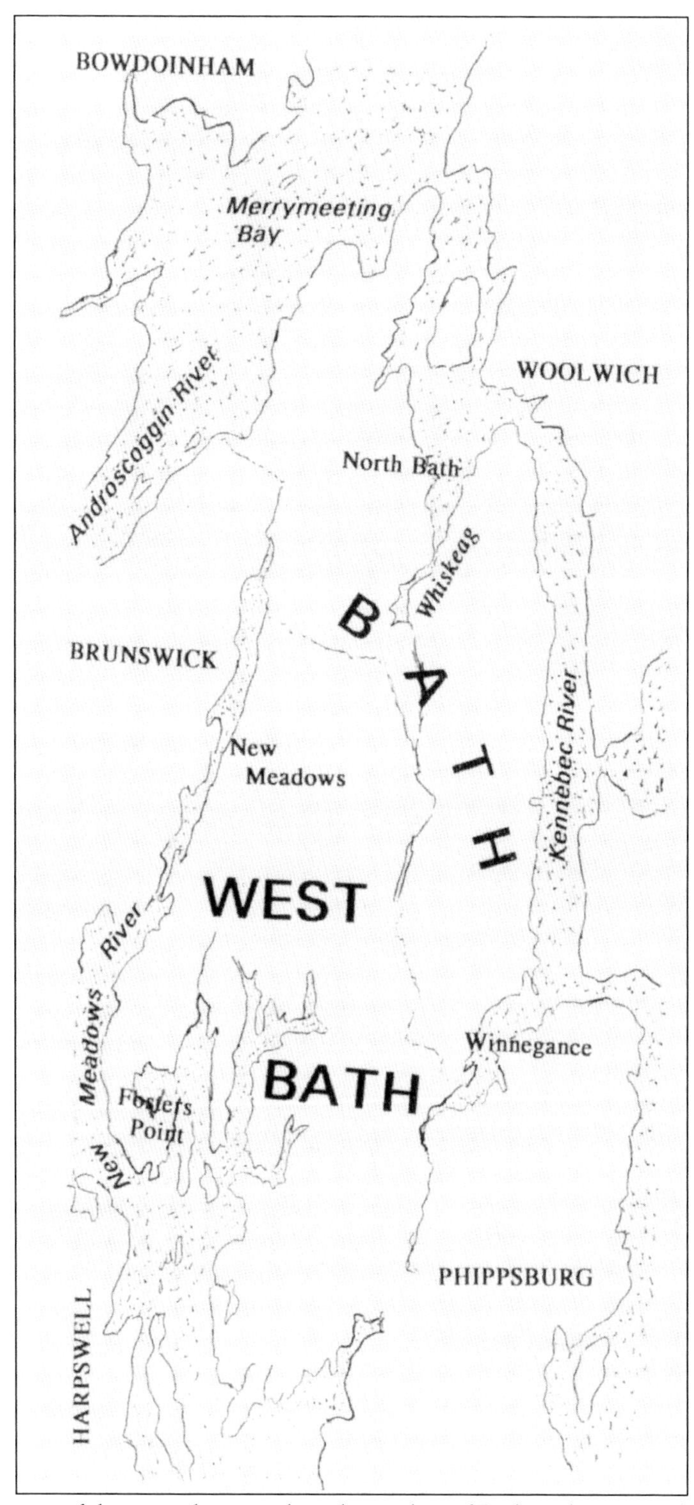

A map of the area, showing the relationship of Bath and West Bath to each other, neighboring towns, and bodies of water.

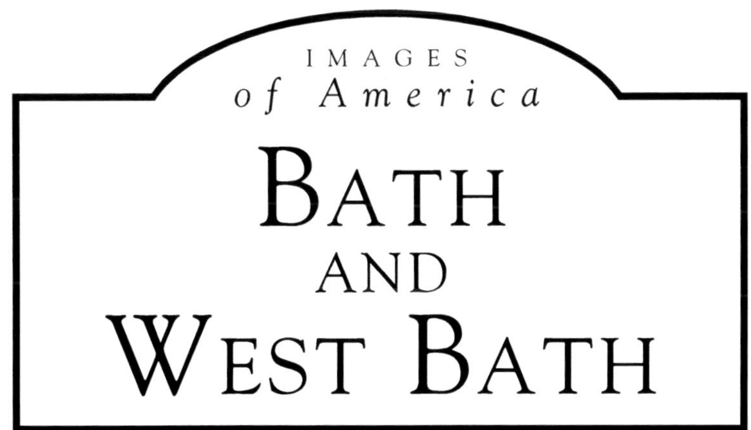

Joyce K. Bibber

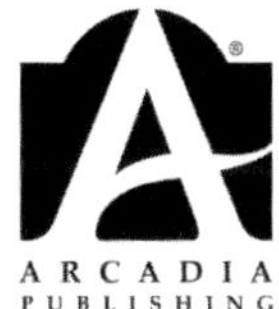

ISBN 978-0-7385-1256-3

Published by Arcadia Publishing
Charleston, South Carolina

Printed in the United States of America

Library of Congress Catalog Card Number: Applied for

For all general information contact Arcadia Publishing at:
Telephone 843-853-2070
Fax 843-853-0044
E-mail sales@arcadiapublishing.com
For customer service and orders:
Toll-Free 1-888-313-2665

Visit us on the Internet at www.arcadiapublishing.com

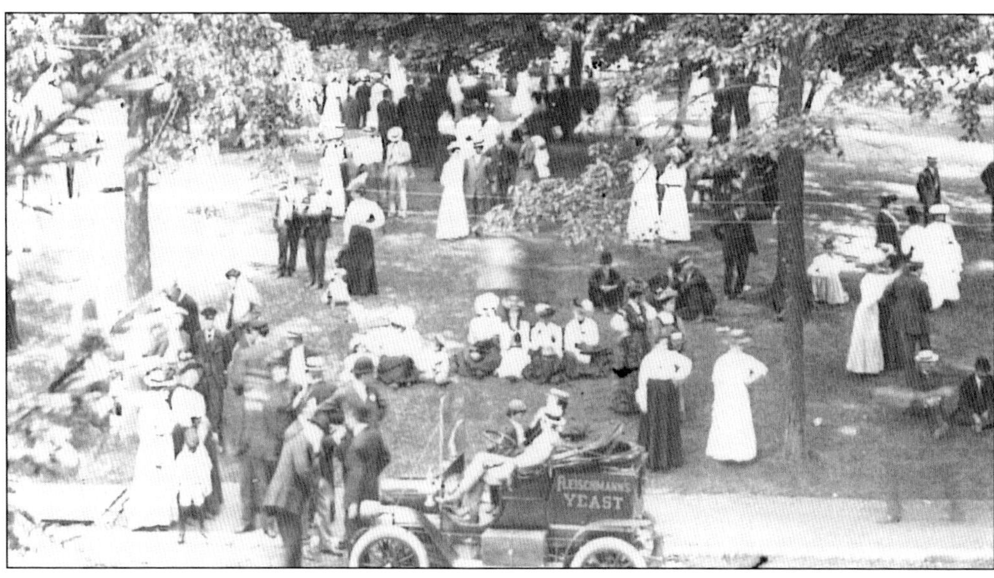

Contents

Acknowledgments 6

Introduction 7

1. All Around the Town 11
2. Homes 29
3. Religious Establishments 39
4. Lumber and Shipbuilding 51
5. Schools 69
6. Public Buildings 77
7. Getting Around 85
8. Work and Play 101
9. West Bath 117

ACKNOWLEDGMENTS

Many people have contributed time and knowledge to the compilation of this book. Among those allowing access to some of their old photographs and postcards were: Viola Bibber (pp. 35u, 62u, 80u, 81, 84, 123); Connie Boardman (76); Charles Cahill (89); Joseph Haines (83, 114); Howard Kirkpatrick (94, 95); Kathleen Labbe (27, 28u, 34, 38, 50, 57, 65, 84, 90, 100, 102u, 105, 107, 113u, 116, 121); Lorraine Lowell (87, 122); Emily McMann (25, 28, 84, 90, 100, 102u, 105, 107, 113u, 116, 121); Barbara Marriner (9, 10, 110, 111, 112, 113, 117, 128u); Alice and Lester Munsey (90, 126); Robert Rice (82, 104, 115); Merritt Scott (48-49, 70); Barbara Swensen (30, 47, 88u, 92, 96, 97u, 98, 99, 109); and Grace Waterhouse (102, 119, 127, 128u). These individuals, and sometimes their families, helped with identifications. More advice came from members of the Bath Area Senior Citizens, who interrupted their activities to make suggestions and even let me borrow photographs from their walls.

I was also permitted to use copies of materials from the collections of the Bath High School Alumni Association (53u, 71, 72, 73, 75, 76u); Kennebec Camera (11, 26u, 37, 102, 107u); the Bath Historical Society (21, 36, 43u, 92); and the Maine Maritime Museum (51, 52, 59, 63, 66, 67, 68). The Maine Historical Preservation Commission provided most of the rest, except 70u; Earle Shettleworth Jr., of the MHPC, was especially generous. Nathan Lipfert, of the Maine Maritime Museum, not only assisted my research in his archives, but also helped me gain access to the Bath Historical Society collections, for which Charles Richelieu did leg work. Beverly Laine made a special trip to share the Bath High School Alumni materials with me.

Less obvious, but important, support came from Carol Hyde and Elin Dozois, both of whom live closer to Bath than do I and who referred me to friends, took messages, provided a bed or a telephone when needed, and even drove or walked around with me to make visits or just to try to match old pictures with today's landscapes.

To all of these go my warmest thanks. If, in spite of their assistance, the book contains errors, it will be because I failed to listen properly or (just as likely) couldn't read my own notes!

INTRODUCTION

Bath, as seen from the river. Bath is located on the Kennebec River, approximately 16 miles north of its mouth. Throughout the nineteenth and into the twentieth century, it was easily reached by sailing vessels and the numerous steamboats which plied the waters between the Kennebec and Portland, Boston, and other points Downeast. In the 1870s, when the following photograph was taken, railroads reached Bath from the east; but a view from the river would have been many visitors' first glimpse of the city.

Visible to those arriving by water were a number of signs of the city's importance. The dark-colored Sagadahoc County Courthouse, on the skyline to the left, indicated Bath's role as the county seat. The light granite structure seen through the masts of the schooner at anchor represented the Federal Government, which maintained a customs office as well as a post office there. Along the skyline at the left ran an impressive hotel, the Sagadahock House, providing quality accommodations for visitors. The waterfront itself was packed with manufacturing

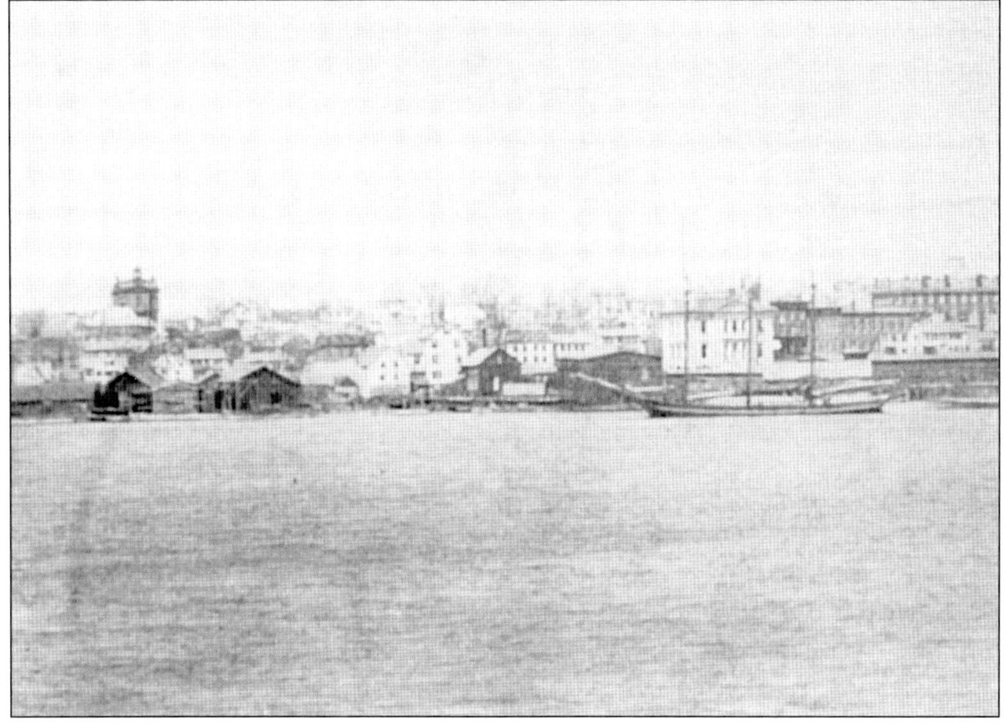

concerns, wharves, ferry slips, and warehouses. Not shown here were the shipyards, which filled the shoreline both north and south of the city center. Bath was a bustling place.

Growth came largely after 1800. Although settled in the 1660s, the region had been a part of Georgetown, across the river, until 1781, when Bath became the first town incorporated under the new state constitution of Massachusetts. Nine years later, at the time the first U.S. census was taken, the entire Bath region held fewer than a thousand souls: six other municipalities in Lincoln County were larger. However, the following decades brought more businesses and inhabitants for the riverside area, and the population increased greatly. Moreover, concentrations of people demanded better streets, with sidewalks, and improved schools.

Residents of the western part of town grew restless, as taxes seemed to be spent more for the benefit of urban dwellers; and in 1844 West Bath became a separate town. The boundary line eventually gave to Bath the river front on the east, from Winnegance north, as well as the northern frontage on Merrymeeting Bay. West Bath, in the southwestern portion of the former town, had about the same land mass, but a much smaller population (603 to Bath's 8,020 in 1850). Development continued as it had begun, with West Bath remaining largely agricultural and experiencing the shrinking population common to eastern rural areas of the period, while Bath grew to become both a city and the seat of the newly formed Sagadahoc County in 1854.

The separation was amicable, and the peoples of the two towns continued to associate as before. West Bath had a Methodist church in its southeastern sector, but did not always keep a pastor. (Since 1924, it has been used only during the summer.) Members of other parishes continued to worship at the same churches they had attended previous to the governmental split. Later, young people of West Bath who desired more than an elementary education went to secondary schools in the city; and residents of all ages made the short trip there for shopping or for various types of entertainment. The city was close enough so that residents might stroll westward to enjoy specialties like clambakes and shore dinners. (A Bath historian has claimed that the "shore dinner" was originated in West Bath.) Above all, as Bath's industrial sector grew, it provided employment for West Bath residents who were not tied down by farms.

Numerous other industries flourished and provided employment, but Bath came to regard itself particularly as a producer of vessels. On an 1858 map there were eighteen separate shipyards along its shores. Those all went out of operation with the decline of wooden sailing vessels; but newer firms made the transition to iron hulls and motorized shipping. Even today, signs welcome travellers to the Shipbuilding City, and high school sports teams call themselves the "Shipbuilders." The industry has touched many lives, is the focus of the city's major museum, and will, of course, be reflected in this volume.

Any book of old photographs must rely both on those present-day individuals willing to share their personal favorites and on the photographers of earlier generations, whose works have been collected. After the middle of the nineteenth century, large towns usually had at least one resident professional. The bulk of their photography was done in studios, as old and young sat for portraits, but there were professionals who took their cameras out to record their cities. In the late decades of the nineteenth century, the most established of those working in Bath, J.H. Higgins and A. Hatch, produced double-image cards for use with the stereoptic viewers commonly present in parlors of the period. Reproduced in sets, enough have survived to enrich our knowledge of the city's past. Both the professionals and amateurs who began to work around the turn of the century made up prints of larger photographs to sell when they could.

At about that same time, however, the picture postcard became popular. Produced in large numbers, postcards were relatively inexpensive and thus appealed to a wide range of purchasers, who took advantage of the new RFD system and used them for short messages. Collecting postcards was in vogue, and there were special albums available to hold them. Professional photographers sometimes took advantage of the new fad for income and to keep their names before the public; but most such cards were the work of a new breed of camera-wielder, who sought both the commonplace and the romantic in order to attract buyers. (Some companies which developed private films obligingly put the prints on cards which served for mailing if one desired.) Postcards are thus excellent source material for the past.

Although ordinary people increasingly had the means of taking pictures, it was not until the 1920s or later that amateurs truly came into their own, filling family albums with pictures taken by relatives placed alongside the formal portraits. Personal snapshots began to outnumber those taken by professionals, who often found it advisable to expand their shops to develop others' films as well as their own.

Examples of many varieties of pictures make up this work. Because of the nature of the materials used, I do not intend this volume to be a complete history of the development of either of the two municipalities included. Rather, it represents a series of glimpses into what the area once was.

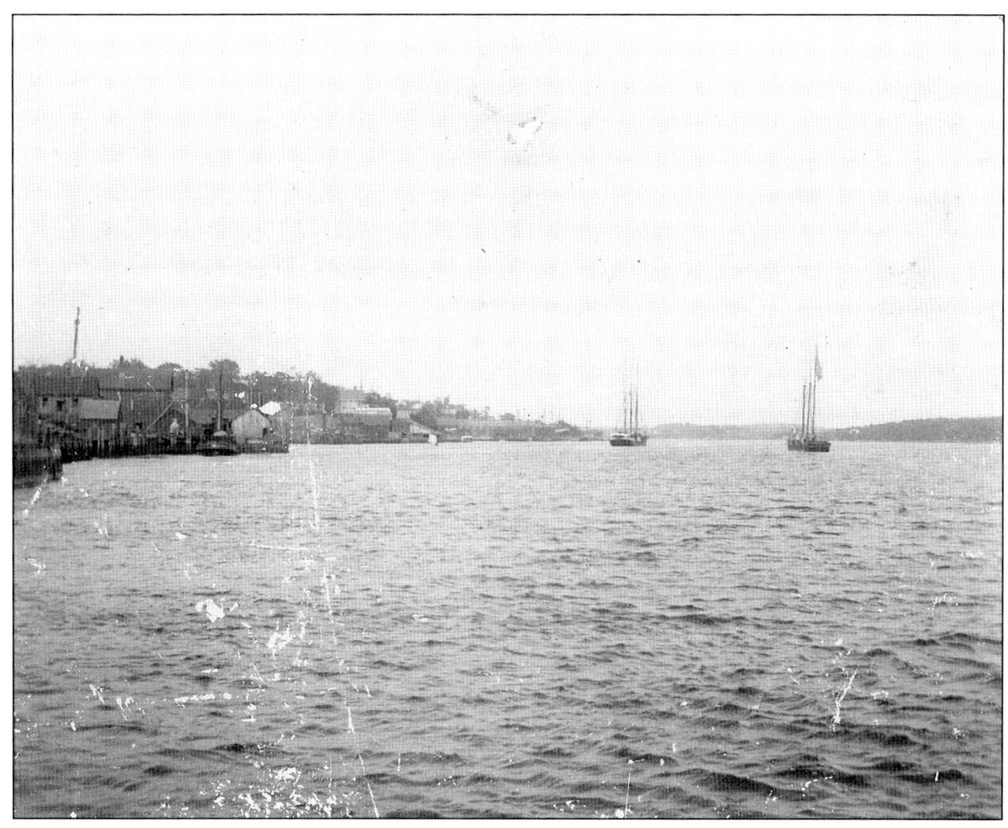

Bath and the river, c. 1900. This view, looking up the river, was taken on the water, and it makes one understand why the Kennebec was not quickly or easily bridged at Bath.

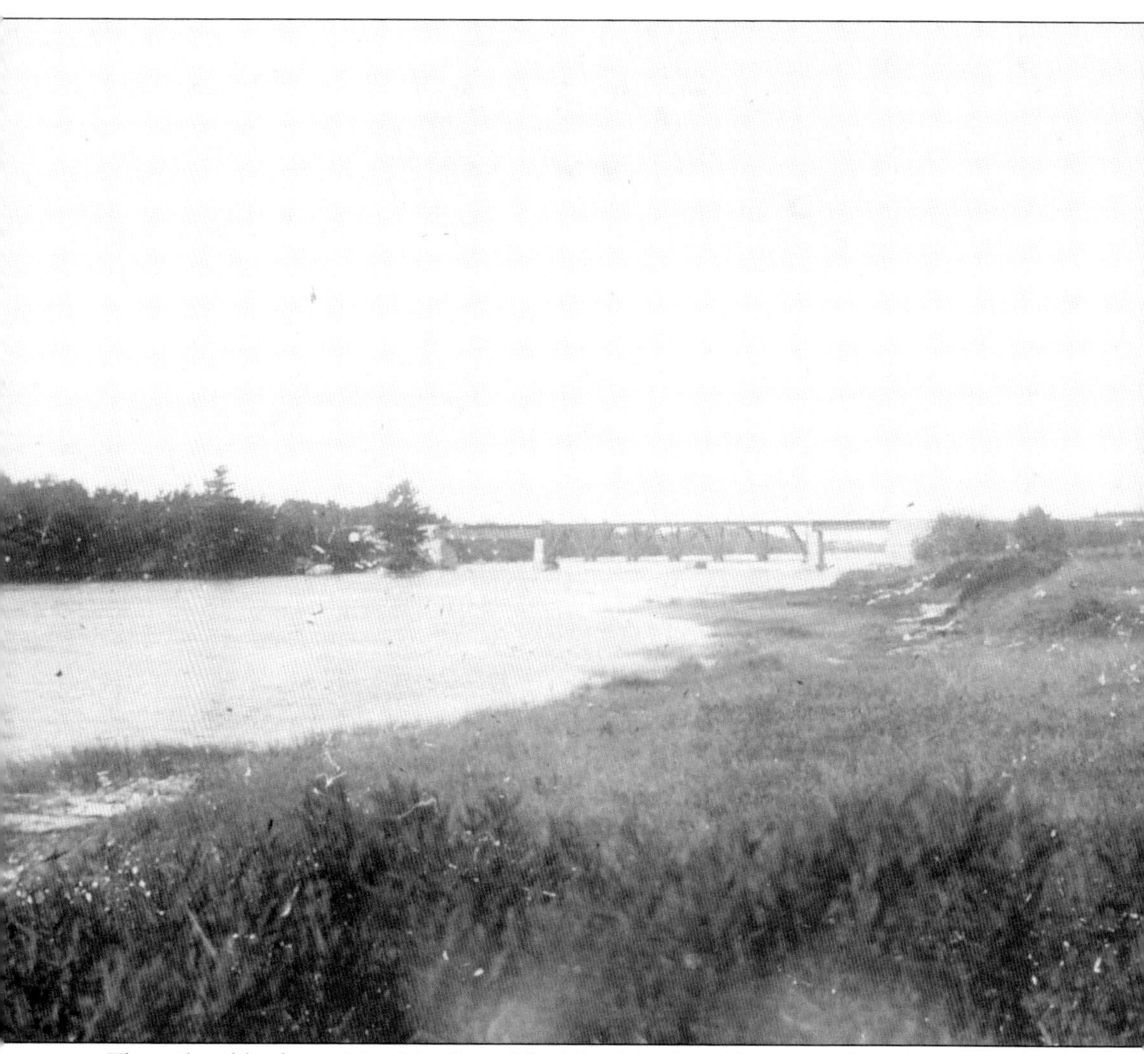

The railroad bridge at New Meadows. The New Meadows River is really a long arm of Casco Bay, but it provided a barrier between West Bath and anything to the east, a barrier which had to be bridged. This view down the river toward the railroad bridge was taken before the new wagon bridge was constructed nearby in 1907.

One

All Around the Town

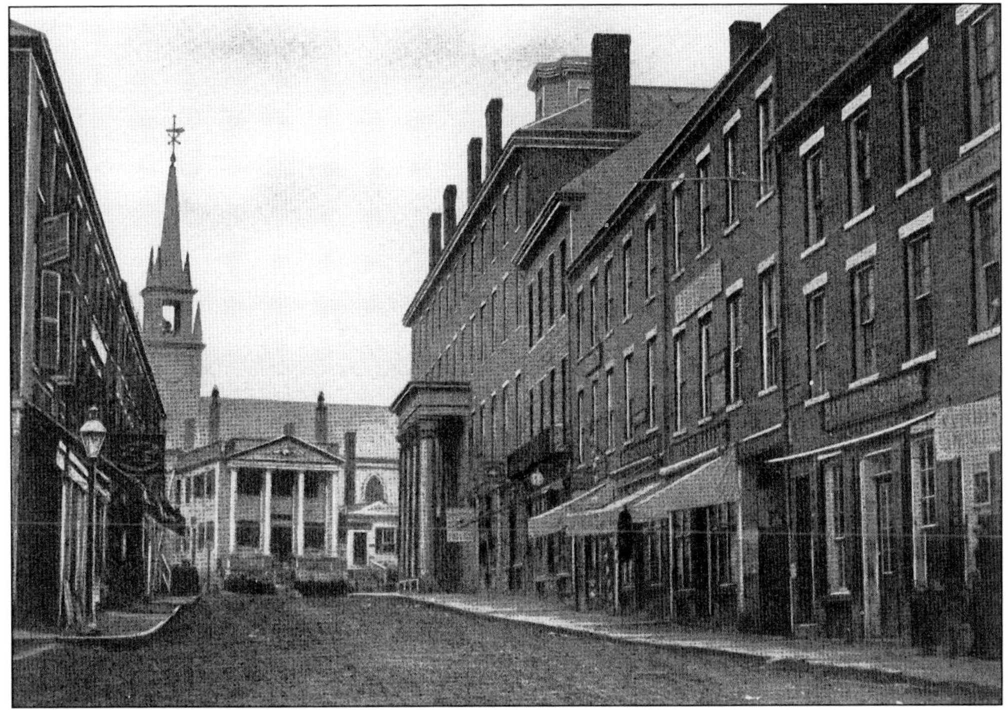

Front Street, looking south, before 1860. This very early photograph shows the First Universalist Church (sold in 1860, then removed) looming behind the columned Bath Bank, begun by the merchant William King. The edifice, which housed customs offices during King's tenure as collector, served as the custom house between the 1830s (when the Bath Bank failed to get rechartered) and 1859 (when the new custom house was constructed). The building itself was replaced in 1878.

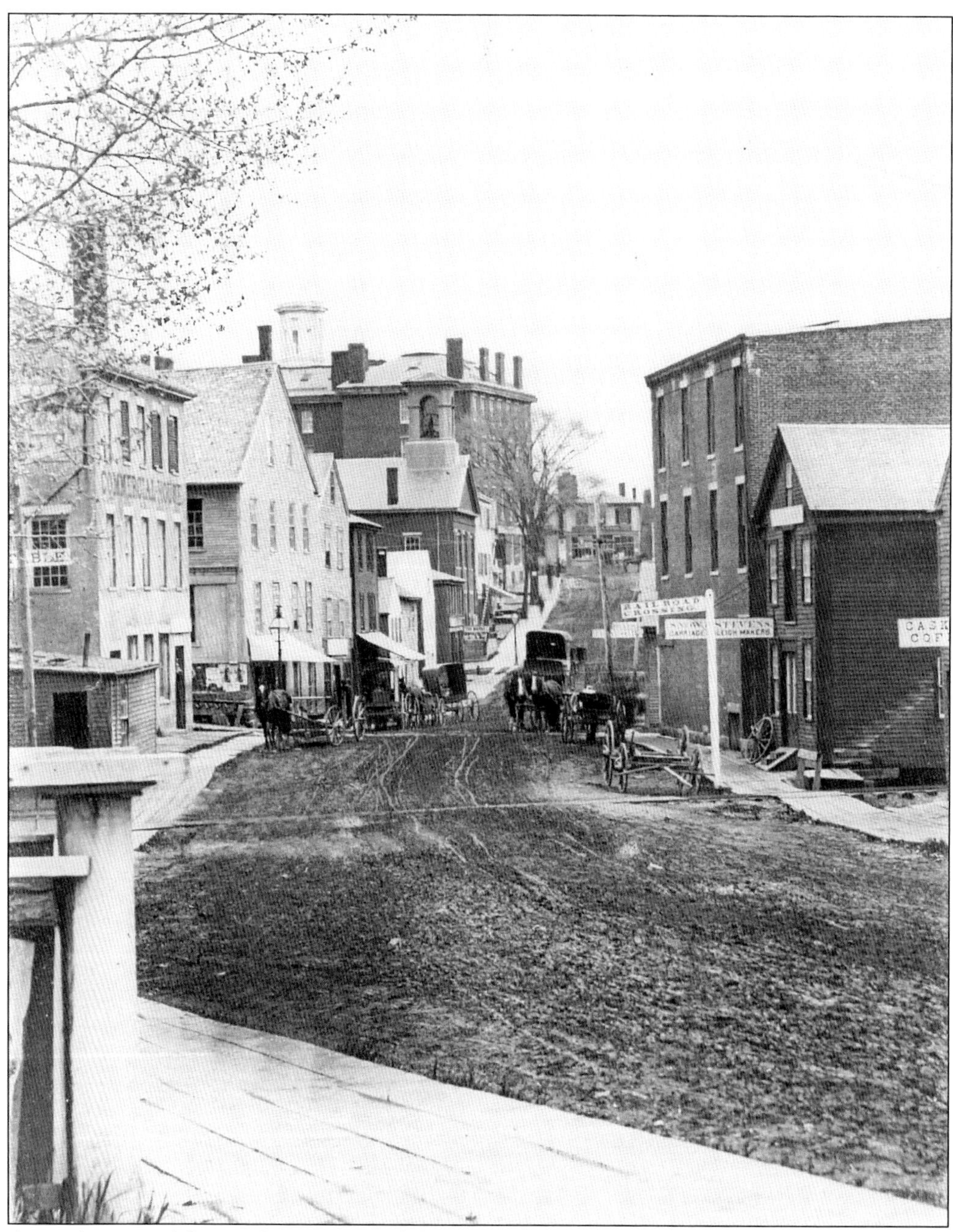

An early view of Center Street. Printed from a rare tintype stereoptic, this photograph shows traffic at the foot of the hill, looking east. Presumably the horseless cart near the railroad tracks represents the work of the Snow and Stevens firm next to it. Every building shown here has disappeared over time.

Looking west on Center Street in the 1870s. This view down that same slope includes the courthouse on the hill beyond, as well as an assortment of carriages and pedestrians. Trees and frame stores are long gone from upper Center Street, but the brick mercantile structures on the left still stand.

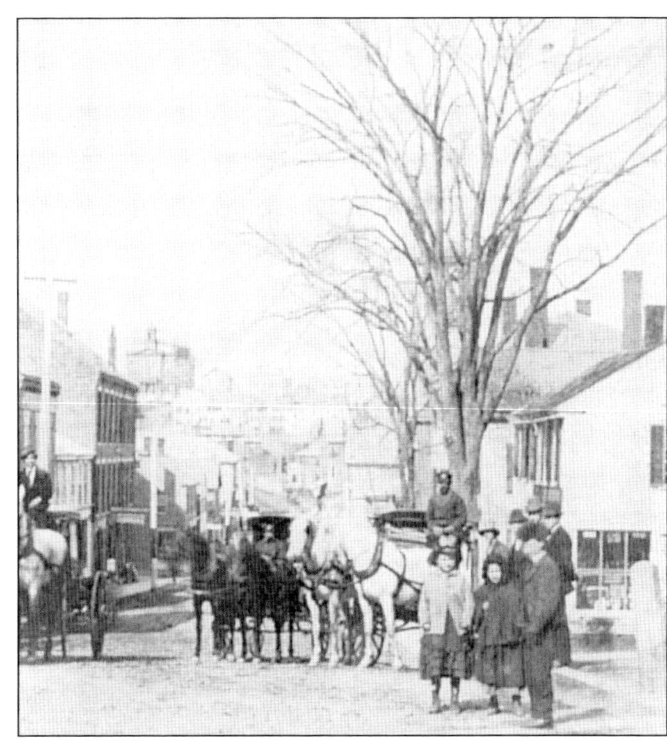

Front Street, near Center. Front Street was photographed in sections. Carriages are drawn up in front of the Sagadahock House (on the left). Notice how narrow Front Street was then.

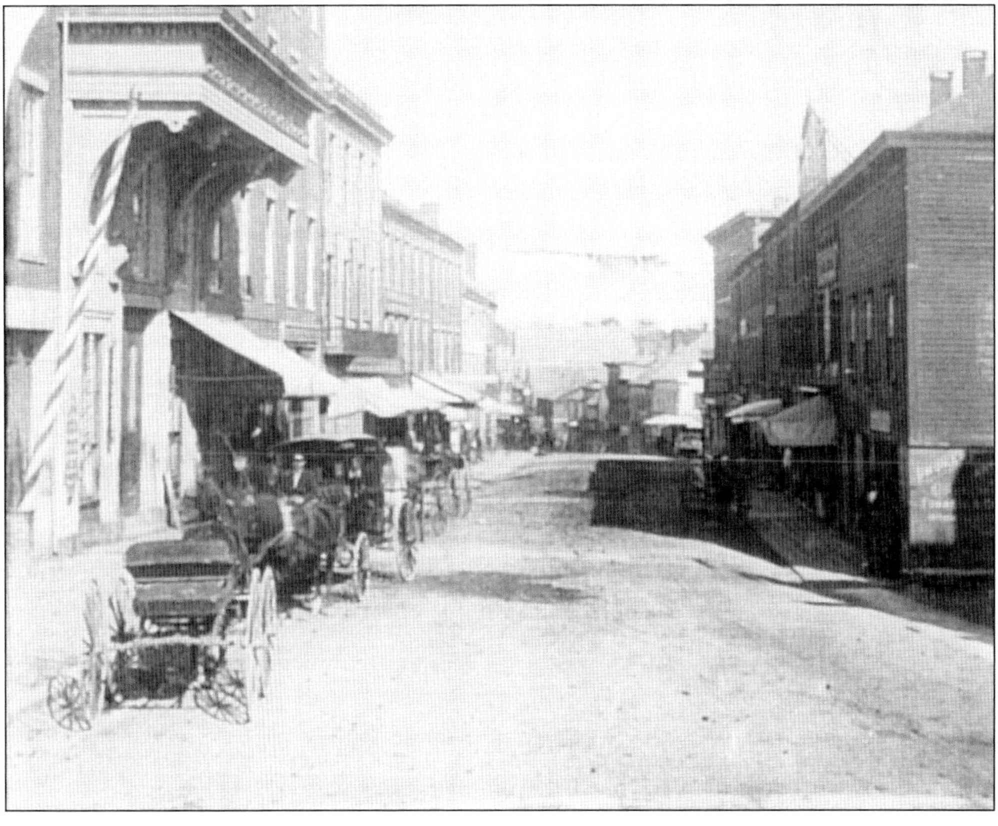

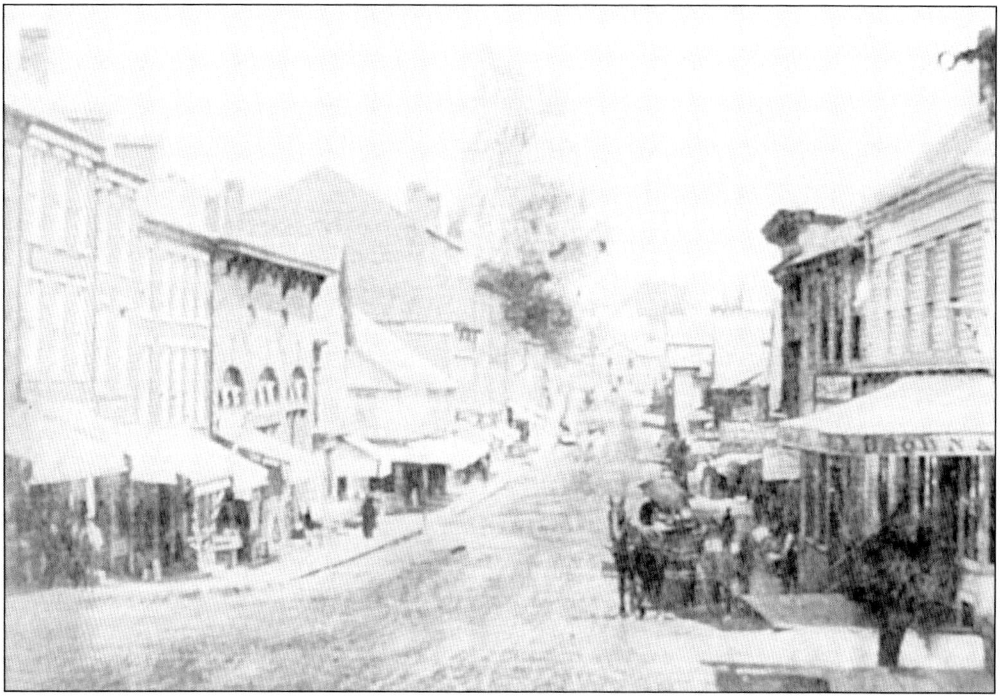

Front Street, farther north. Most of the structures north of Broad Street were wiped out in the fires of 1893–94.

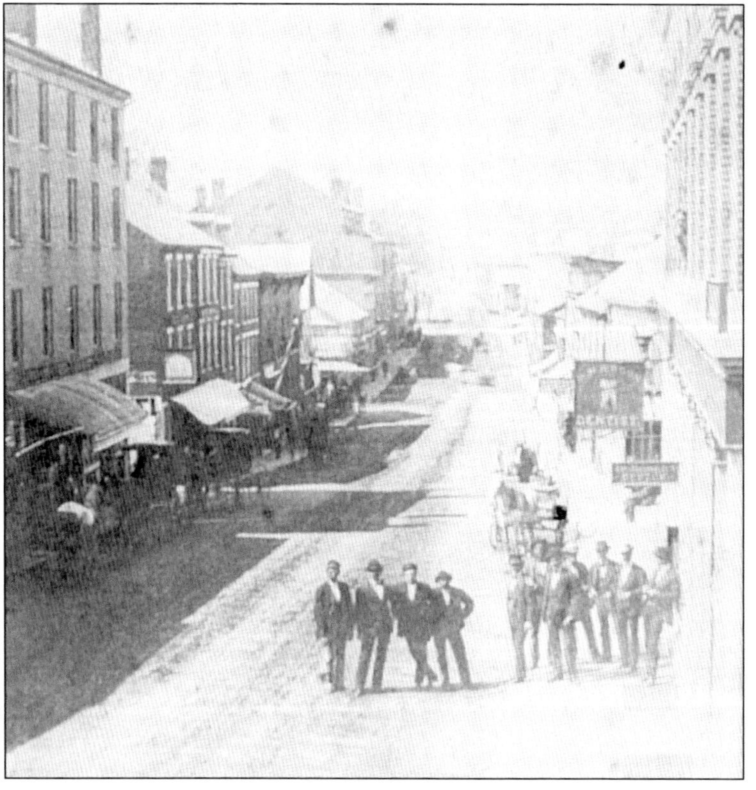

A detail of Front Street. Yes, men of the 1870s were likely to pose when a camera appeared; and no, Mr. Ragon, the dentist, did not stress tooth preservation.

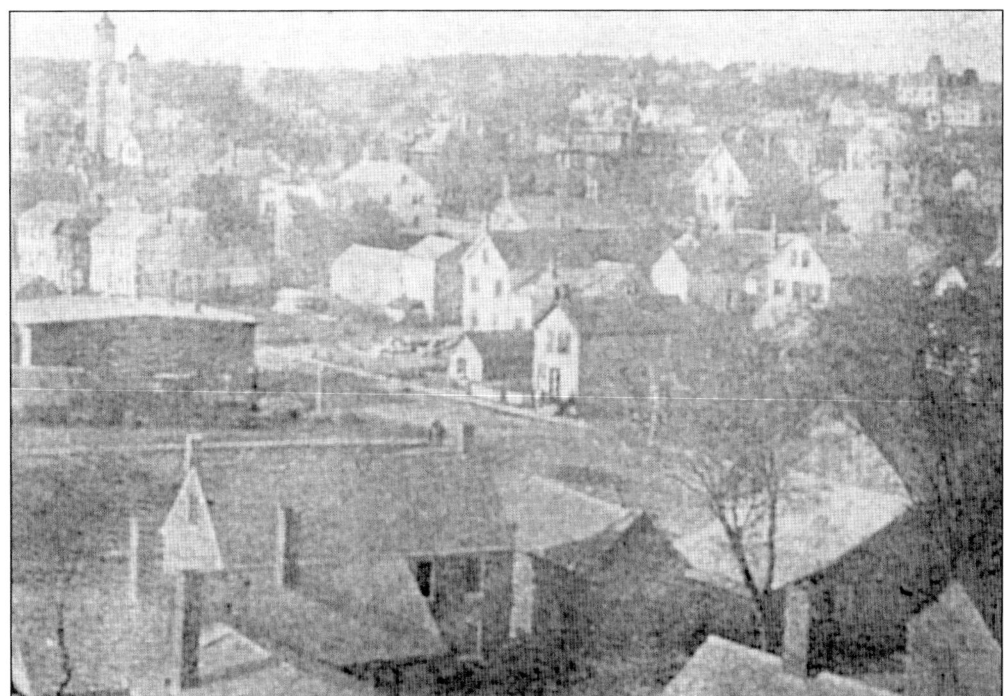

The South End. This "general view" of the South End was taken from atop one of the three-story buildings on Front Street. The photographer's studio was in the Church Block, which replaced the church shown on p. 11; and he often varied his perspective by climbing into steeples or towers.

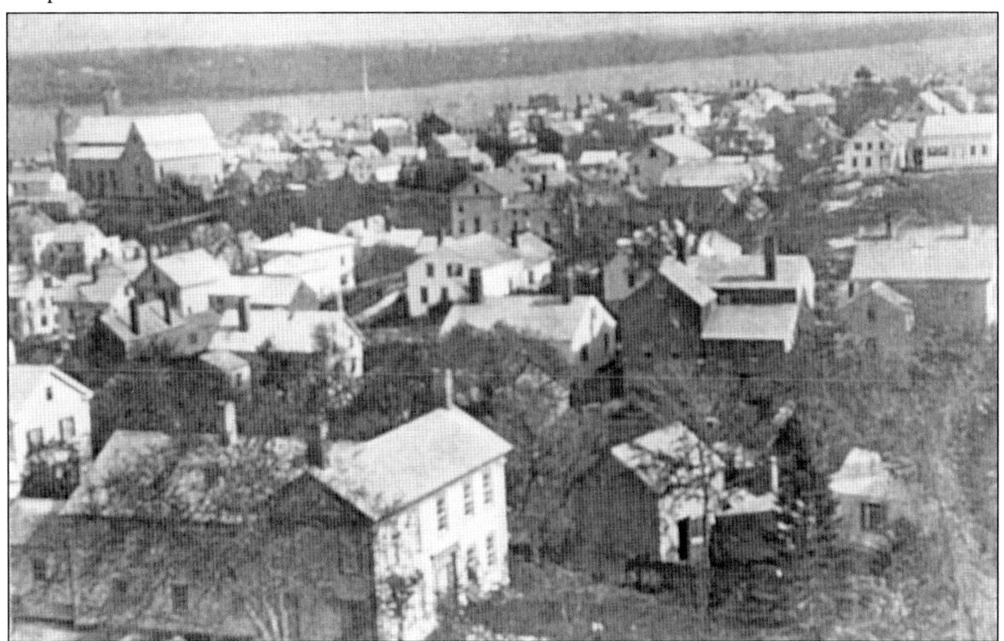

The South End. This overview of the South End may have been from the Sagadahoc County Courthouse. Nearby homes stood where the Leeman Highway would later cut through. The rear of the Methodist church, near Wesley Street, can be seen on the upper left.

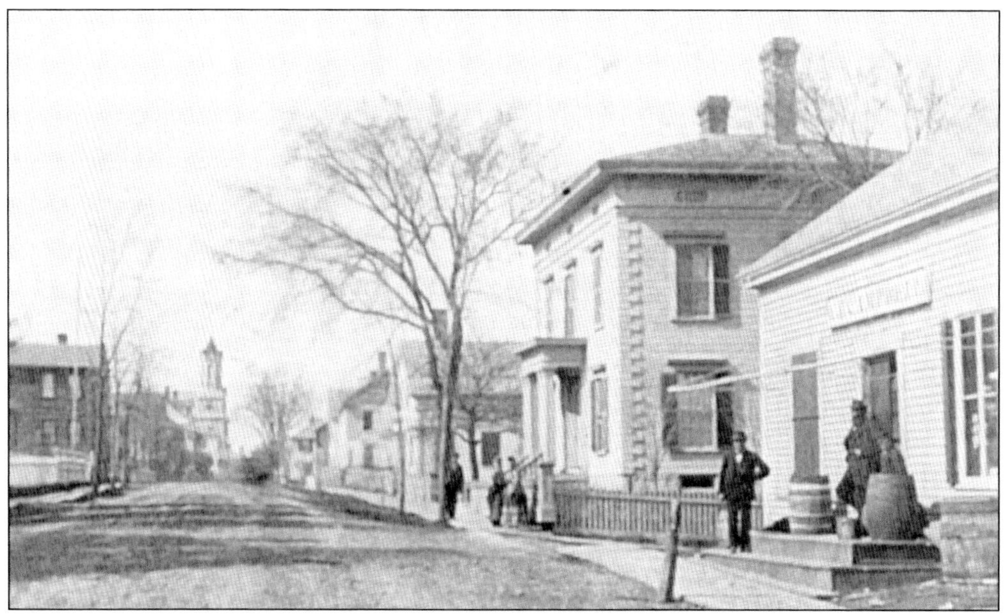

Washington Street. The river side (shown here on the right) of Washington Street in the South End has been absorbed by Bath Iron Works. One can orient oneself by the old Methodist church in the distance: its replacement still stands on the site, although no longer a church. C.W. Campbell, whose sign is on the house at the right, was a grocer.

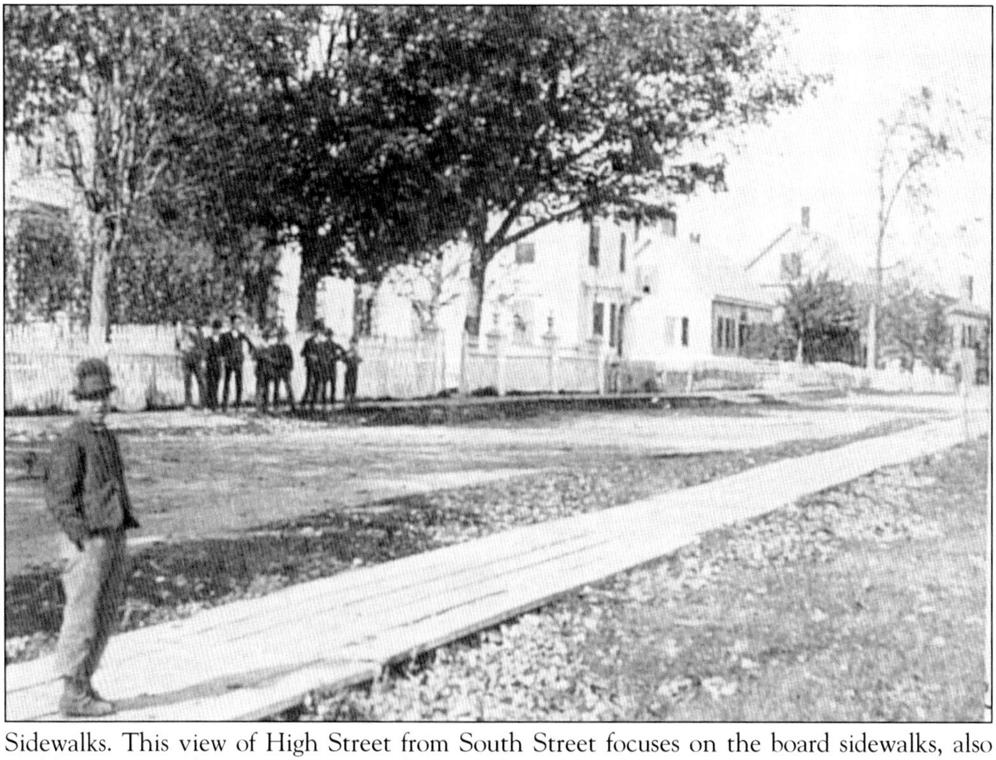

Sidewalks. This view of High Street from South Street focuses on the board sidewalks, also visible in many other street scenes of the period. Bath had 25 miles of sidewalks in 1878, most of wood. All streets were then made of dirt.

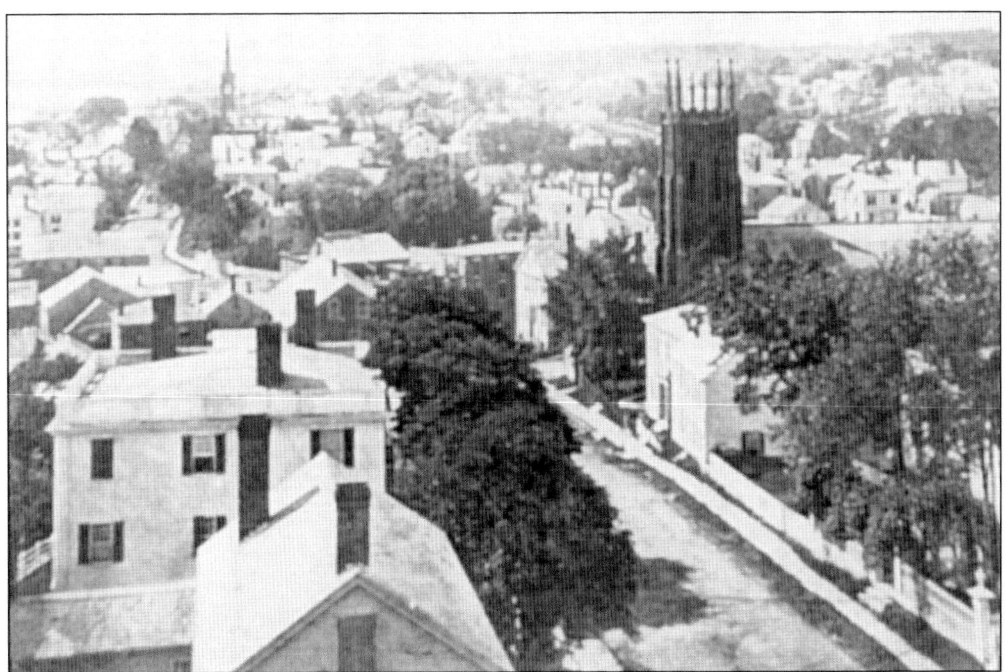

Looking south along Washington Street. From the steeple of the Elm Street Baptist Church, the photographer could peer down on the Central Church and its tower.

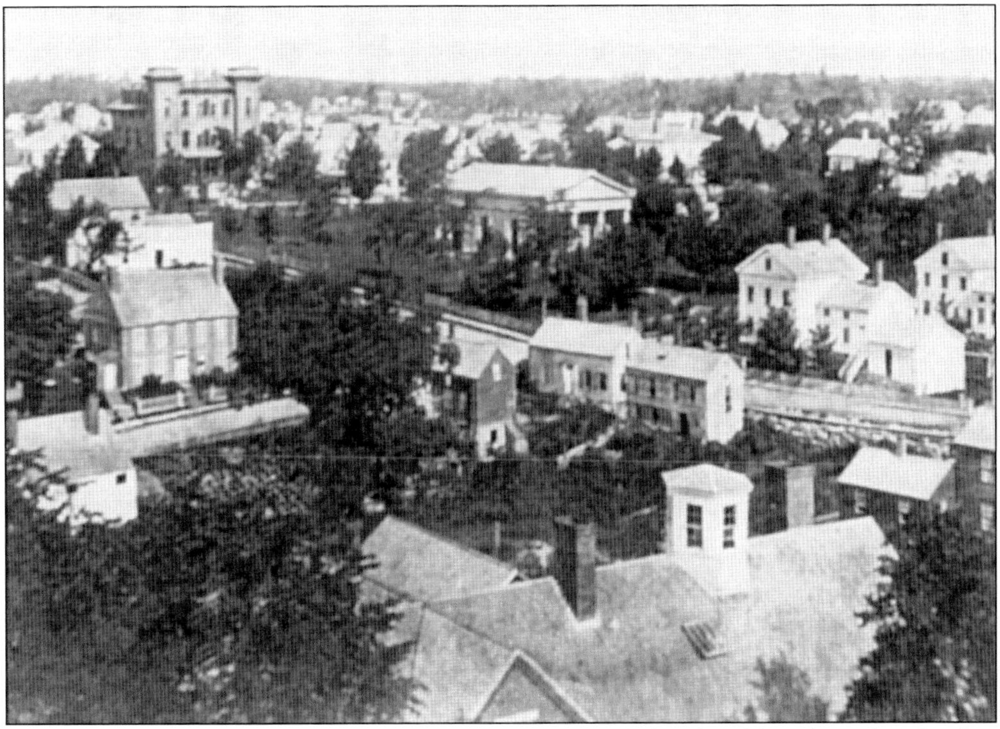

A view to the west. Another shot from that location includes the old Bath High School as well as the temple-like Swedenborgian church (the Church of the New Jerusalem) among various residences.

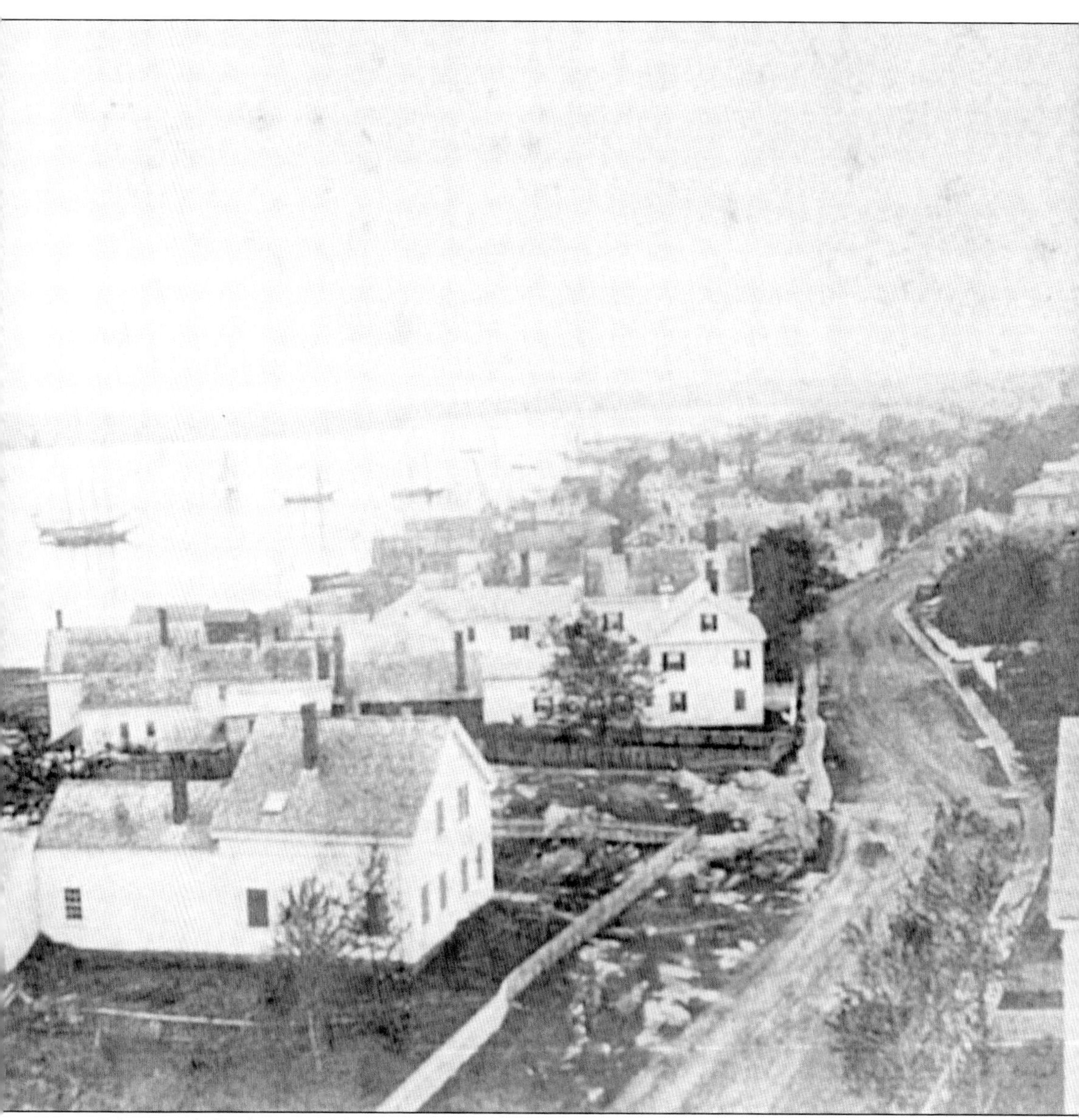

The North End. Part of the North End, looking toward the downtown, could be seen from the steeple of the Beacon Street Methodist Church. Nearby houses and prominent ledges are still recognizable.

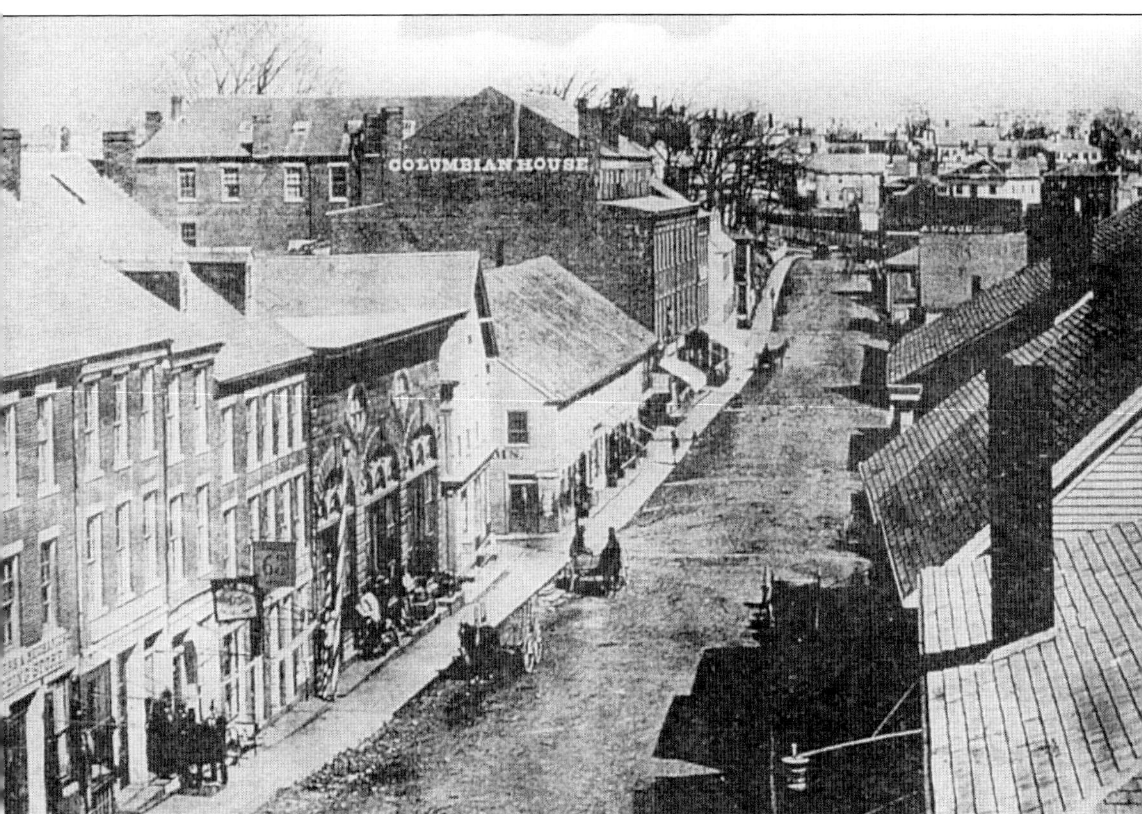

Front Street in the 1880s. Postcards provide opportunities to note changes along the city streets. This view of Front Street first appeared as a photograph, and was only later made into a postcard. Until it burned in 1893, the Columbian House was an important hostelry; its function rooms included a theater.

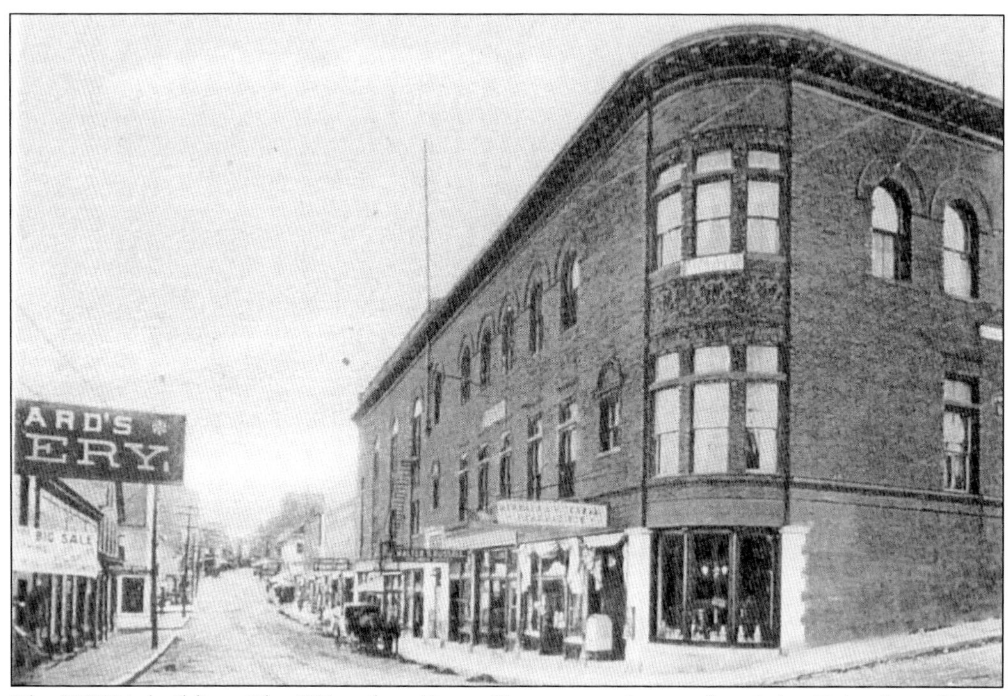

The YWCA building. The "Y" and an Opera House next door replaced the Columbian House and its theater. Both were financed by entrepreneur Galen Moses.

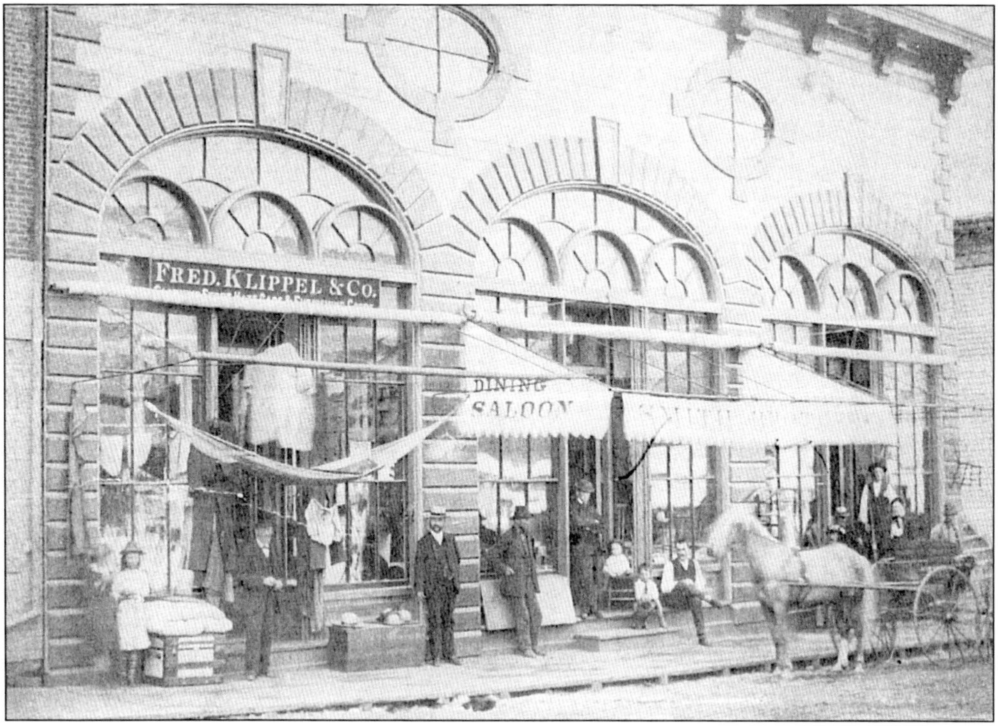

Front Street businesses. Fred Klippel's clothing store and the Smith Brothers' Dining Saloon occupied this unusual wooden building which burned in 1890.

The Sagadahock House. Built in 1848–49, this was the largest hostelry in the city. Note the numerous chimneys, indicating fireplaces in each room. It stood on Front and Center Streets until January 28, 1894, when a fire that started in its stables destroyed the hotel along with buildings next to it and across Front Street.

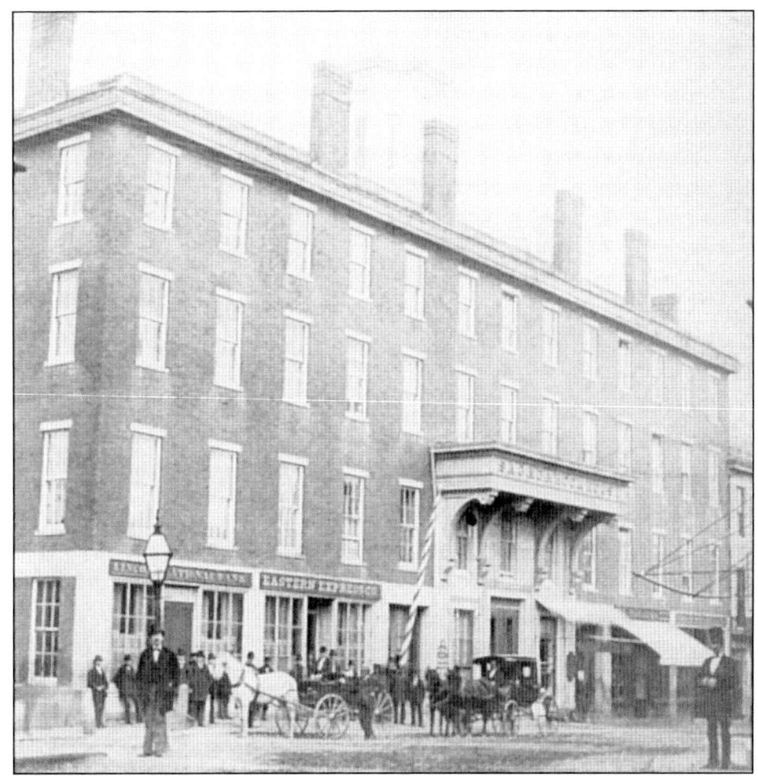

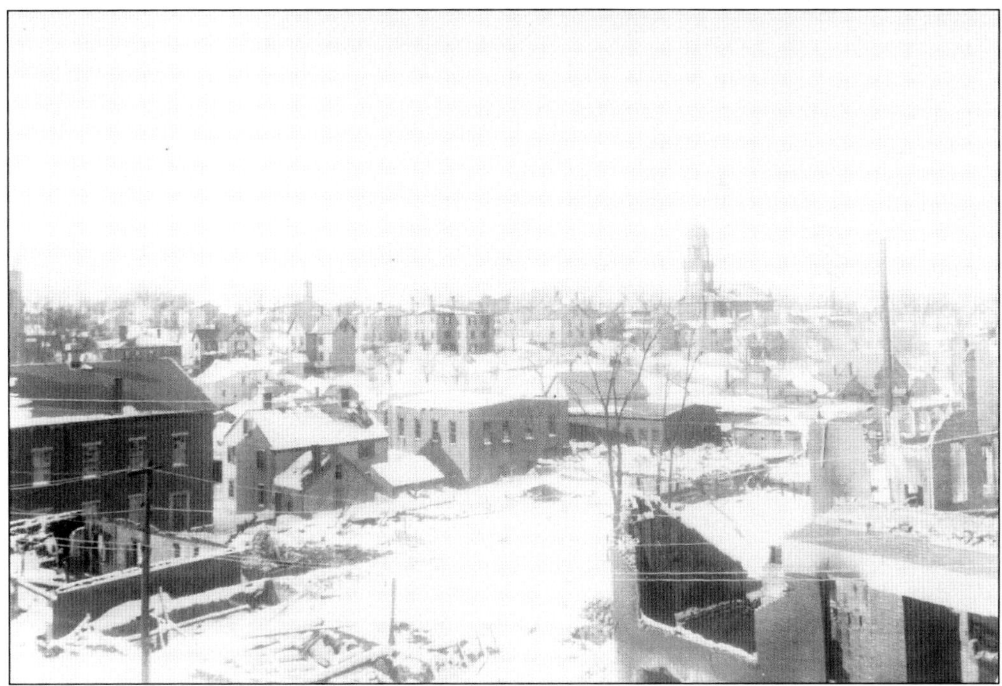

Damage from the 1894 fire. This view is toward the northwest, with the City Hall still standing on the left and hotel ruins in the lower right. Part of the reason for the fire's damage was a break in the water mains preceding the disaster.

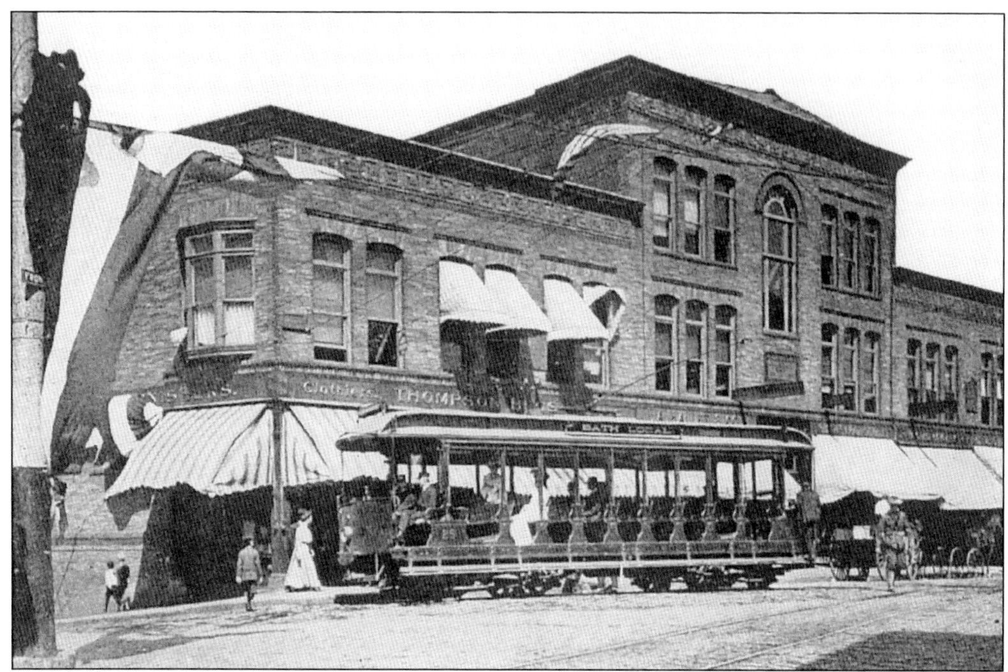

The Sagadahock Block. The building then erected on the site of the hotel was lower and housed more shops, including Thompson's clothing store.

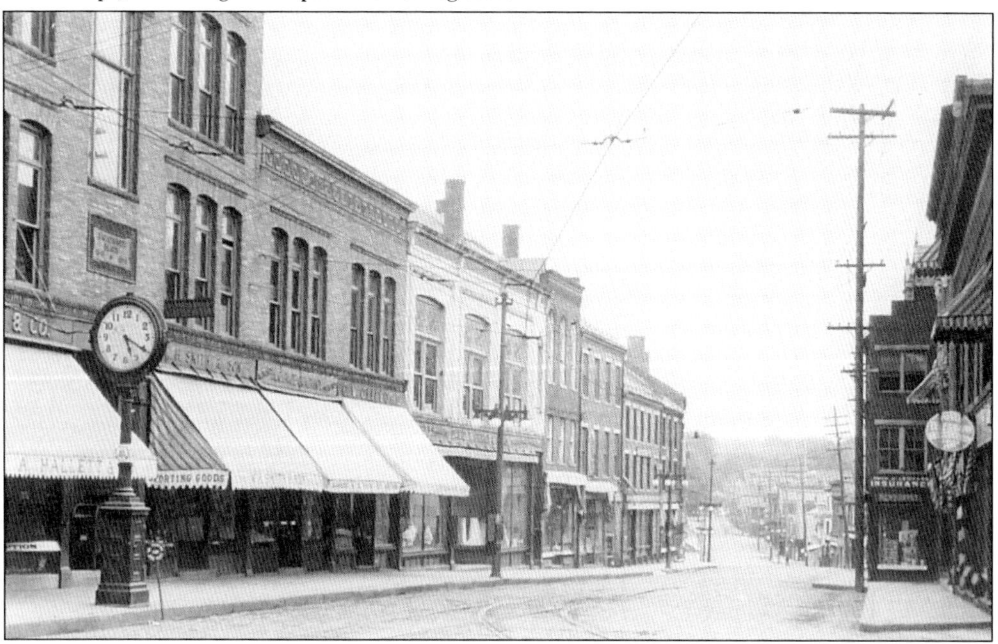

Front Street at 5:30 am. Such quiet would occur only in the early morning. The clock in front of the drugstore has had its location changed slightly in recent years; but local outrage at a rumored sale showed how important it seemed to residents, and it stayed in the city. Over the years, when buildings on the right side of Front Street burned or were torn down, their replacements were set back and the street widened. The crow-stepped building on the left, built in 1839, was razed in 1959 to even out that side.

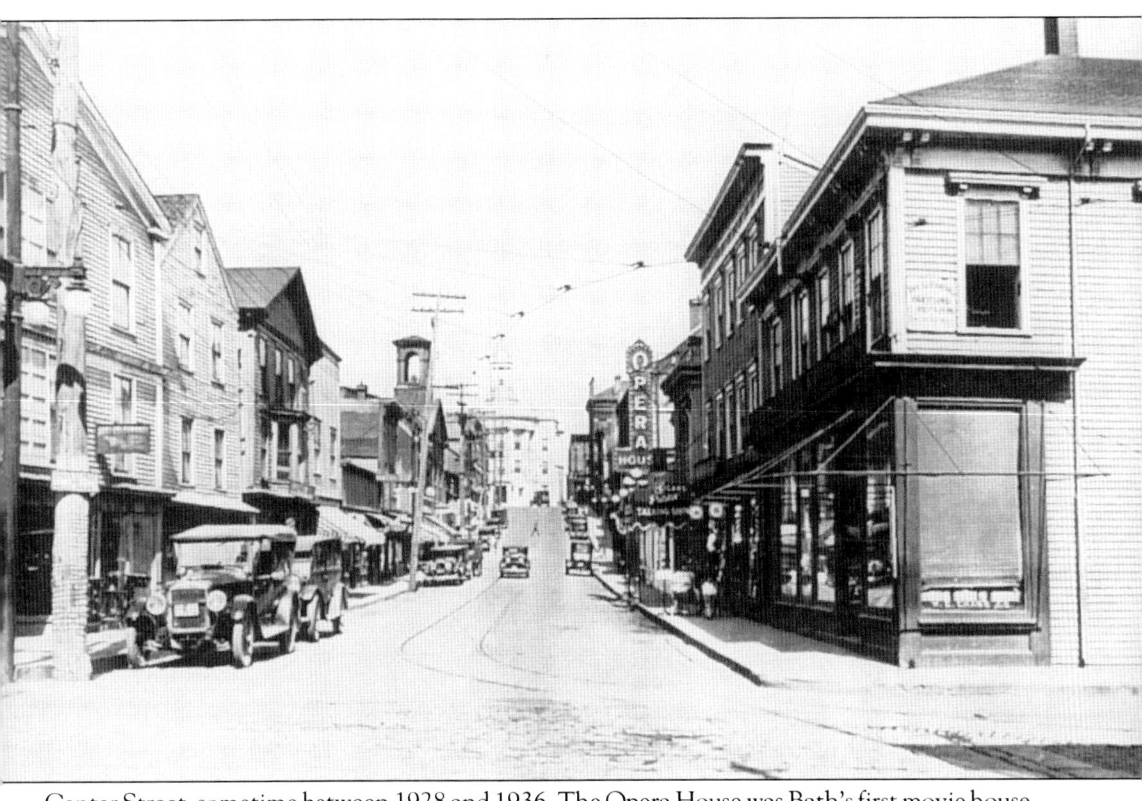

Center Street, sometime between 1928 and 1936. The Opera House was Bath's first movie house, erected in 1913. Center Street had changed considerably since the earlier view on p. 12.

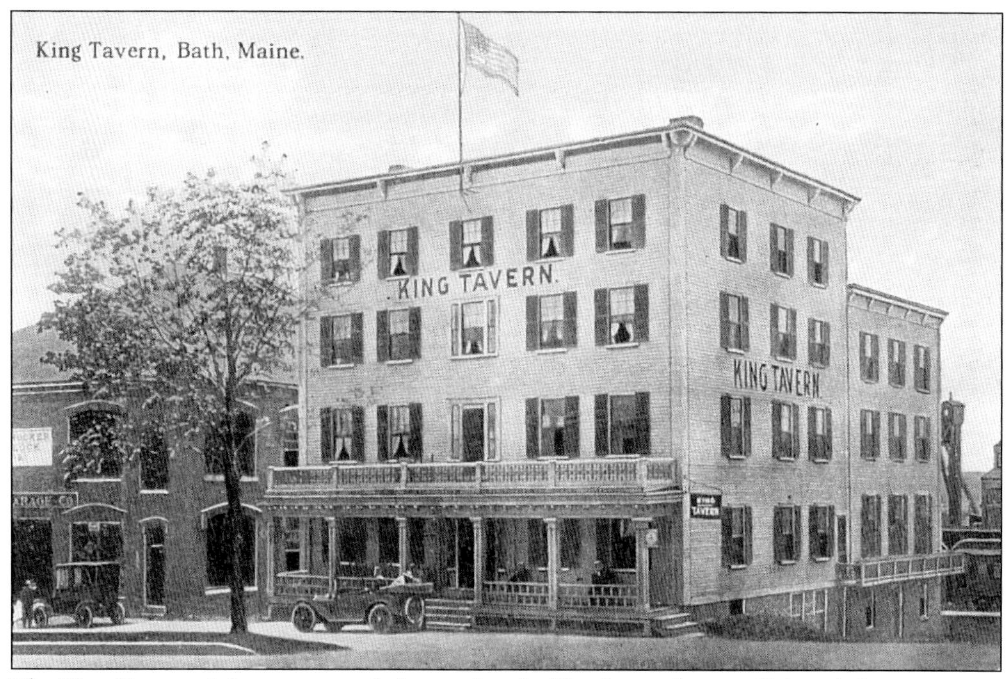

The King Tavern. A busy port needed many hotels. The former home of Maine's first governor, enlarged by him from one-and-a-half stories to three, was moved off its original site, given a fourth floor, and named the Shannon House. It was renamed the King Tavern in 1910, but was taken down in 1926 to make way for access to the new bridge. To the left stood the city's first Ford dealership, also removed for the access road.

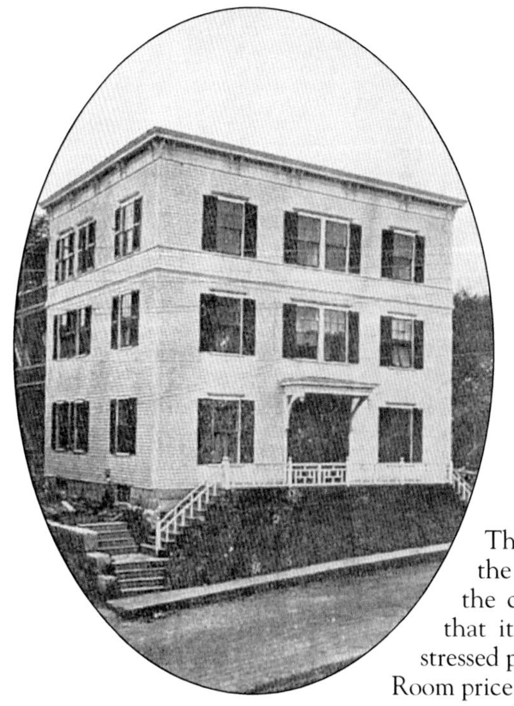

The Park Chambers. One of the smaller hotels was the Park Chambers, on Summer Street, opposite the city park. Advertising cards not only insisted that it was "A good place for Ladies to stop," but stressed proximity to "Steam Boats, R.R. and Electrics." Room prices varied from $1.50 to $5.00 a week.

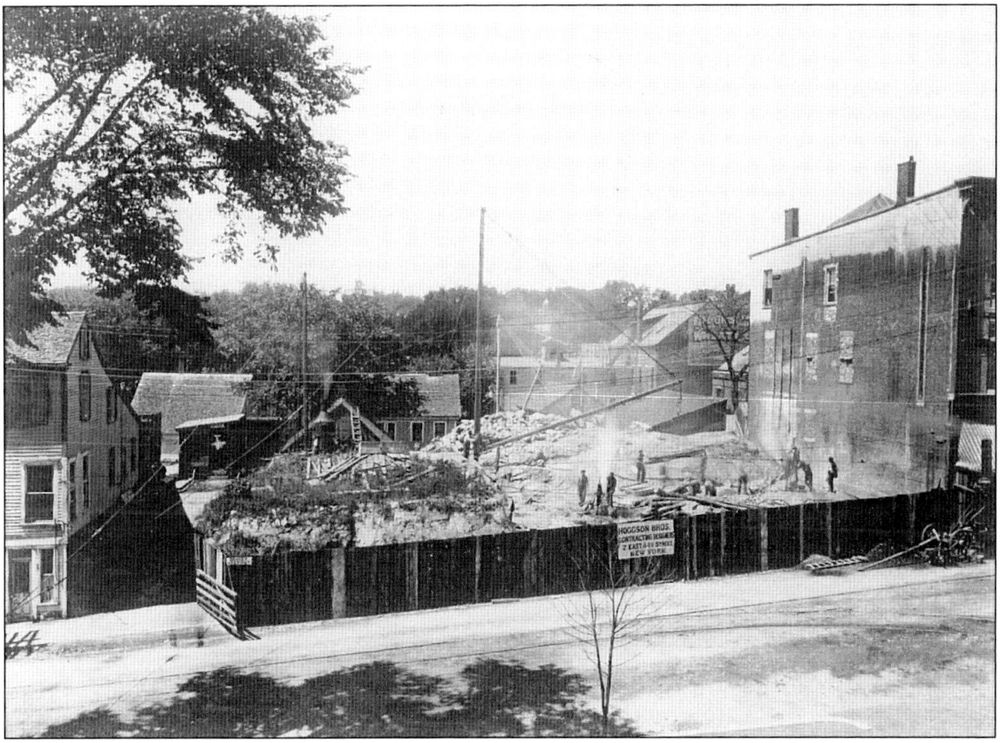

"Progress." The city's downtown area has been the scene of continual rebuilding, as shown by the number of old structures no longer extant. Many were, of course, lost to fires; but others simply gave way to a desire for something newer. This Front Street site once held the three-story Neal Block (which can be seen on p. 88), removed early in the century to allow construction of Bath National Bank (recently Key Bank). Note the flour advertisement on the gable of the brick block on Center Street: the lettering has faded, but is still legible in the 1990s.

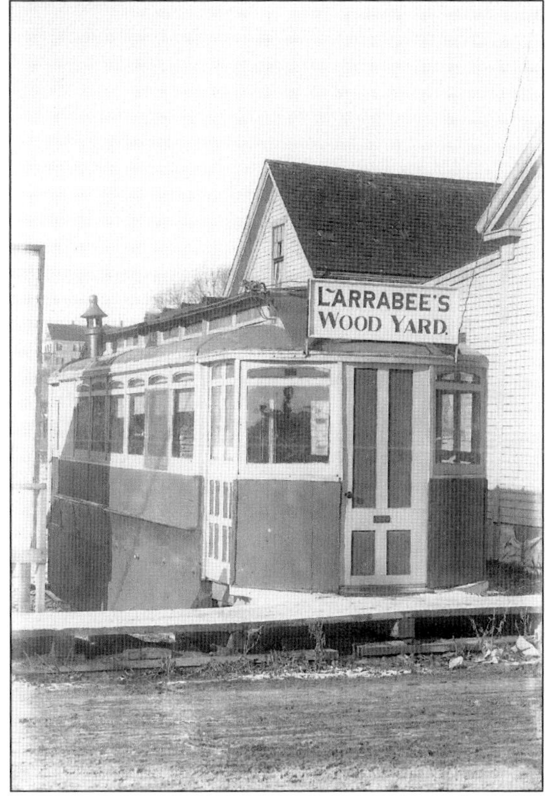

Larrabee's Wood Yard, c. 1907. Not all commercial buildings were conventional. Edward Larrabee's Front Street company office began its existence as a railroad car. The firm operated for more than two decades, starting about 1899.

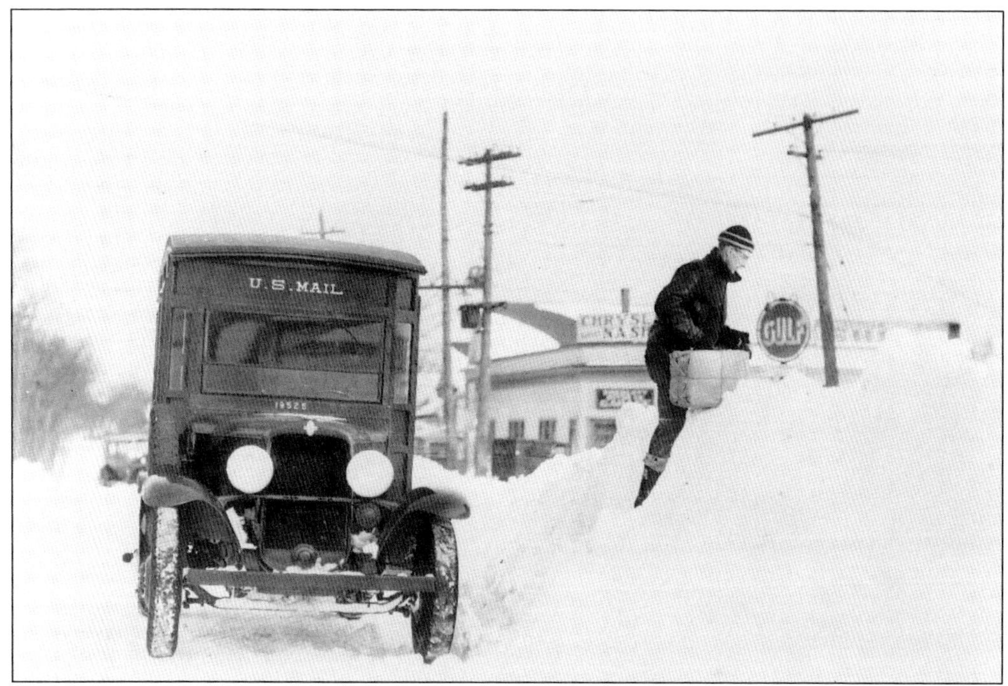

The mail must go through. Photographers found warm weather most appealing for cityscapes, but Maine winters demanded recording, too. Although he had a truck to carry his load, this mailman still found delivery more than a little difficult.

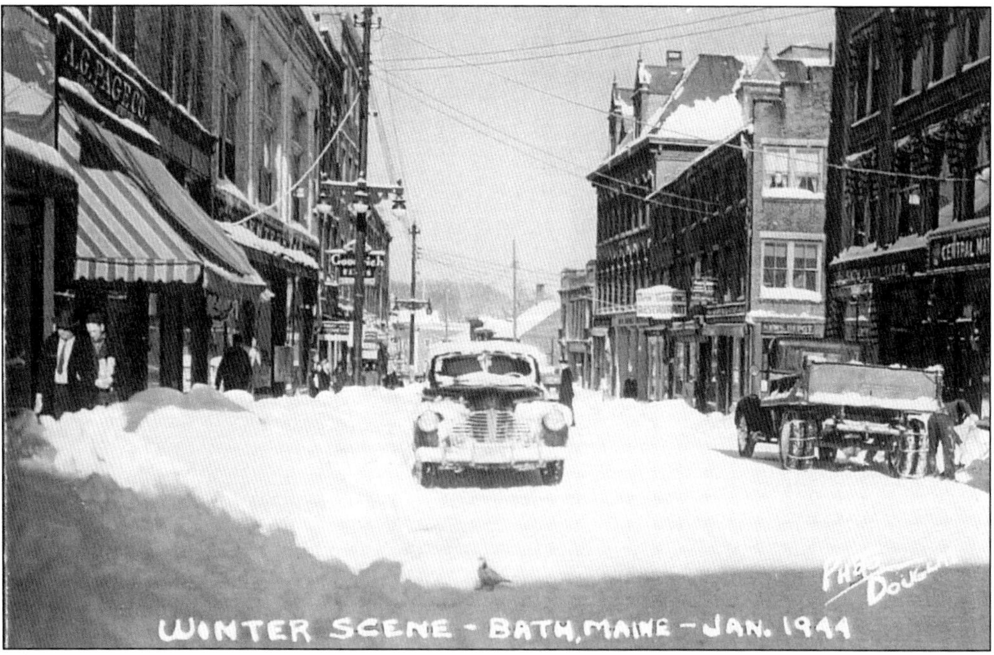

Clearing Front Street, 1944. The dump truck on the left, with chains on its rear wheels, is from the highway department. The worker nearby is shoveling snow—which will probably be dumped in the river—into the truck to clear the street. The photographer, Herbert Douglas, recorded activities in Bath for decades.

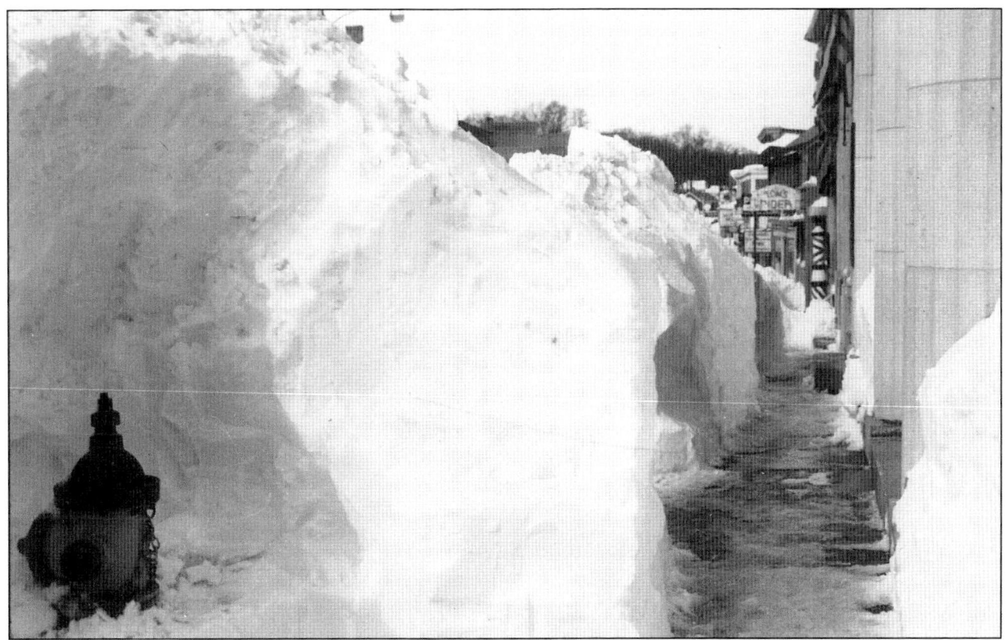

The Blizzard of February 1952. Any big storm slowed the highway crews. Two days after this snow fell, an amateur photographer recorded the barely-opened streets on her way to work. Only a narrow path was provided pedestrians at Front and Broad Streets, but fire hydrants had been cleared.

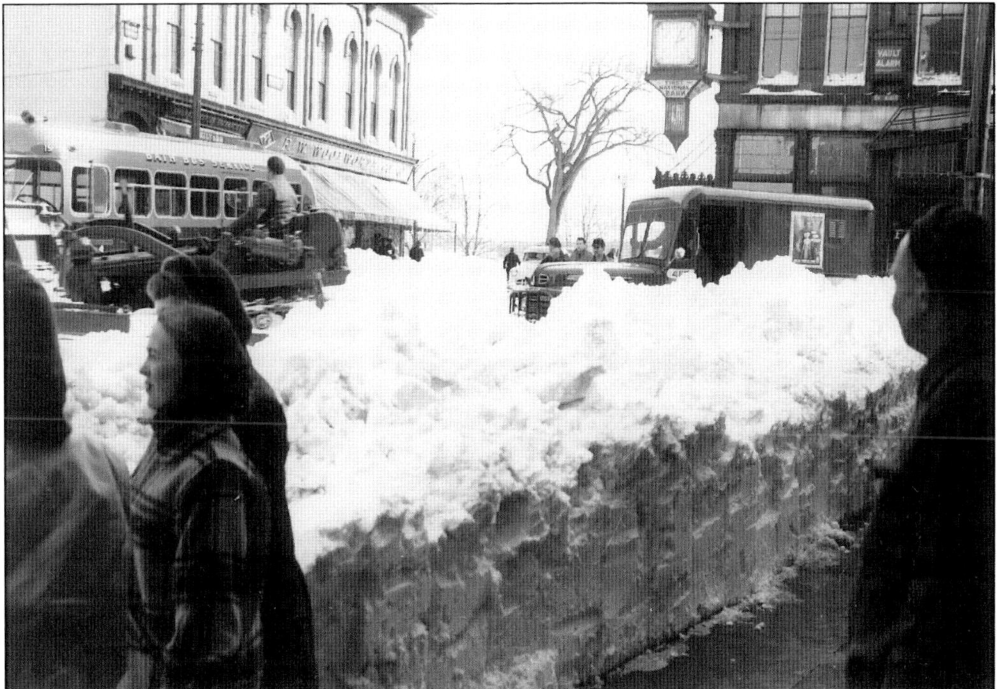

Front and Center Streets. Caterpillar-tread snow machines endeavored to clear passage for autos, buses, and delivery trucks. The First National Bank's clock was still in place then, and Woolworths would occupy the building across Front Street for about four more years.

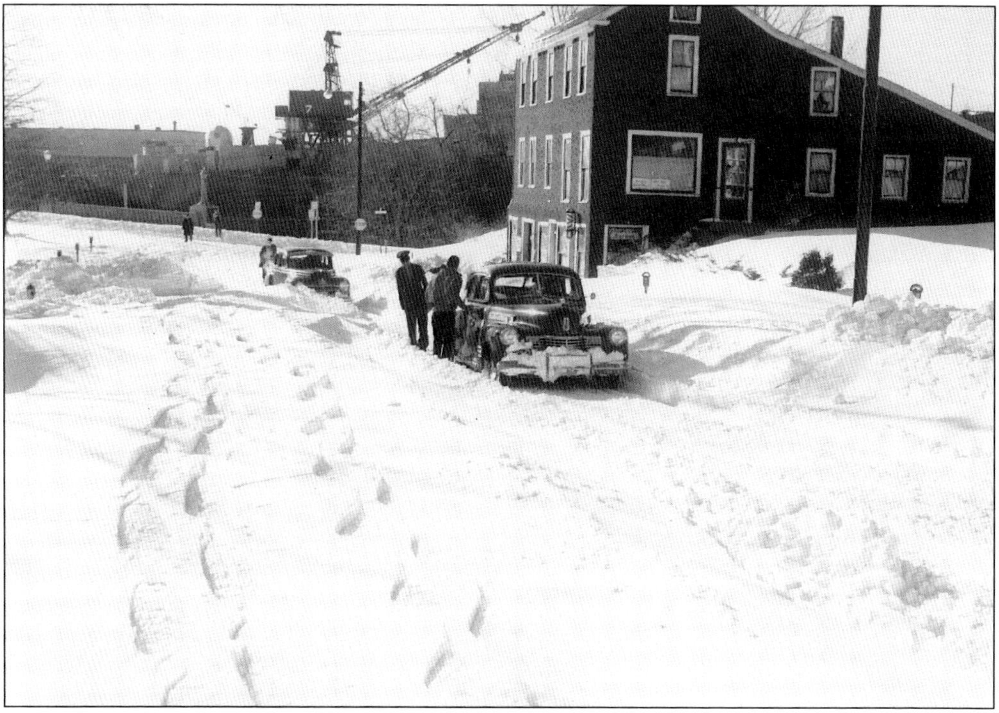

Front Street, near the bridge. How little snow had actually been displaced can be seen farther down Front Street. Nearly buried parking meters (in use between 1947 and 1967) stood useless, as no one could possibly park. Snowshoe tracks on the left indicate that a much older means of travel over snow had been utilized. The building on the right is remembered by many as the best source of recapped tires during wartime shortages, and by others as the site of a diner. Bath Iron Works is south of the bridge.

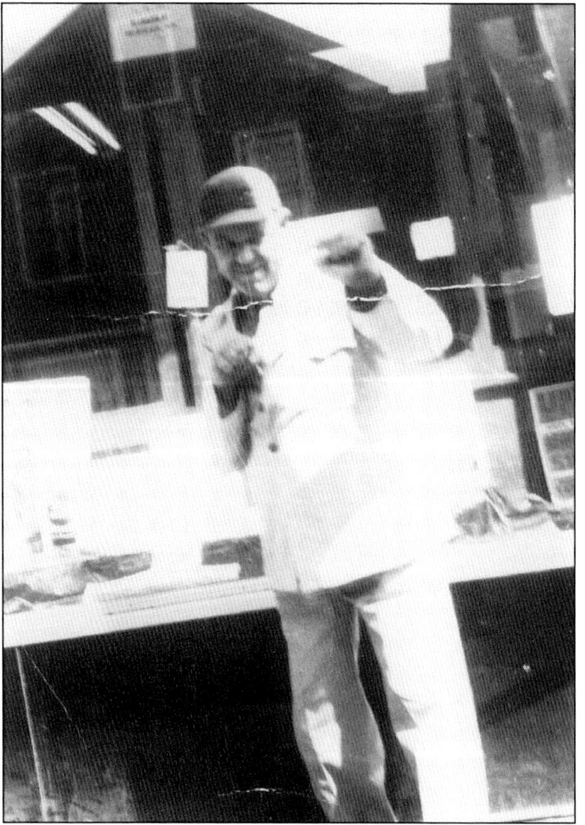

Norm Roderick. Every town has individuals who are known to all. In mid-twentieth-century Bath, one such character was Norm Roderick, an ex-boxer who did odd jobs, while "waiting for my ship to come in."

Two

HOMES

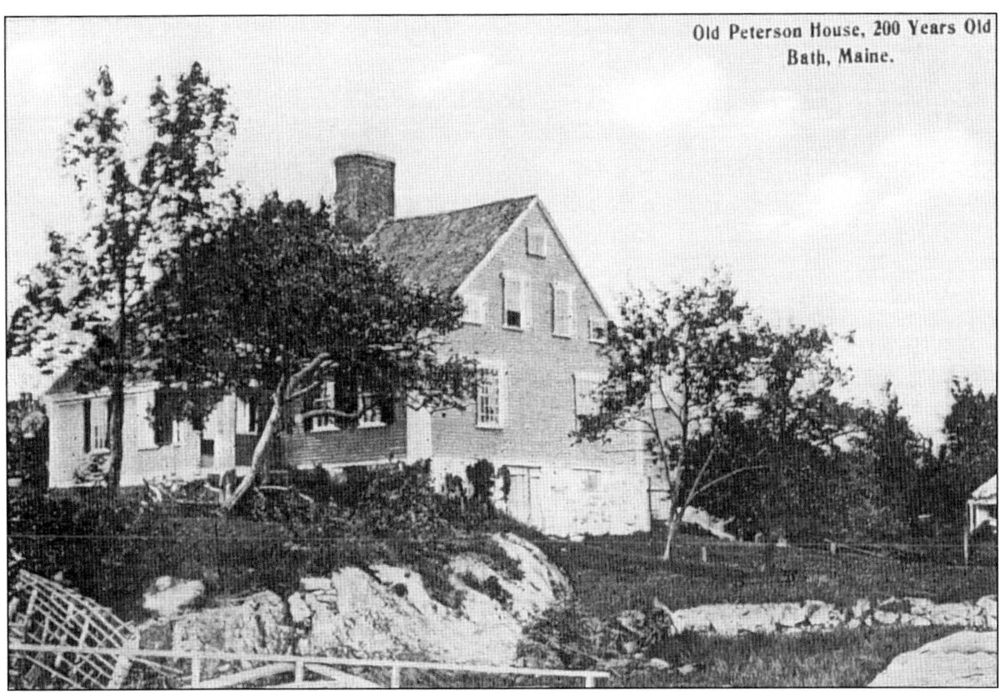

The old Peterson Place. As in most successful urban areas, Bath's earliest homes were replaced by bigger houses when the city grew. By the early twentieth century, photographers were seeking out the few remaining older buildings as "picturesque." This elongated Cape Cod cottage stands on a spit of riverside land at the foot of Harward Street, although with its roof line now pierced by dormers and other trim added. Built by a man named Turner and sold to a Peterson in 1797, it was far enough north to escape most industrial development, but did overlook a shipyard in the 1850s.

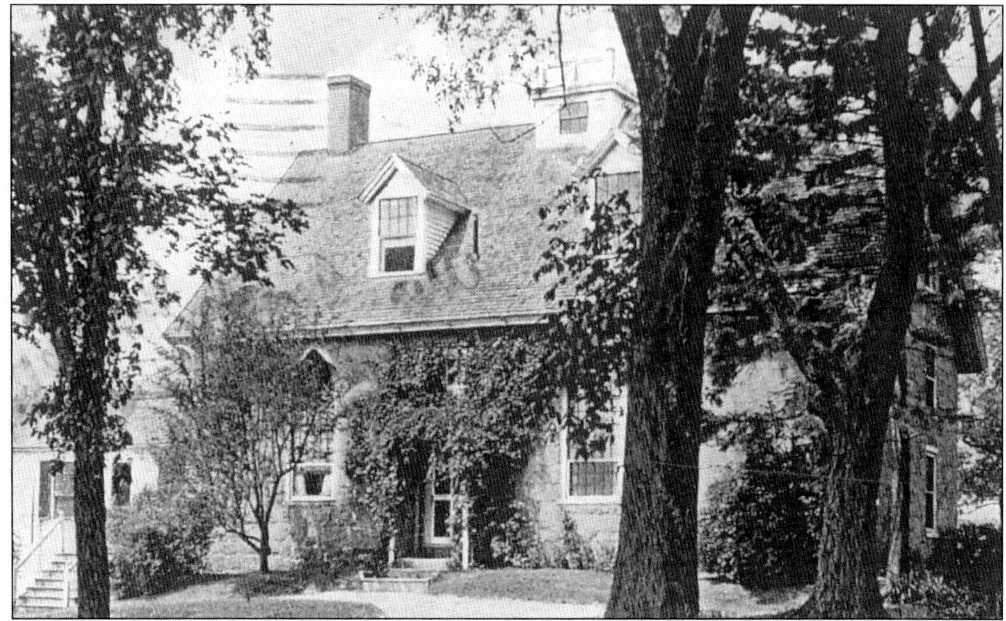

Stonehouse Farm. William King owned a farm in North Bath, purchased in 1808, in addition to his large home near his wharves. The farmhouse is unusual: built of stone, it had tall Gothic-arched windows decades before that style came back into fashion. It may have been built to the taste of an earlier owner.

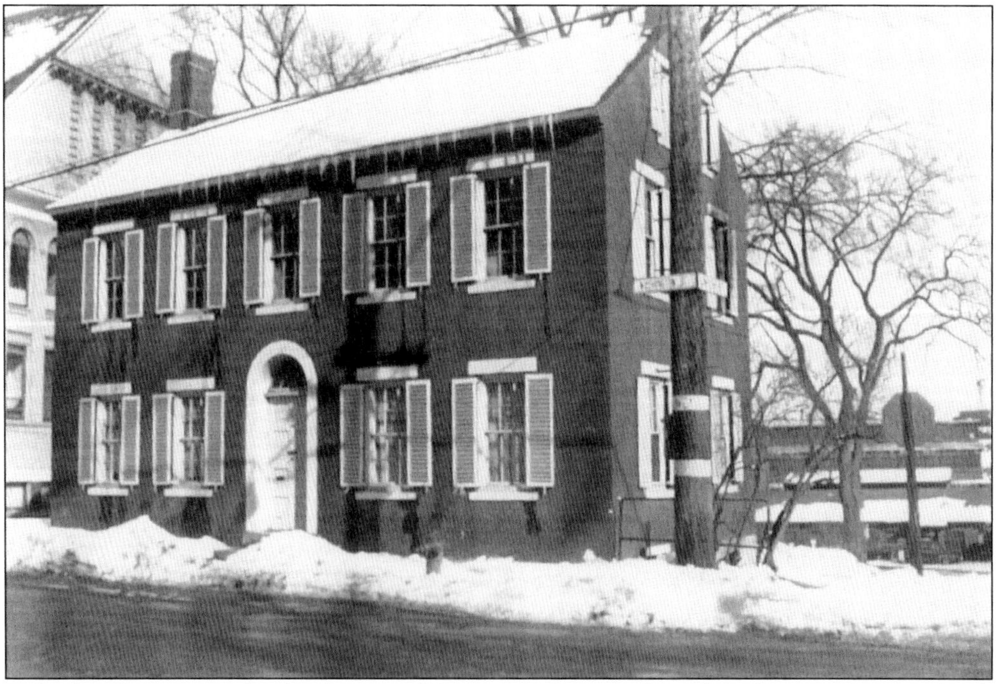

Federal style. Among the few houses of King's era that stood until fairly recently was a brick Federal at Washington and Union Streets. When Bath Iron Works (seen in the background) expanded to Washington Street, this house was one of those in the way.

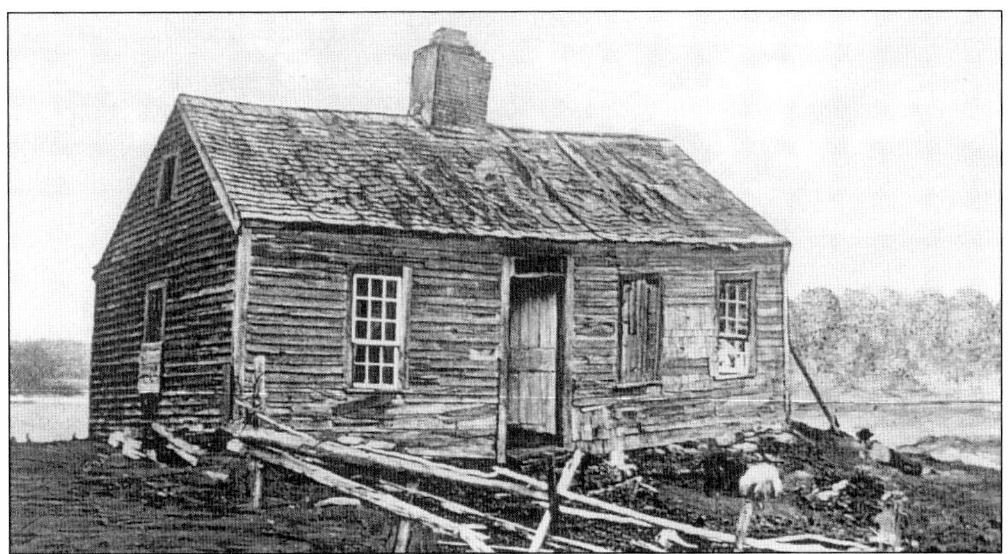

A hermitage. Whereas other homes won mention in early histories, this shack, depicted on postcards, did not. Neither poverty nor anti-social living is a matter of civic pride. Nevertheless, Mr. Michaels was remembered by neighbors for an act of kindness, albeit a possibly misguided one. In 1883, a man discovered in the act of burglary shot the policeman who made the discovery and fled. When the fugitive was finally apprehended in the woods of the North End, it appeared that "the hermit" had been providing him with food.

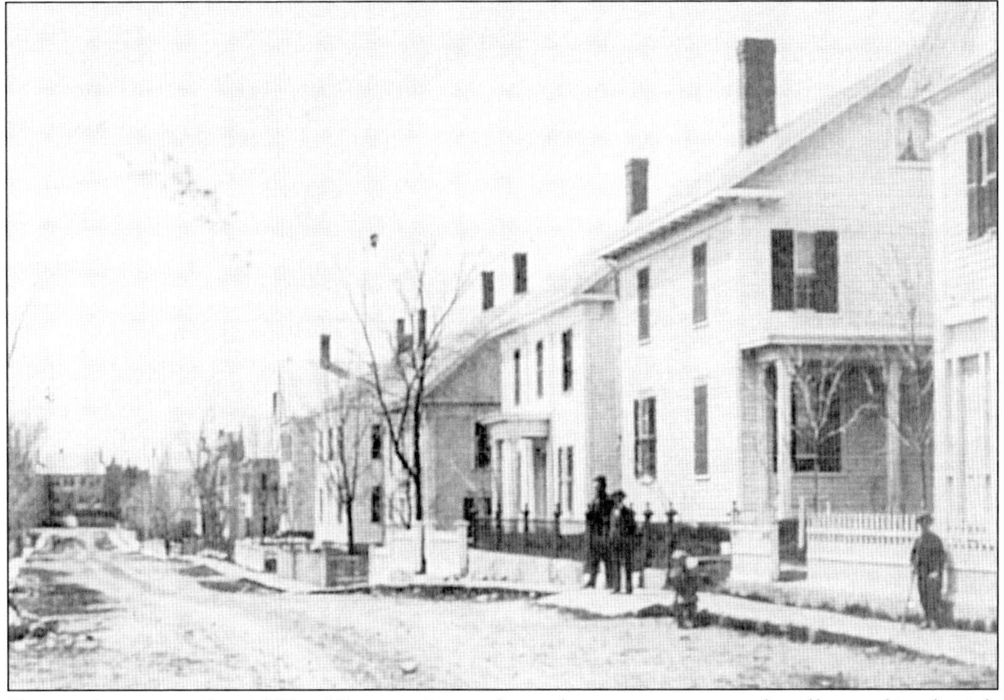

Green Street in the 1870s. The city's residential streets were, and still are, lined with solid, well-built houses, most dating to the mid and late-nineteenth century, when Bath's greatest growth occurred. This area has more vegetation today, but has otherwise changed little in appearance.

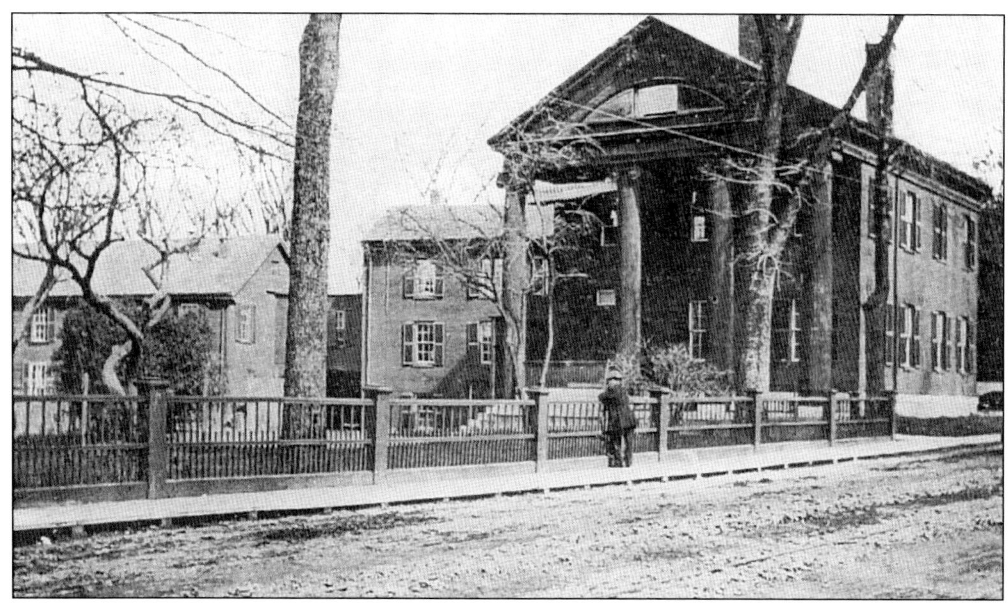

The McLellan residence. Fortunes produced by the expansion of shipping and shipbuilding were often displayed in housing. In 1841 J.H. McLellan had this brick version of a Greek temple (with numerous non-Greek characteristics) erected on Washington Street. It was later owned by C.W. Morse, and still later became a funeral home.

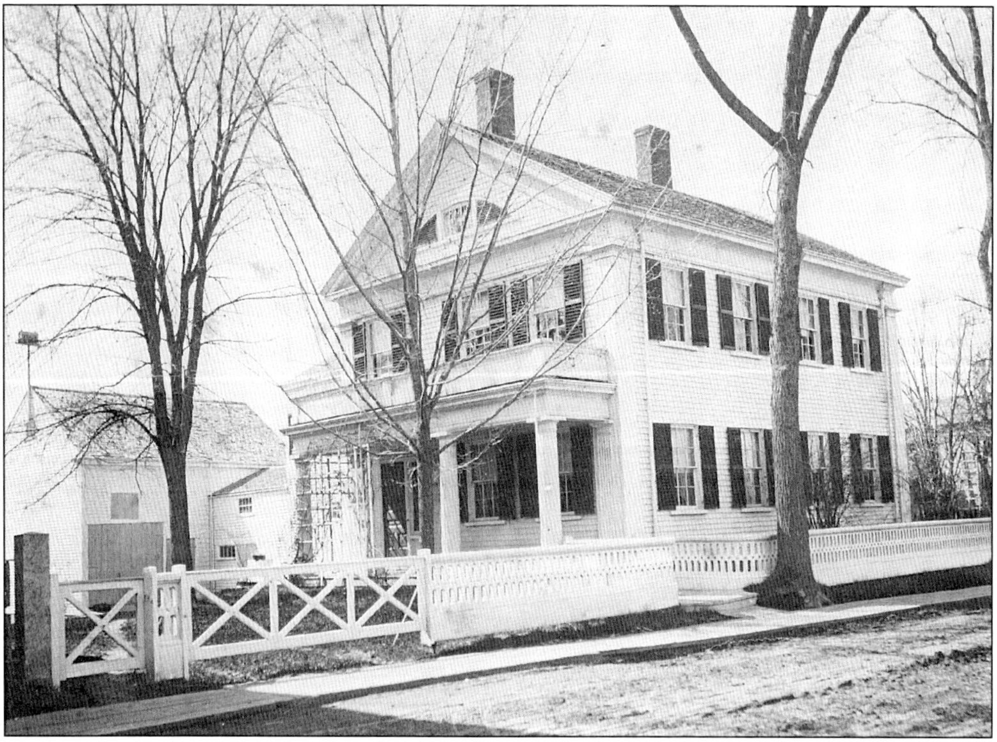

The Preble residence. Greek Revival-style architecture is especially well represented in the city. This house on Middle Street received a few alterations after this early photograph was made, but remains recognizable.

The Israel Putnam home. Another version of the Greek style on Washington Street was the home of Dr. Israel P. Putnam, who filled numerous roles in city government, including that of mayor. Note the atypical elliptical motif in the gable end of this and the two opposite homes. This house later became the home of the Cosmopolitan Club.

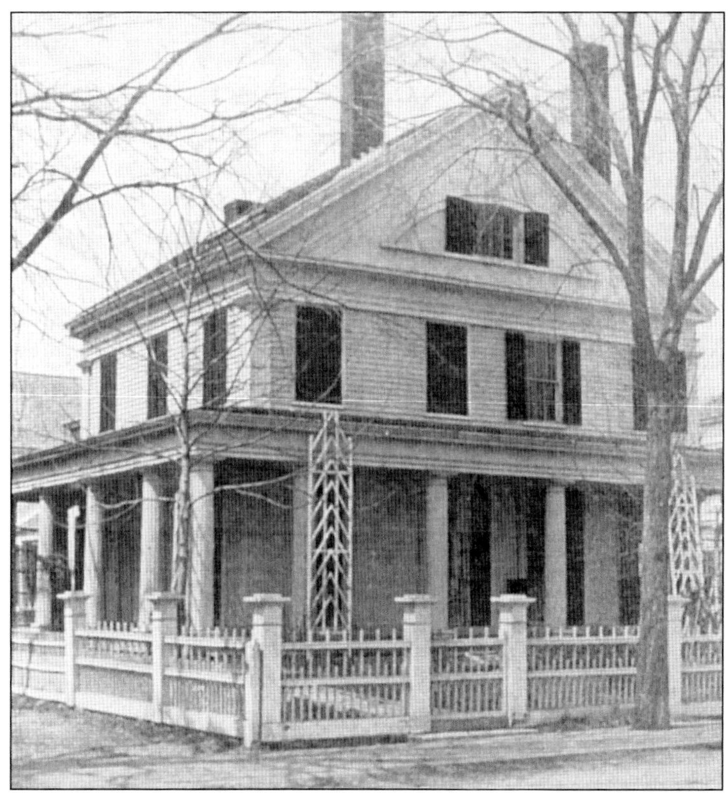

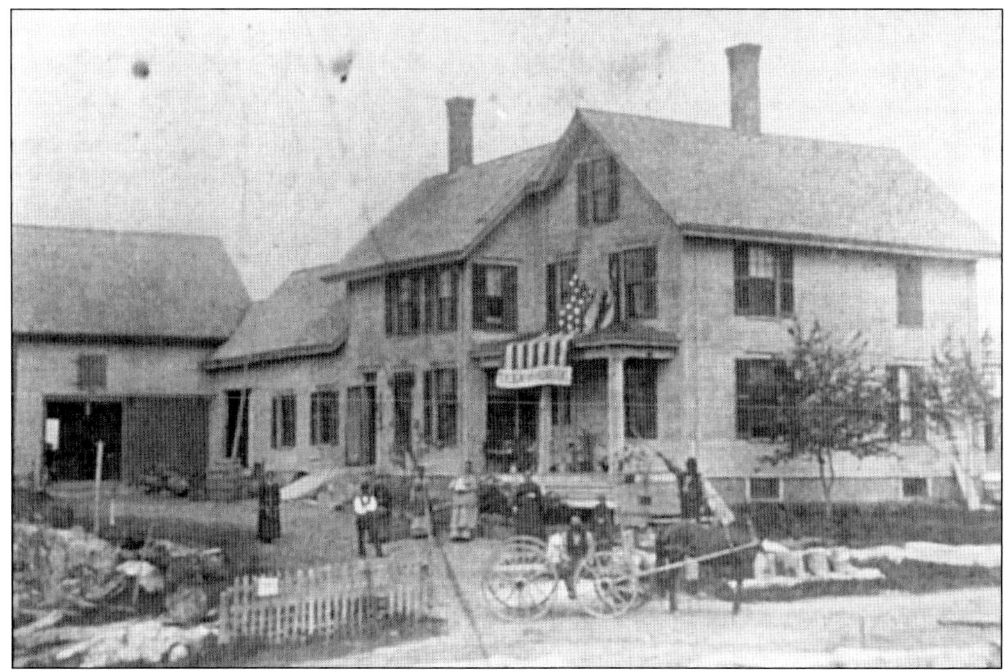

Tilden supporters. The majority of Bath's political leaders after 1860 were Republican, but Democrats were active, as evidenced by the Tilden banner draped on this front porch. Samuel Tilden nearly won the disputed Presidential election of 1876.

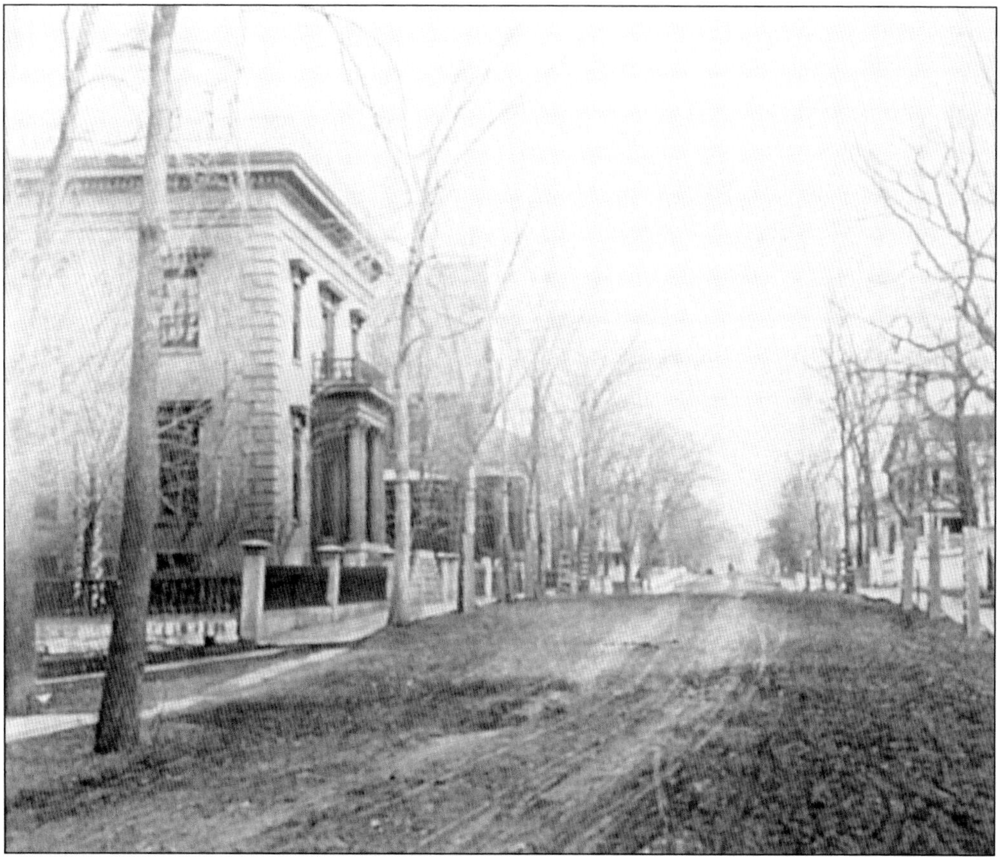

The James Drummond house. After the mid-nineteenth century, Bath acquired numerous square Italianate homes built of wood and brick, and often including a cupola. Drummond's brick house, built on Washington Street in 1852, gained an addition and was used as the Masonic Temple seventy years later.

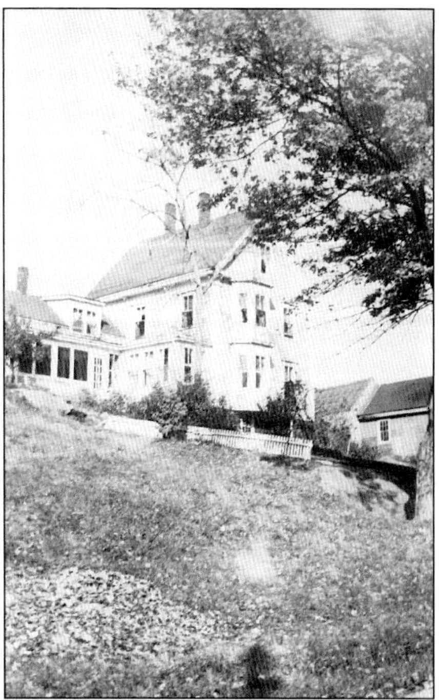

A farmhouse. Italianate features, like brackets and bay windows, were added to other basic shapes. This tall home in the North End was part of a farm overlooking the Kennebec River.

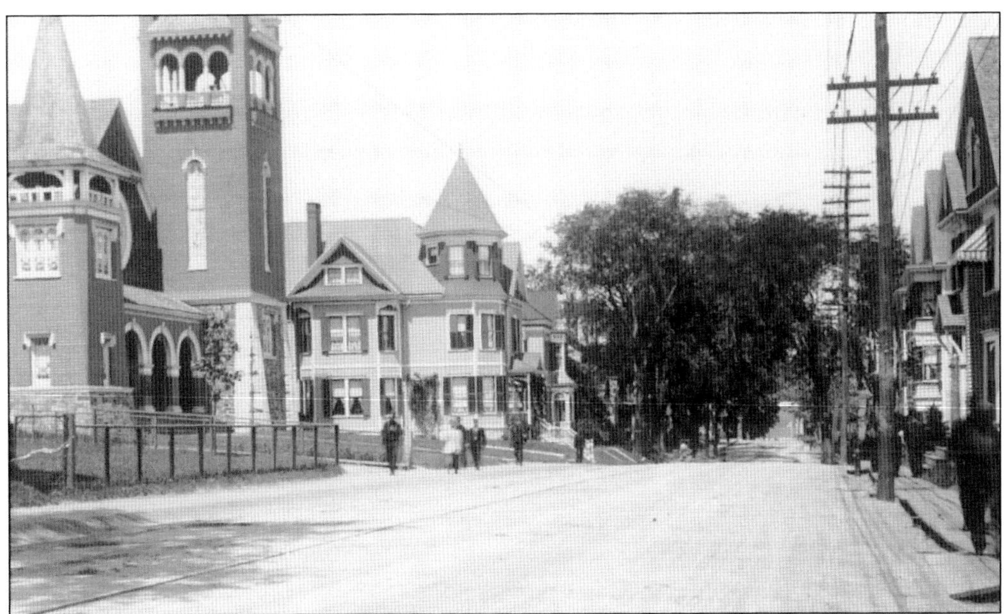

Queen Anne style. Later in the nineteenth century, the Queen Anne style added interesting house shapes, including towers, to the streetscapes. The building next to the onetime Methodist church has been altered, but still stands.

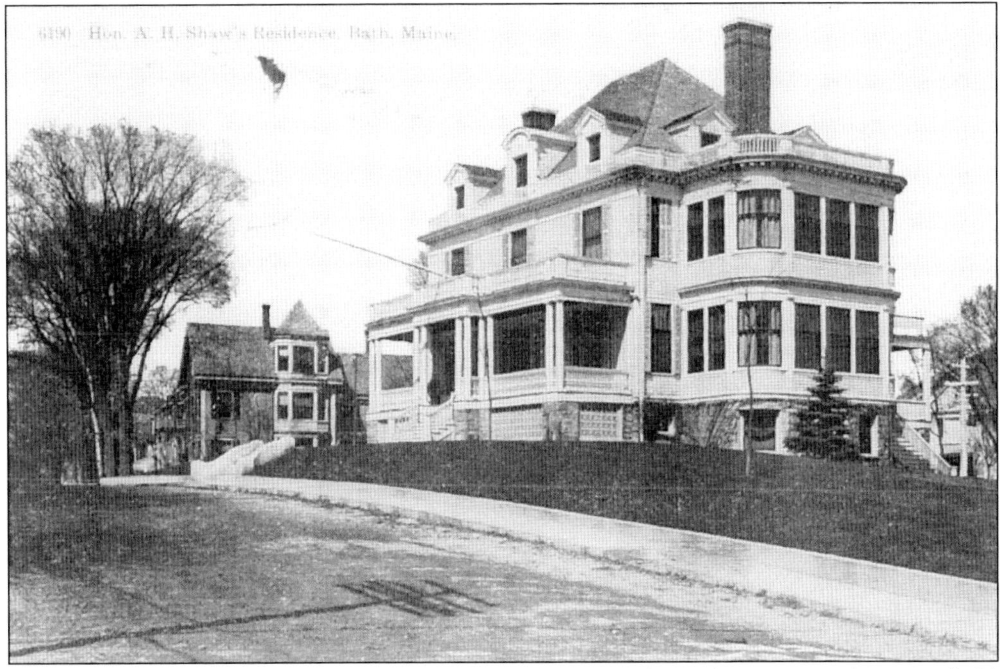

Neo-Colonial style. The "tower" added to the William Pendexter house on High Street (left) reflects a blending of Queen Anne and later ideas; but the extravagant dwelling on the corner of Center Street, built for lumber dealer and banker Albert H. Shaw in 1900, was primarily Neo-Colonial. In 1936, with the addition of a large ell to the rear, it became the Hotel Sedgewick—serving as a hotel until it burned in 1973. The concrete retaining wall challenged passing schoolchildren to walk its length.

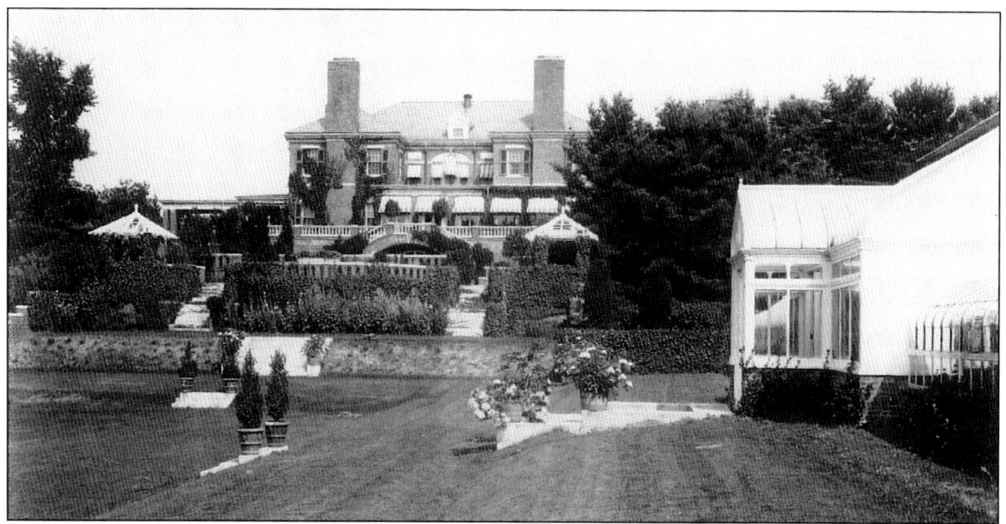

Elmhurst, 1914. This view from the formal garden of the house which John S. Hyde, president of Bath Iron Works, had Portland architect John Calvin Stevens design indicates that "Neo-Colonial" could look palatial. The site lent importance to a house which was only two stories in height (not counting the basement, which held a swimming pool). The conservatory at the right was only one of the outbuildings: the estate included a farm.

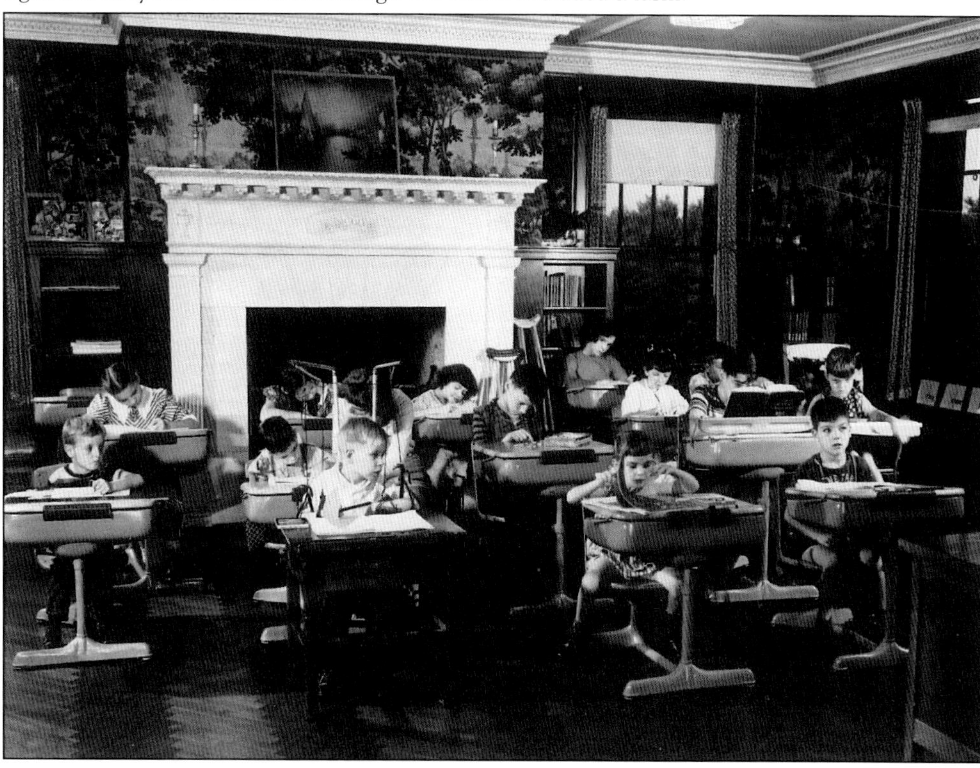

An interior view of Elmhurst, 1947. After Hyde heirs donated the property to the Pine Tree Society for Crippled Children and Adults, the once formal rooms served as classrooms. The desks, the fluorescent lights, and the small crutches fail to mask the elaborate woodwork and parquet floors.

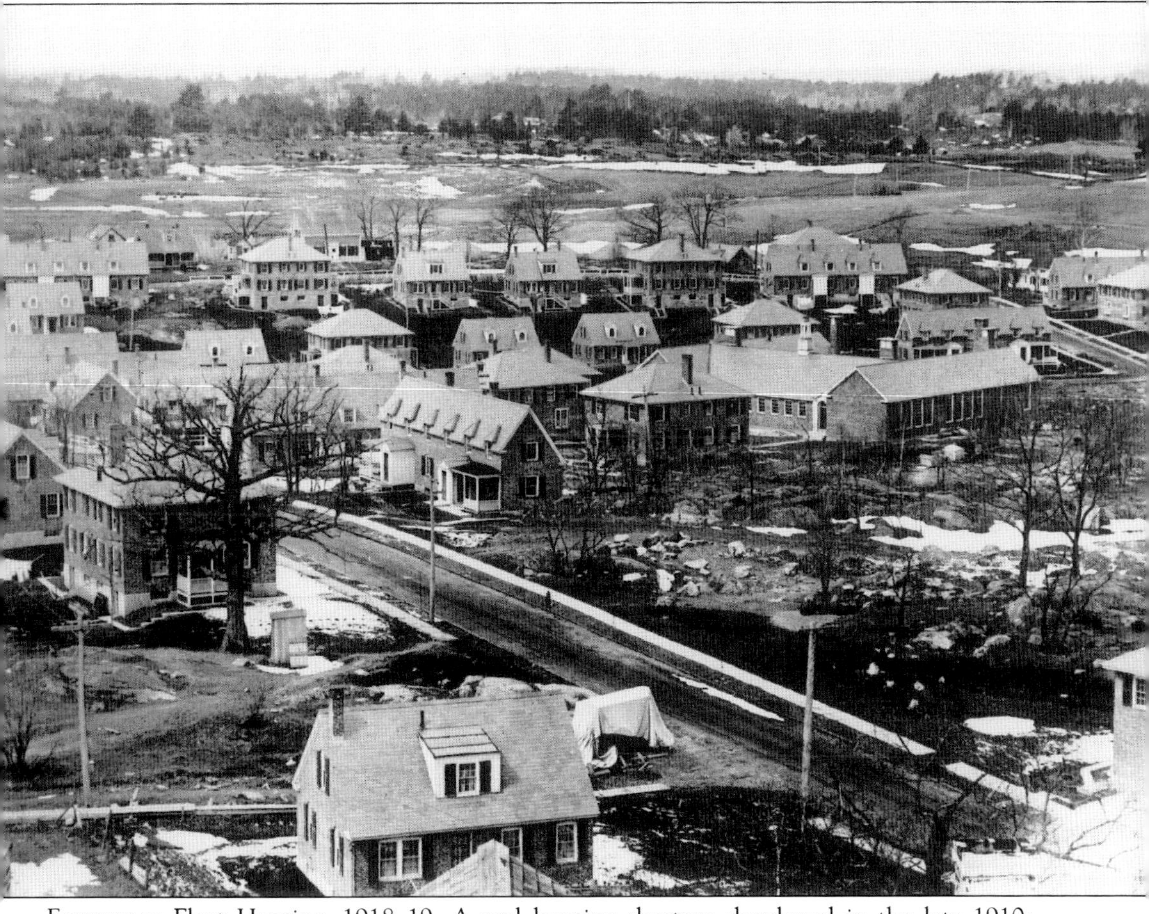

Emergency Fleet Housing, 1918–19. A real housing shortage developed in the late 1910s, when government contracts swelled the shipyards' work forces. Among other solutions was a development of brick rental houses, some singles and some duplexes, at the North End. A modern schoolhouse (Dike School) can be seen at the right center. Begun in the fall of 1918 by the Emergency Fleet Corporation, the houses, like the ships ordered after the declaration of war, were not completed before the Armistice. In the 1920s the development was considered a "white elephant" and sold into private hands. Eventually the homes became resident-owned.

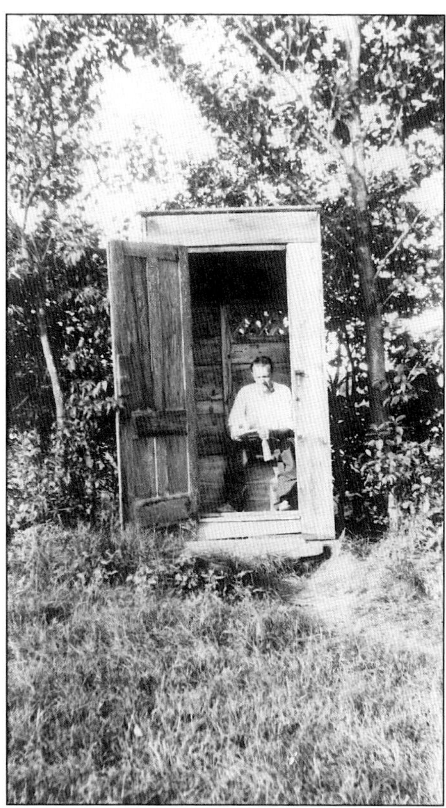

An outhouse in the 1940s. After city sewers were laid in the early twentieth century, even inexpensive in-town housing was built with indoor plumbing. In more rural areas, earlier facilities remained in use, as indicated by this obviously posed snapshot from a North End family album.

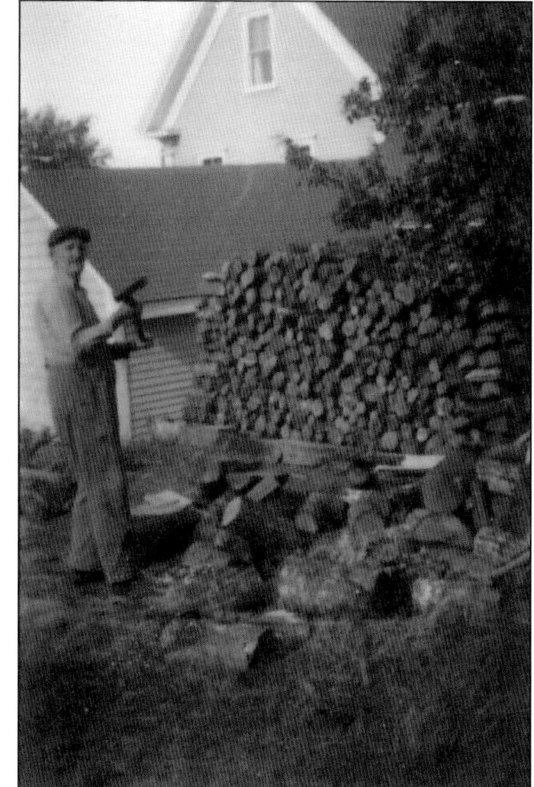

Woodchopping, c. 1944. Bath imported so much coal that a section of its waterfront was dubbed the "coal pocket," but those who had it available still burned wood. Oscar Trott of the North End is shown here splitting sawn lengths into firewood.

Three

Religious Establishments

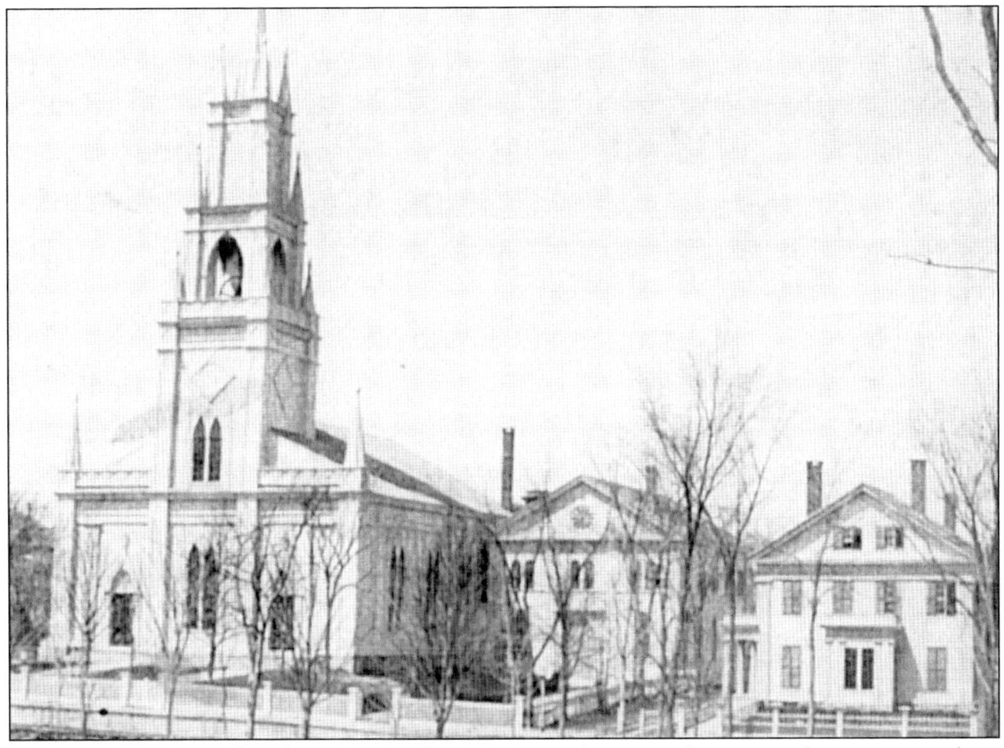

The Winter Street Church. An area of growing population with new residents arriving from diverse backgrounds might be expected to produce both variety and conflict in religious ideas; and so it was in Bath. Not only were new sects formed, but older ones splintered, producing a large number of religious edifices. In the early 1840s the Congregationalists were unable to agree on doctrine. One part of the congregation then proceeded to erect a new building on Winter and Washington Streets in 1843. The work of local builder Anthony Raymond, the Winter Street Church combined the basic shape and light color of a Greek Revival building with numerous Gothic Revival details. When the congregations reunited and relocated in the 1970s, this building became the home of the Sagadahoc Preservation Society.

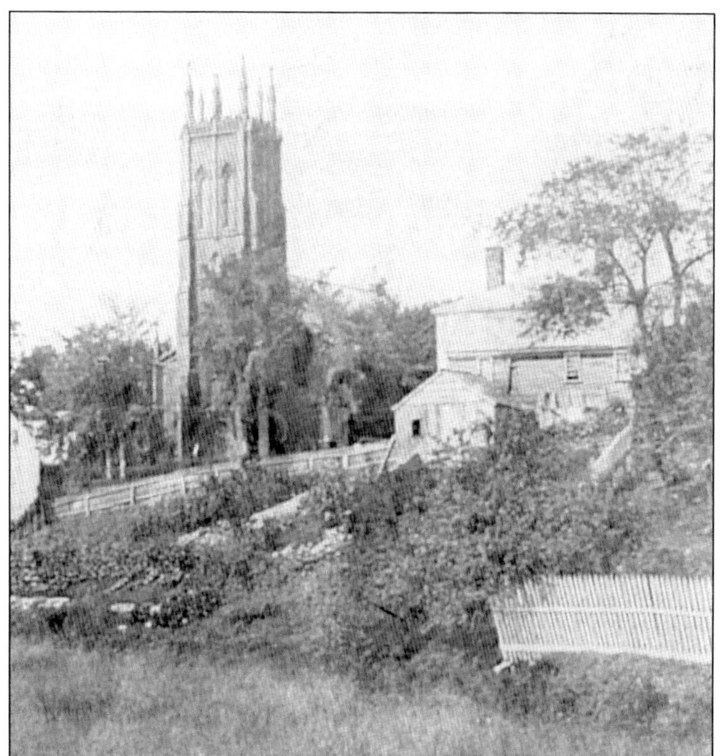

The Central Church facade in the 1870s. This church, more wholeheartedly Gothic in concept than the Winter Street Church, was erected in 1847 by the dissidents and located a block and a half away, also on Washington Street. Designed by Arthur Gilman, it had a tall spire atop the tower until 1861. The front could be seen from the inlet at Water Street.

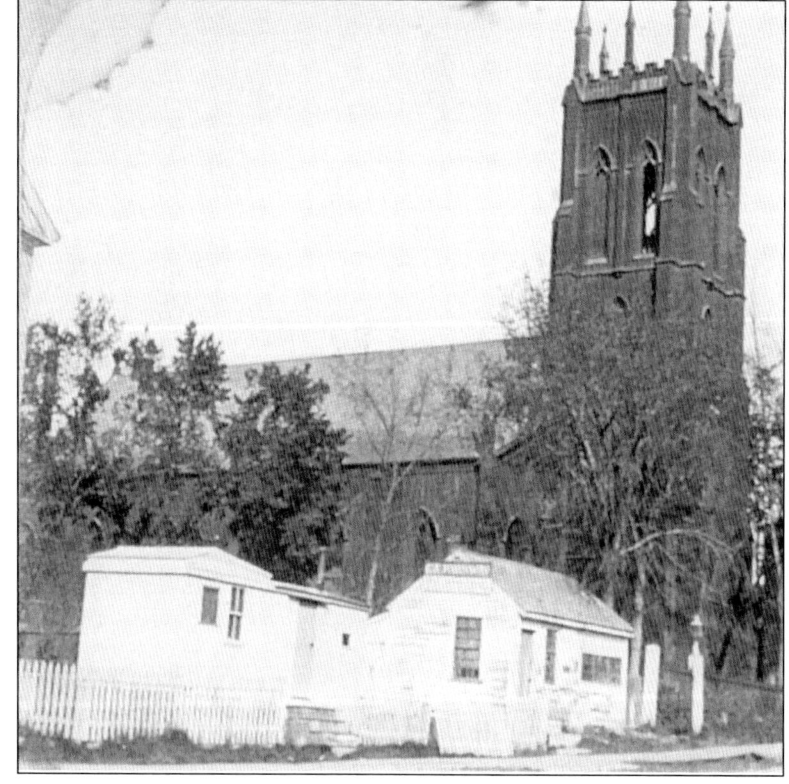

The Central Church and a paint shop. The dark paint on the Central Church was very much in keeping with its Gothic styling. Even without the spire, its soaring lines presented a real contrast with the low paint shop of C.R. Johnson next door. In the 1970s the church building became a performing arts center.

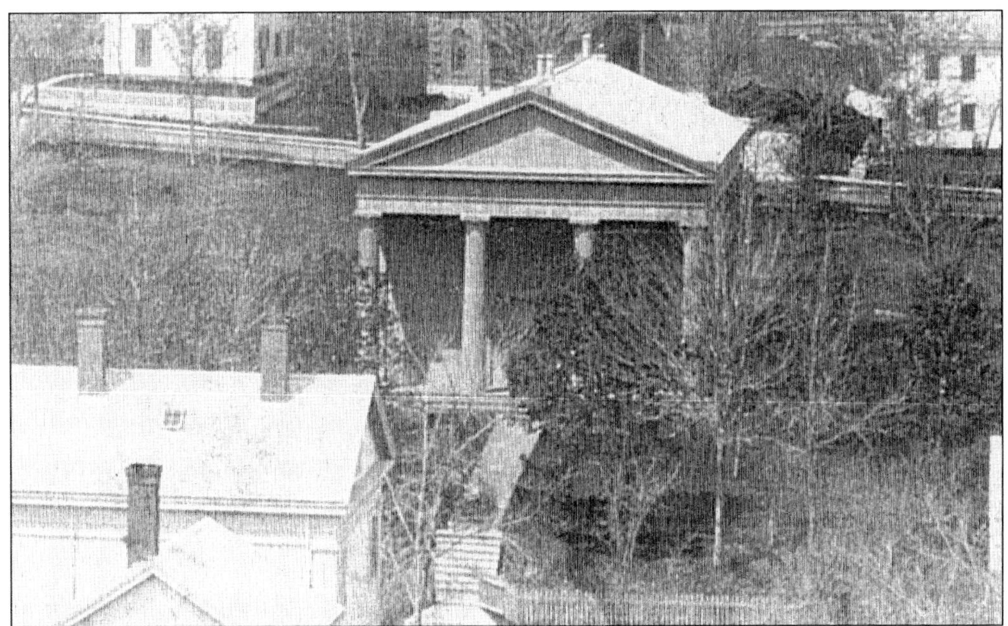

The Church of the New Jerusalem. A few local individuals had been interested in the writings of Emmanuel Swedenborg for decades before a church was organized. They erected Bath's most temple-like church building on Middle Street in 1843. Although parts had to be rebuilt after damage from heavy snow in 1922, it retains its classic form.

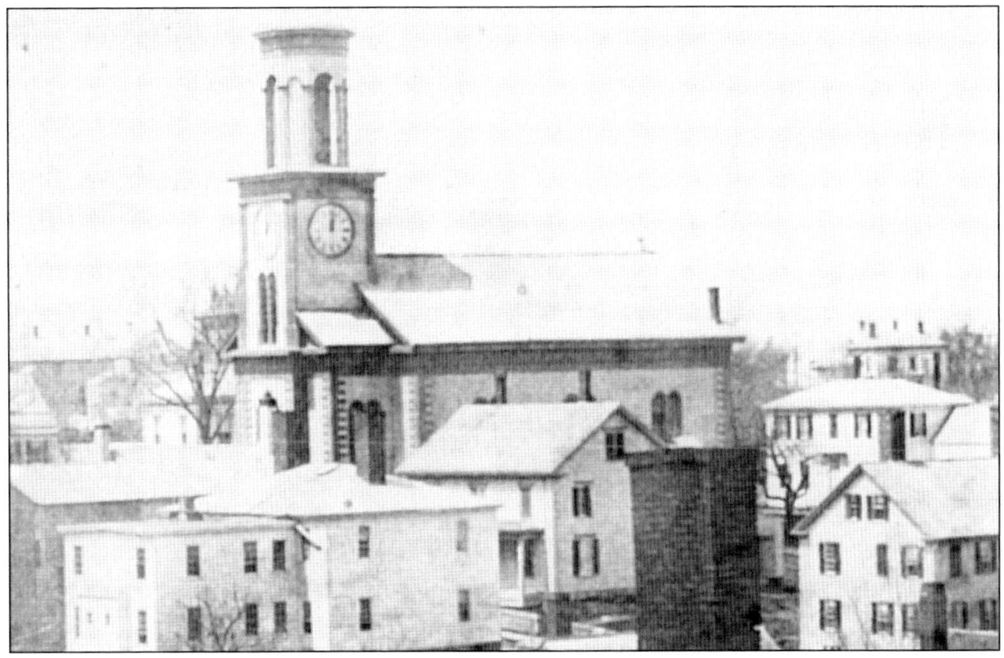

The Elm Street Baptist Church. The first Baptist church in town was built on Elm Street in 1816, then was replaced on its lot by this larger building in 1853. In 1855 a new town clock was installed in its tower. Setting the clock became a problem after the U.S. adopted standard time in 1884, as Bath operated on "sun time," about a half hour earlier than the "standard." Permanent resetting to the new time came only in 1891.

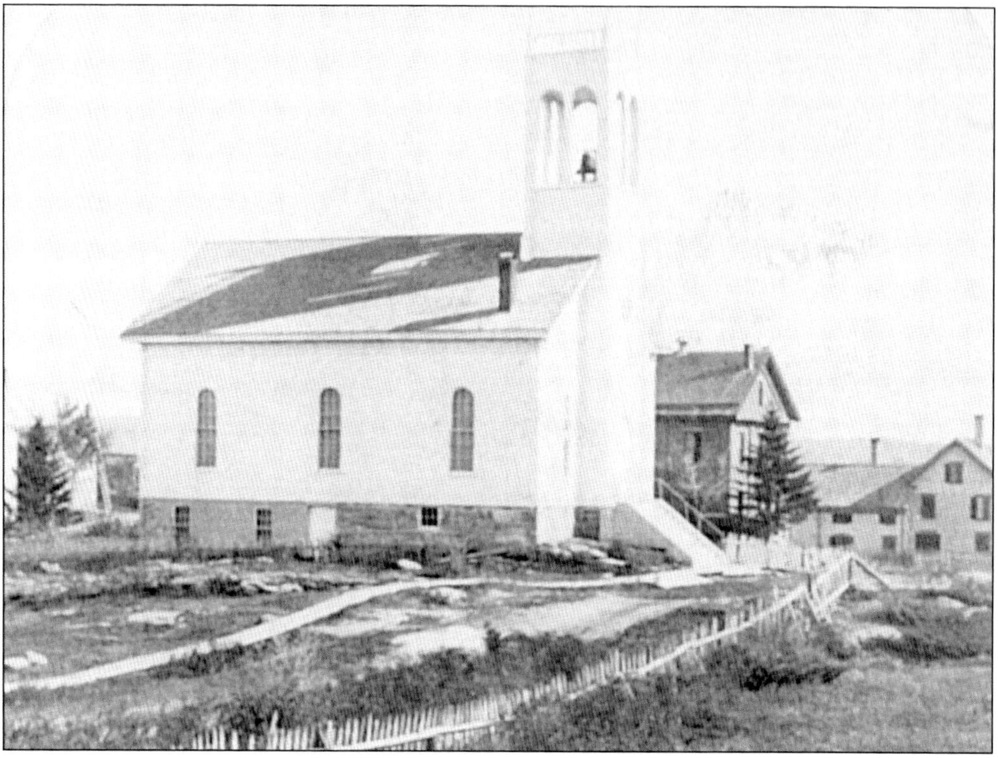

The Corliss Street Free Baptist Church. The name was misleading, as the church was erected on Weeks Street in 1868, next door to the Weeks Street Grammar School, which was built thirteen years earlier. The church entry was relocated to a new tower on its east side in 1908.

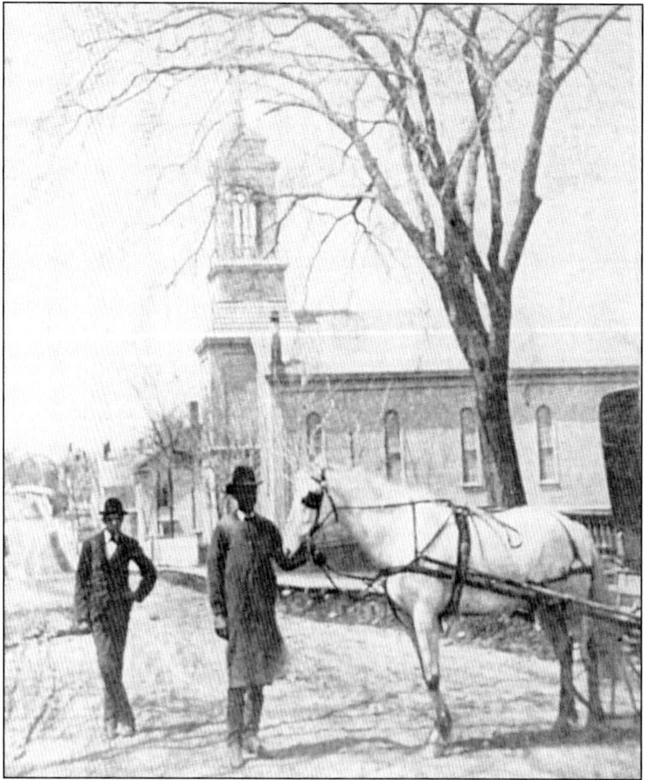

The North Street Freewill Baptist Church. Erected in 1869–70 to replace an earlier structure damaged by wind, it served that congregation for five decades, then was sold to Christian Scientists in 1922. It was later replaced by a new edifice.

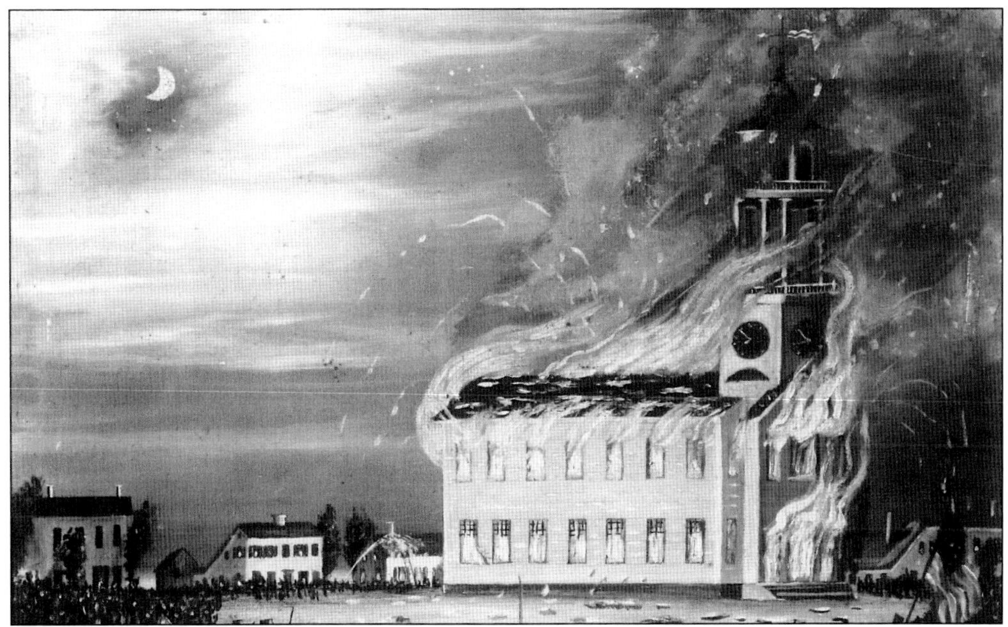
The burning of the South Church, 1854. The leasing of the unused South Church by Roman Catholics in 1853 led to one of the state's most violent examples of the bigotry and anti-Catholicism fostered by the "Know-Nothing" political party. The building (which then held the town clock) was attacked and burned. This is one of a pair of paintings made soon afterward.

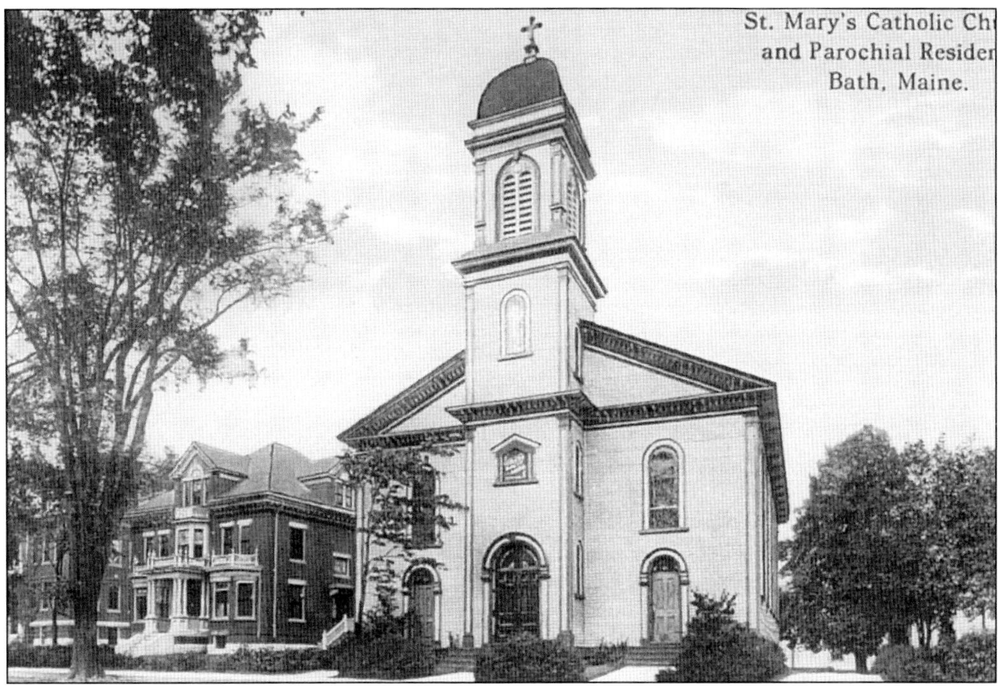

St. Mary's Catholic Church. Erected in 1855–56, the building was purchased by the city and razed to allow an expansion of the high school after a new church was constructed elsewhere in 1968.

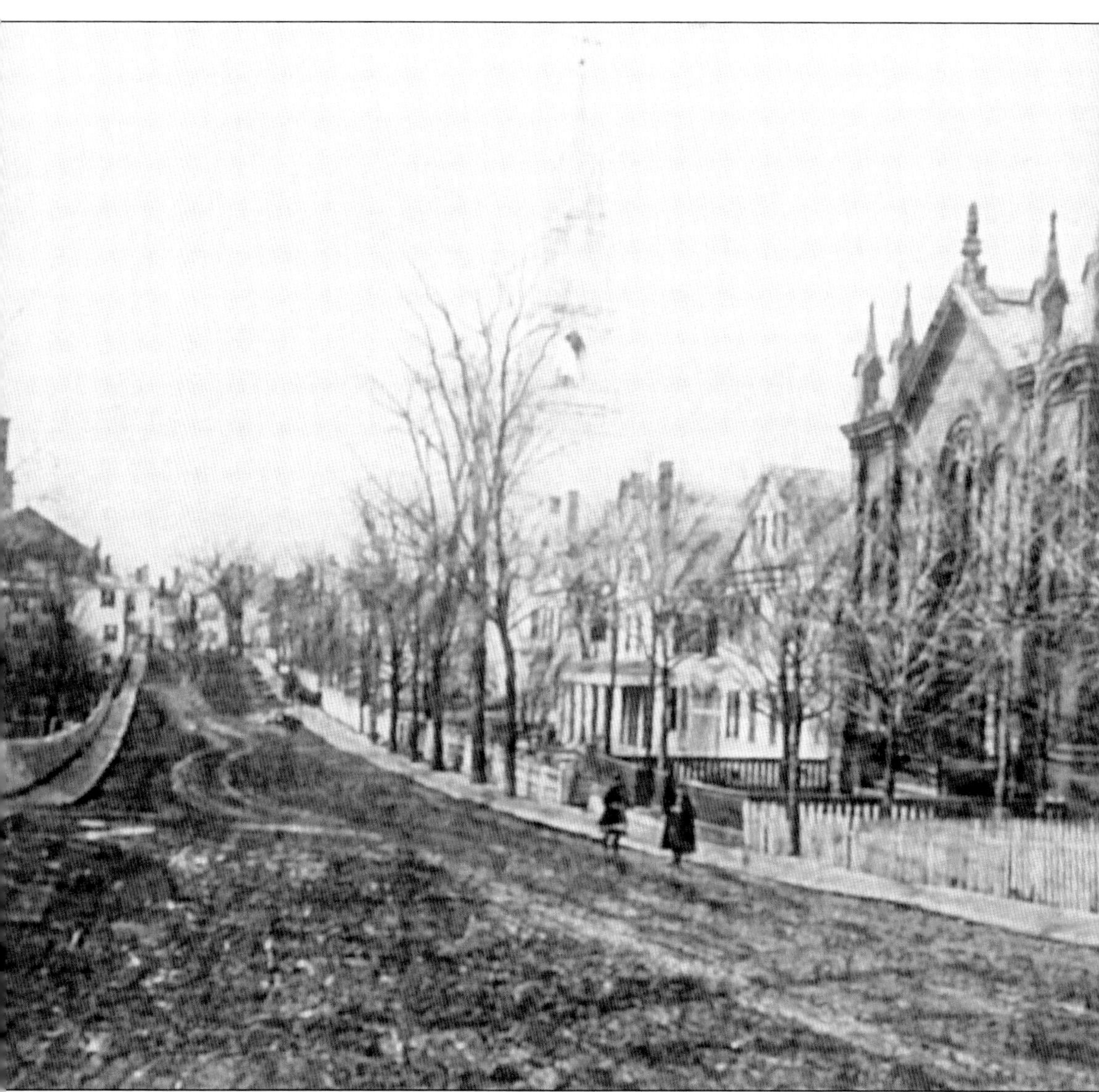

The Second Universalist Church. When Universalists sold their church on Front Street in 1860, they moved to what had been Corinthian Hall, the former home of the Bath Elocution Society. The Washington Street building was remodeled to be the Universalist church, and stood until removed to make way for a modern structure in 1963. To its left, the Elm Street and Winter Street Churches can be seen.

The old Wesley Methodist Church. This church stood at Wesley and Washington Streets from 1869 to 1898. The huge edifice was designed by a Bath native, Francis Fassett, who by then had his office in Portland.

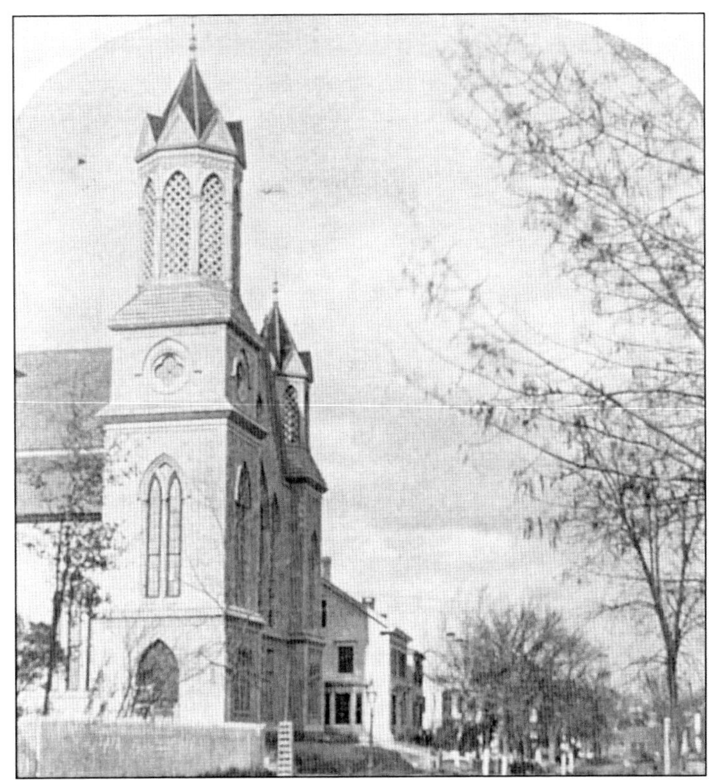

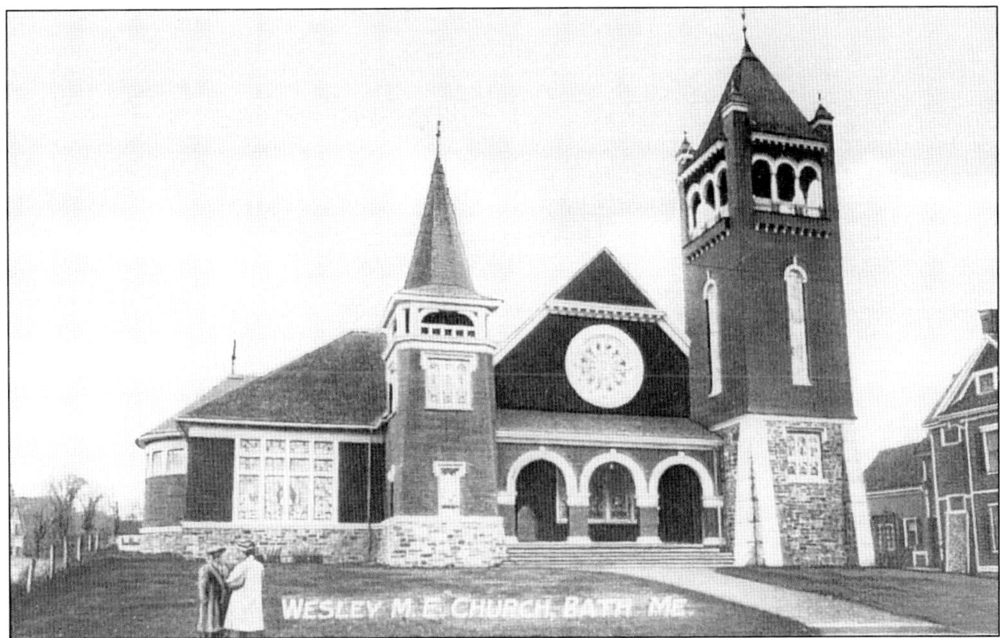

The new Wesley Methodist Church. After the older Methodist building burned, along with much of its neighborhood, it was replaced in 1898 by this structure, which still stands on the site, although no longer a church.

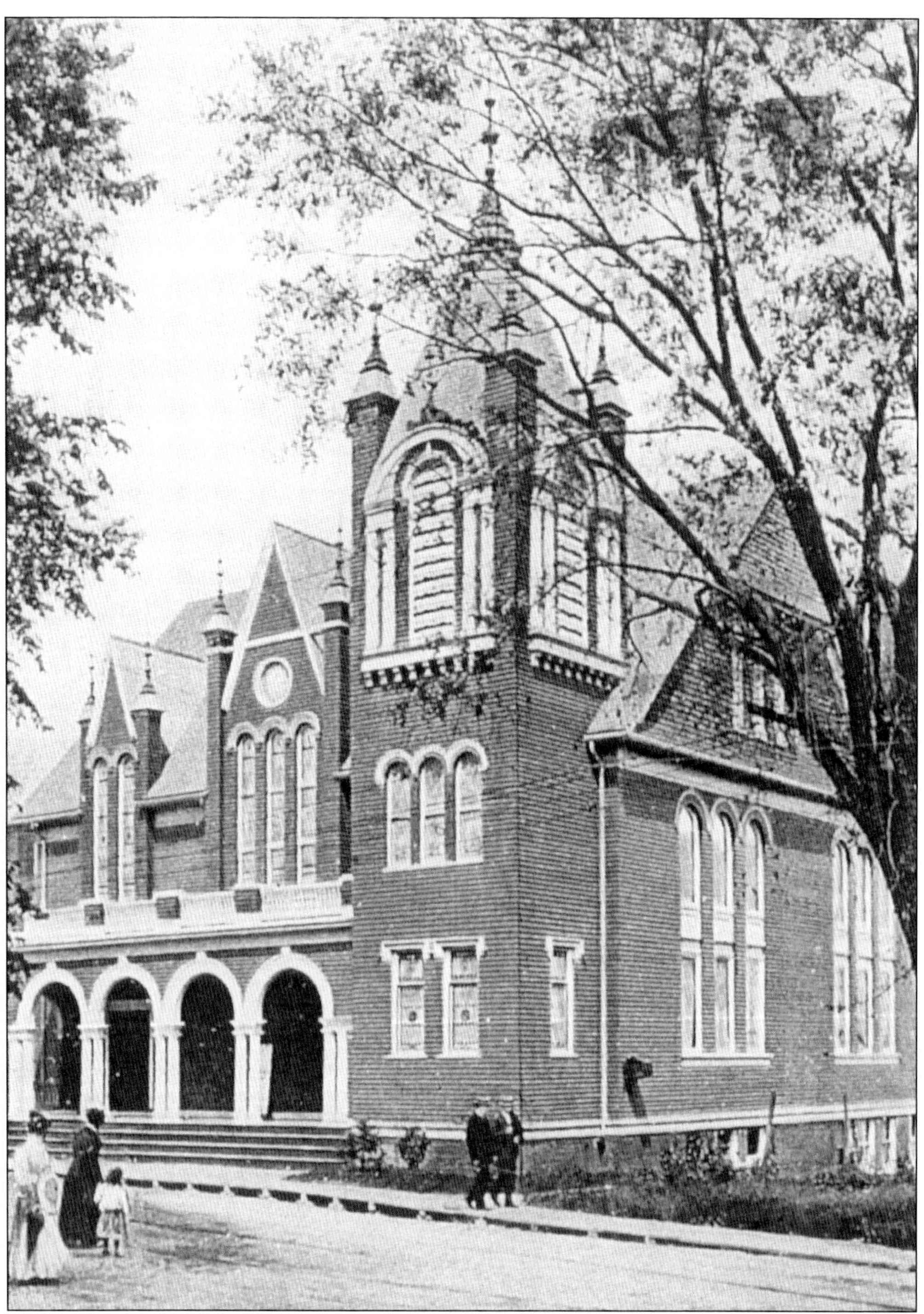

The People's Church. A series of revival meetings and the resulting conversions in the late 1890s led to the formation of the People's Church and the construction of yet another Washington Street religious structure. After the congregation disbanded, the building served as a recreation hall for BIW workers before being razed for a parking lot in 1960.

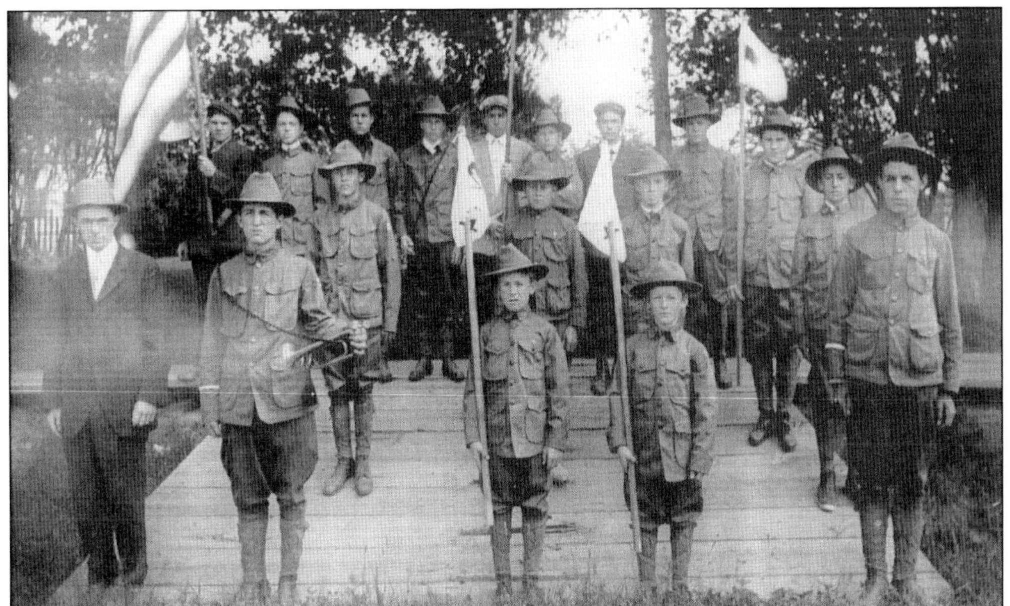

The Corliss Street Church Boy Scouts, May 30, 1911. Open to the neighborhood boys who attended the Baptist Sunday School, this active association encouraged participation in a variety of sports, as well as camping. From left to right are: (front row) Carrol Deering, Bill Tanguay, ? Oliver, ? Oliver, and Stanwood Cutting; (middle row) Laton Jackson, Walter Elliott, Les Robbins, and ? Blackwood; (back row) unknown, Carl Albee, ? Ingraham, Reggie Stacy, Howard Deering, John Coombs, ? Rines, Lee Sheldon, and Carrol Davis.

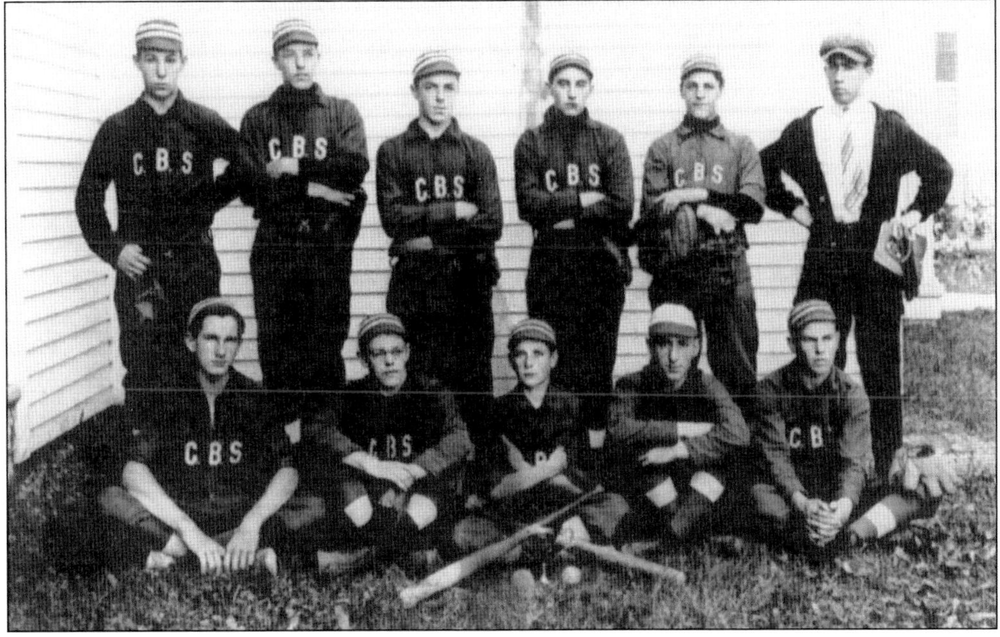

The Corliss Street Church Boy Scouts' baseball team, 1915. From left to right are: (front row) Bernard Snowden, Bennie Murray, Harold Fielding (the bat boy), Thatcher Pinkham, and Bernard Knights; (back row) Arthur Bowker, Laton Jackson, Brim Jewett, Parker Reed, Lee Sheridan, and Walter Knights (manager).

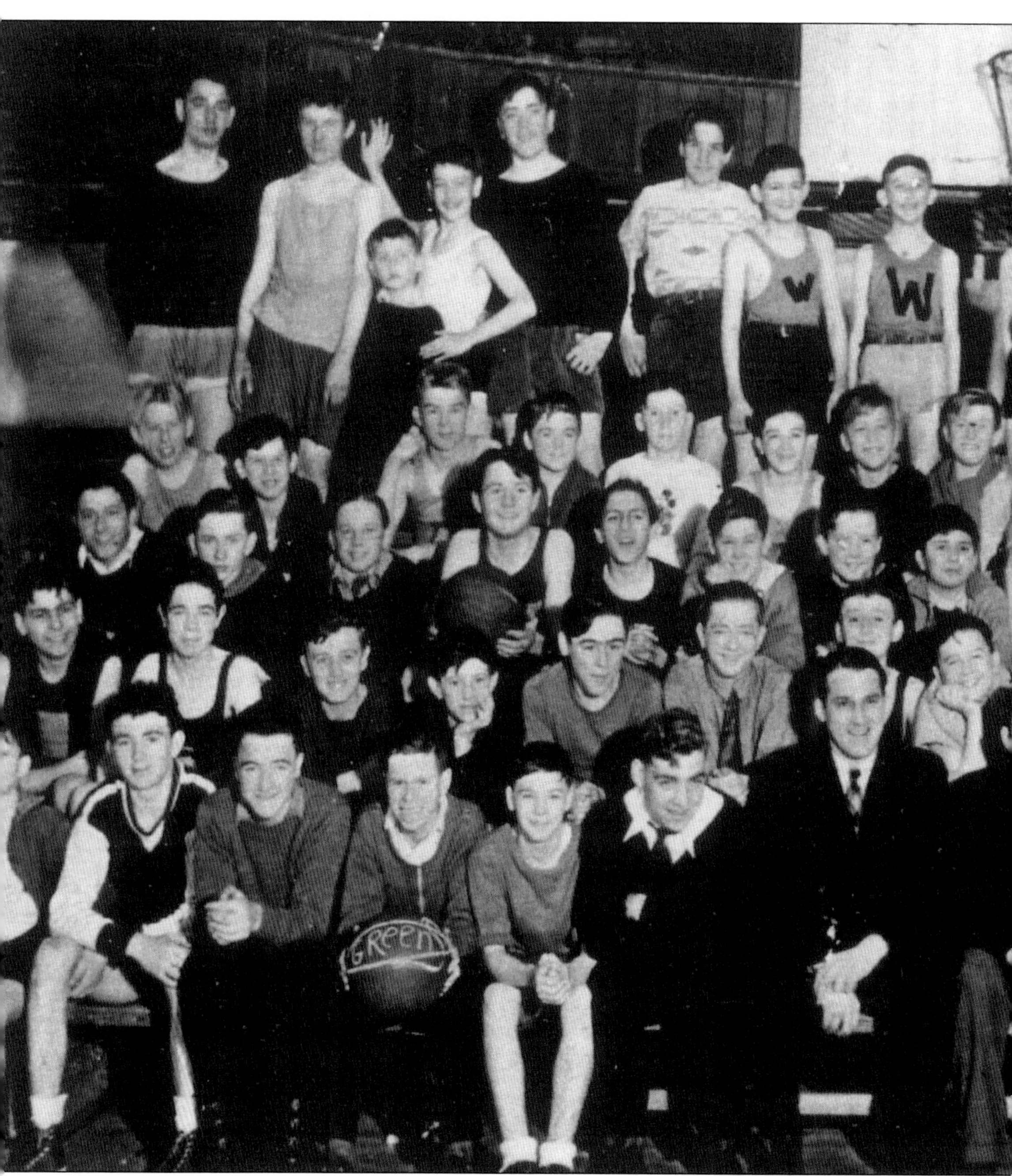

The YMCA Grammar School League of 1934–35. Organized activities for youth could also be found at the "Y." This photograph includes both players and supporters. From left to right are: (front row) ? Sutherland, Clyde Stilphin, Dave Cavanaugh, Jim Ourie, unknown, ? Stover, "Big Daddy" Bill Perkins, Ray Small, ? Footer, Edward Hogan, unknown, Henry Gallant, "Shrimp" Arsenault, Dickie Cummings, Frank Curran, Jim Skaling, and "Cappy" Neale; (second row) Harold McMahon, Ernest Prest, Larry Boardman, unknown, Ed Stilphin, Bob Lee, Emerson Webster, Jim Morse, unknown, Jerry Desmond, Wesley Plummer, Morton Holbrook, Winnie Stilphin, unknown, Maurice Glidden, unknown, and Harry Thayer; (third row) Epie Johns,

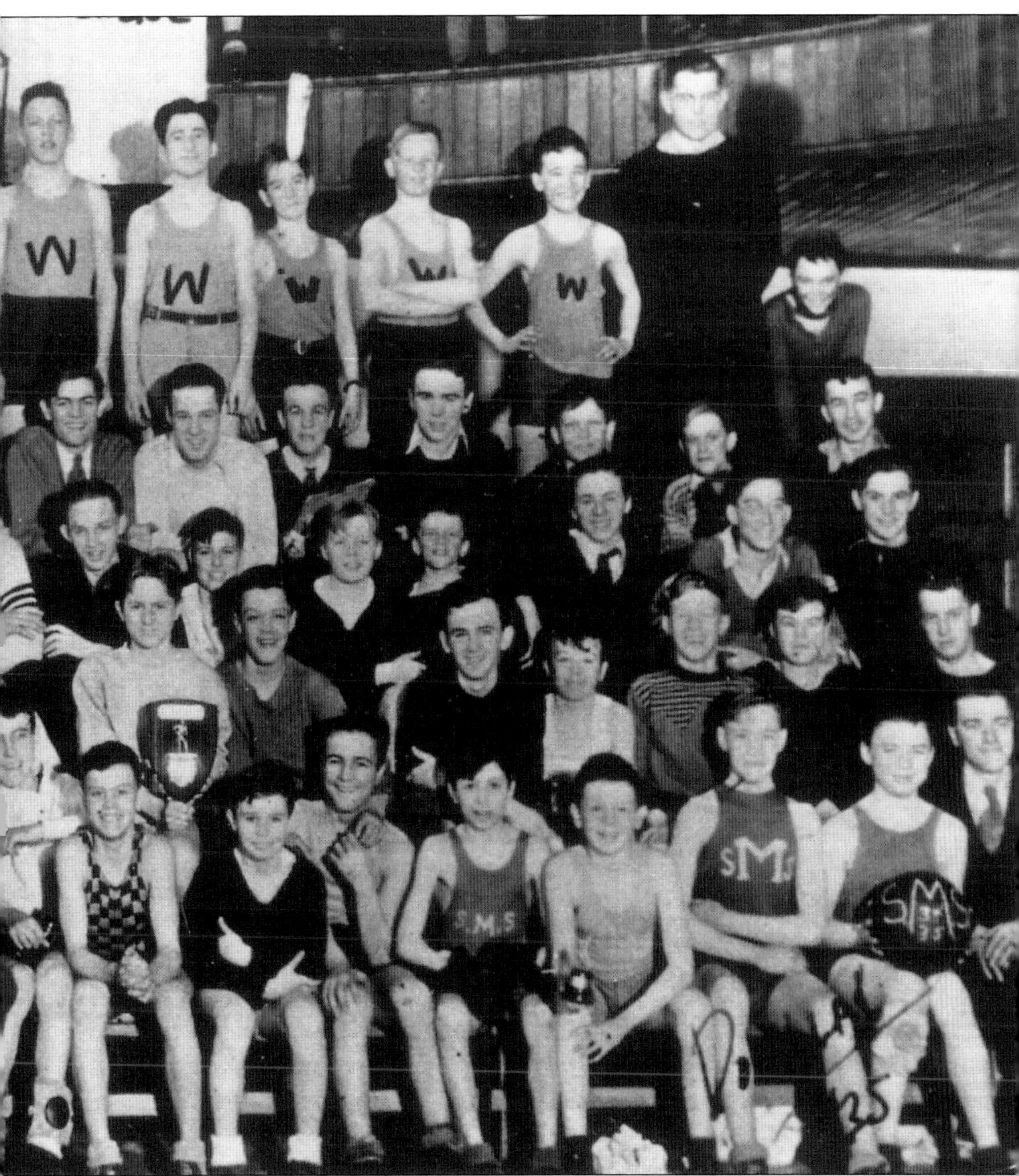

John McLaughlin, Henry Middleton, Larry Curtis, John Mary, Eddie McCabe, Earle Brown, Norman Alkyzin, Phil Oliver, Ed Atkinson, Norm Seekins, unknown, "Flea" Pomerleau, Herb Clossen, Francis Storer, and Peter McVicar; (fourth row) Ardenne McFadden, unknown, Maurice Puffer, unknown, unknown, unknown, unknown, unknown, Hank Gally, T. Robbins, Fred Hamlin, Manley Ellis, Maurice Skaling, Robert Sutherland, Warren Hogan, and "Turkey" Rideout; (top row) Art Warner, Harpo Staples, Clarence Warner, Merritt Scott, Ernie Brown, John Kakos, George Wilson, ? Staples, Jim Knight, Freland King, Everett Comeau, Don Knight, John Borque, Monty Eaton, and Jimmy Pero.

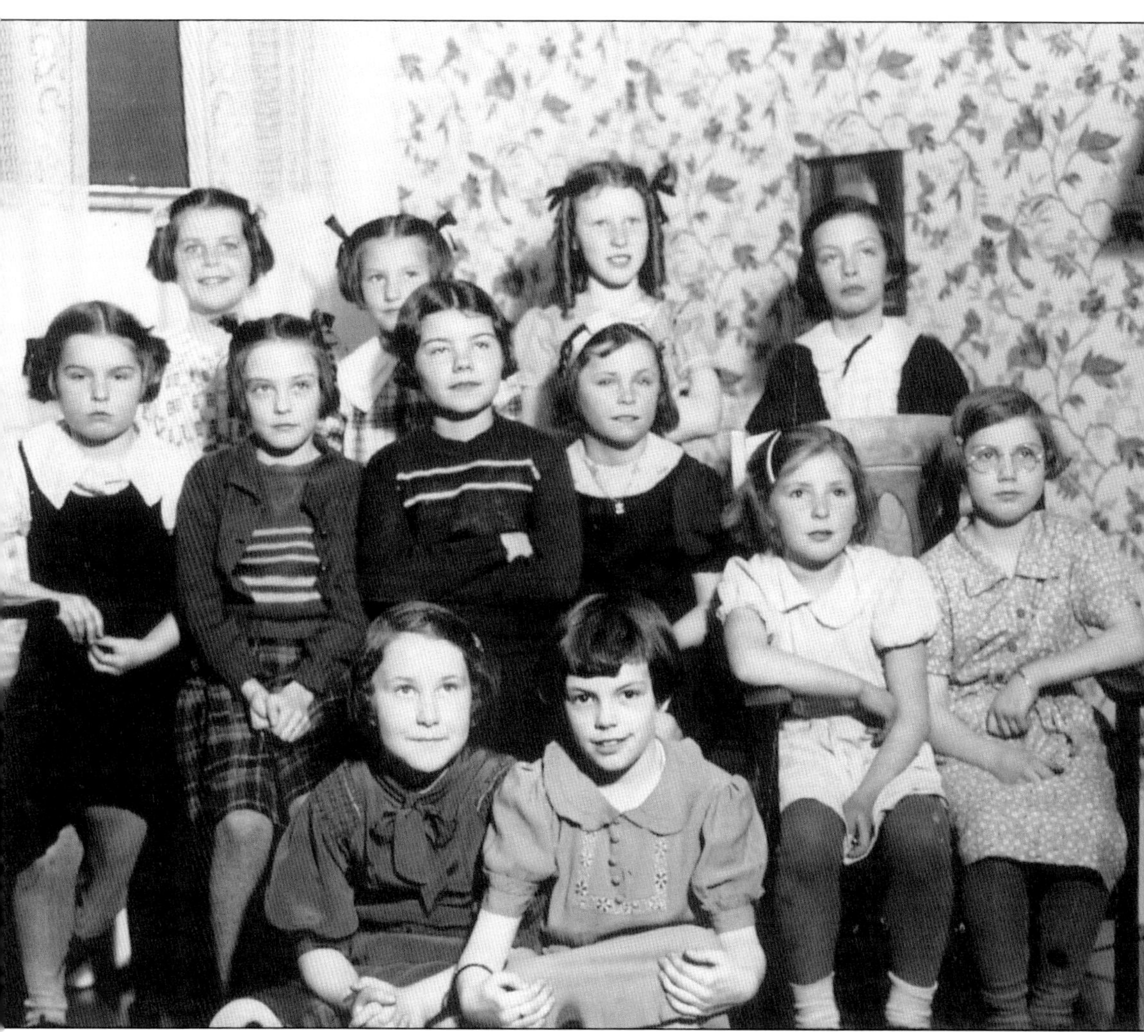

The Kandoo Club, 1937. This club, associated with a Sunday school class at the Beacon Street Methodist Church, included, from left to right: (front row) Helen Plummer and Barbara Pressey; (middle row) Velma Rogers, Carolyn St. Martin, Marilyn Hart, Doris Belanger, Laura Hauser, and Eunice Doughty; (back row) Kathleen Clark, Nola Belanger, Barbara Banforth, and Valerie Nickerson.

Four

LUMBER AND SHIPBUILDING

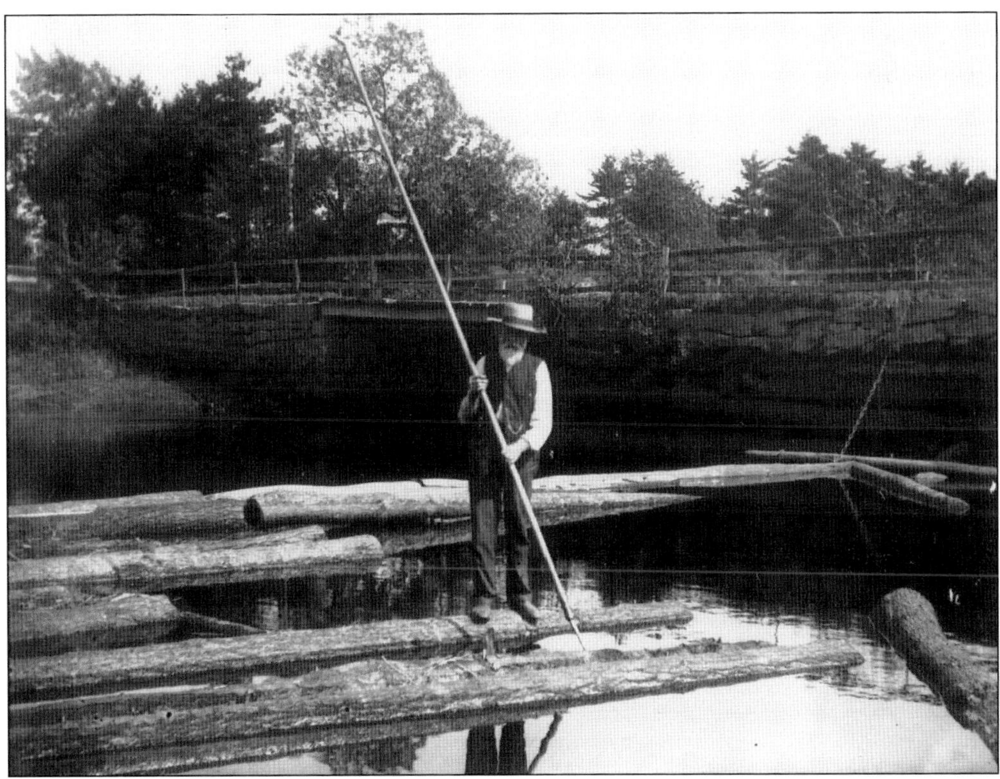

Logs on the millpond. Lumbering was one of the earliest industries to develop in Maine, and the Bath area usually had at least one mill. The availability of timbers helped contribute to the development of Bath as a center of shipping. The Rogers Mill was built in the nineteenth century on the site of the 1764 sawmill built by Dummer Sewall at Whiskeag Stream, in the north part of town. Mr. Rogers is shown here lining up logs.

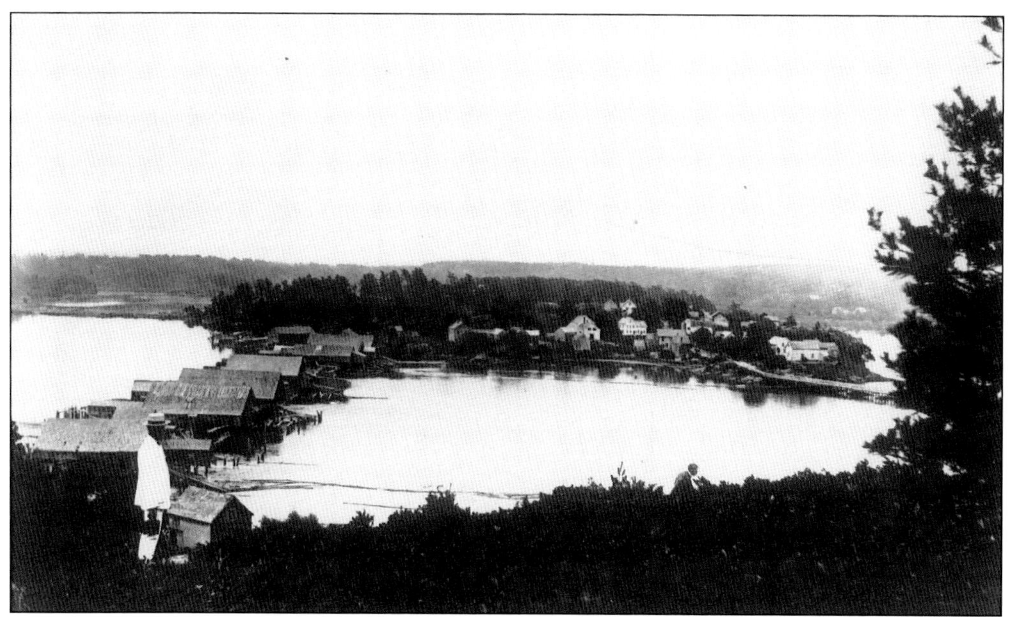

The tide mills at Winnegance. Because the Whiskeag was the only sizeable stream in the area, would-be mill operators had to harness other types of power. On the southern edge of Bath, at the area called Winnegance, a tidal inlet was utilized. The row of mills on the left made use of the flow of the tides until replaced by steam-powered equipment.

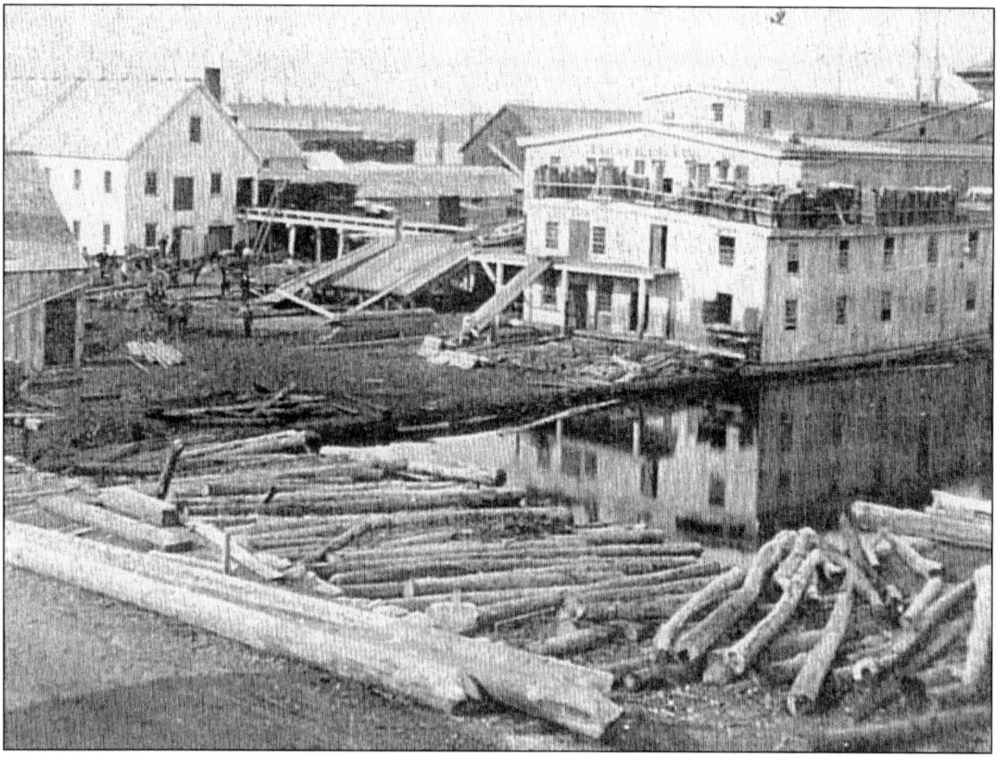

Treat, Lang, & Company. Steam was the power source for this lumber mill, located in the early 1870s on the part of Water Street that would later be home to Bath Iron Works.

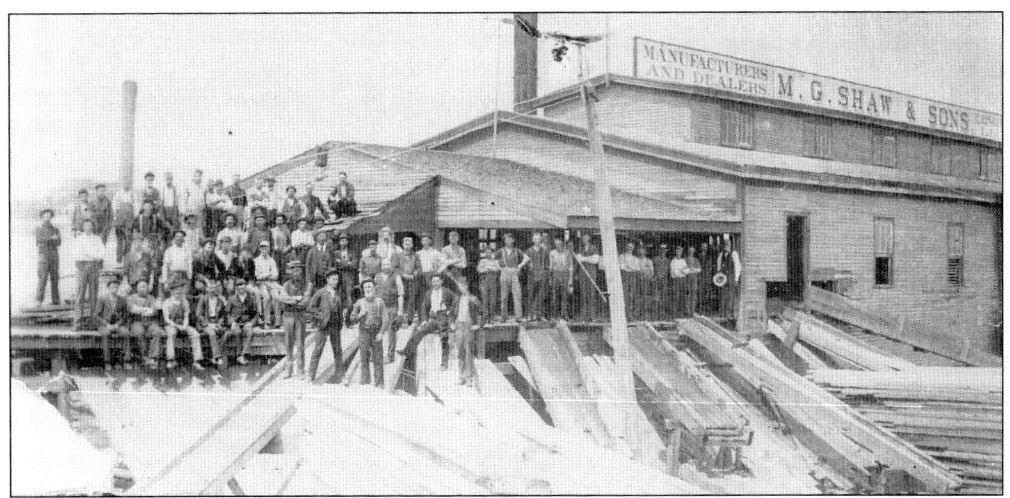

M.G. Shaw & Son in the 1880s. Located on Trufant's Point, on the southern part of Washington Street, Shaw's mill employed from seventy-five to one hundred men and produced a prodigious number of sawn boards and smaller items for construction and household use.

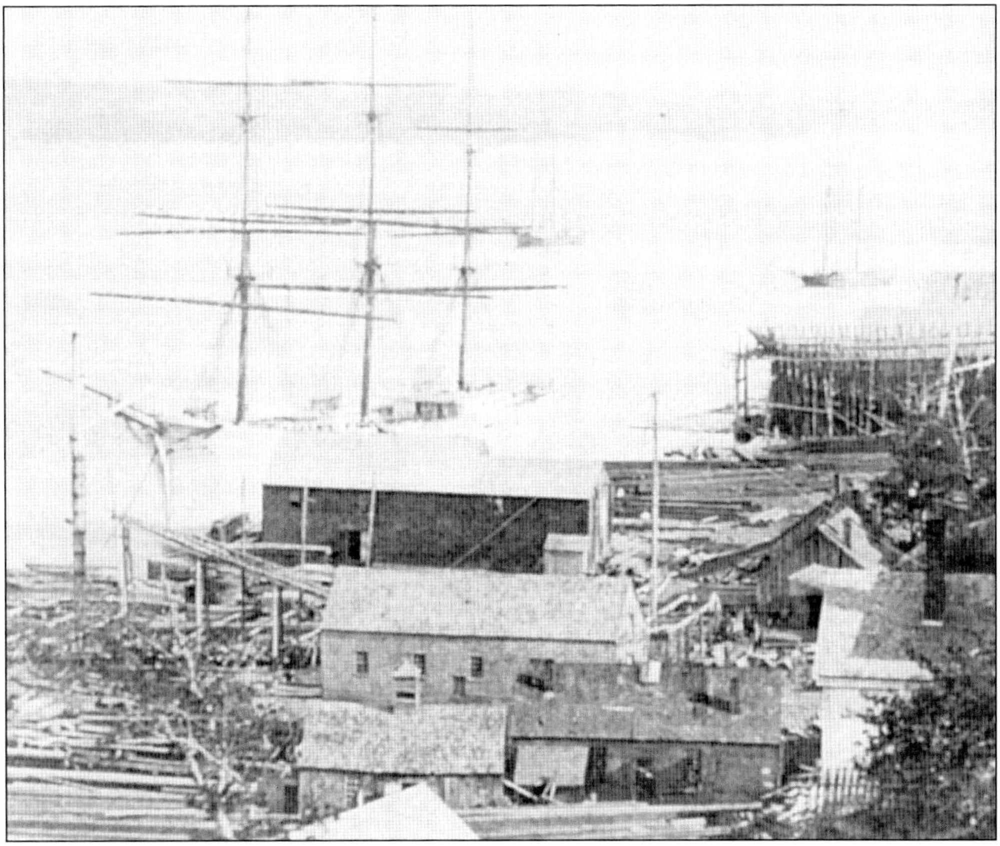

A view of the docks and shipyards. Nearly twenty shipyards can be counted along the river in an 1852 map of the city; and, with varying ownership, many sites remained operational for decades. In the 1870s, the sight of a completed ship at the wharf, small schooners in the bay, and vessels in various stages of construction on the shore would have been commonplace.

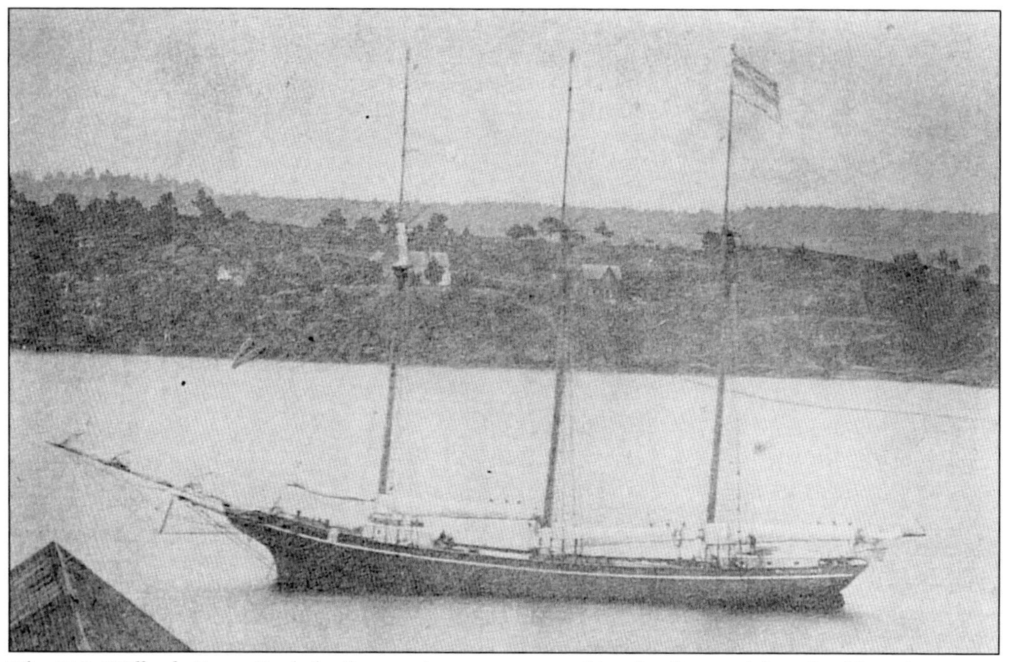

The *B.J. Willard*. Some Bath-built vessels were operated by the firms of their builders, but more and more were built to order for individuals from elsewhere. The 367-ton *B.J. Willard* was considered very large when constructed and became one of the first three-masted schooners operated out of Portland. Shown here just after her 1872 launching, she was soon loaded with Kennebec River ice, bound for Philadelphia.

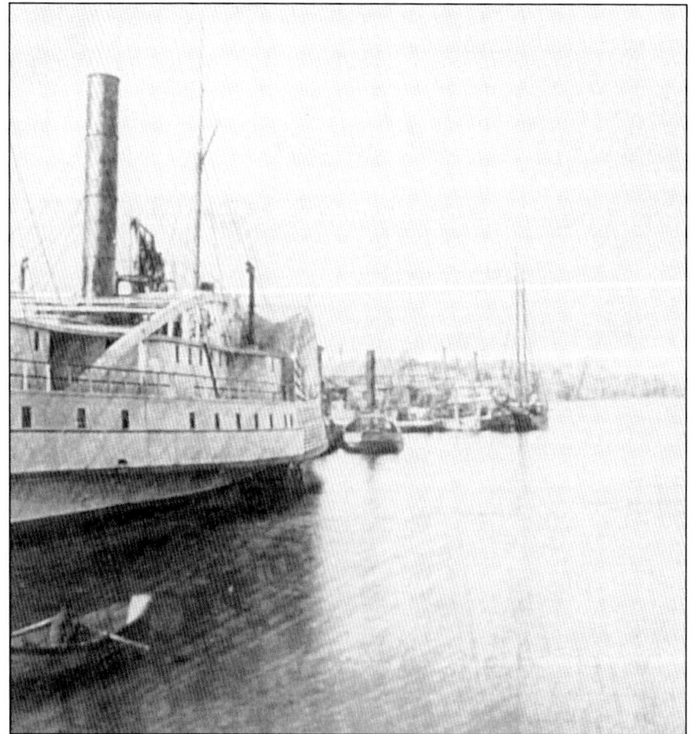

The *Eastern Queen*. In the second half of the nineteenth century, a variety of motor-powered vessels came from local yards, including steam vessels like the *Eastern Queen*, which maintained connections between Bath and Boston in the 1870s.

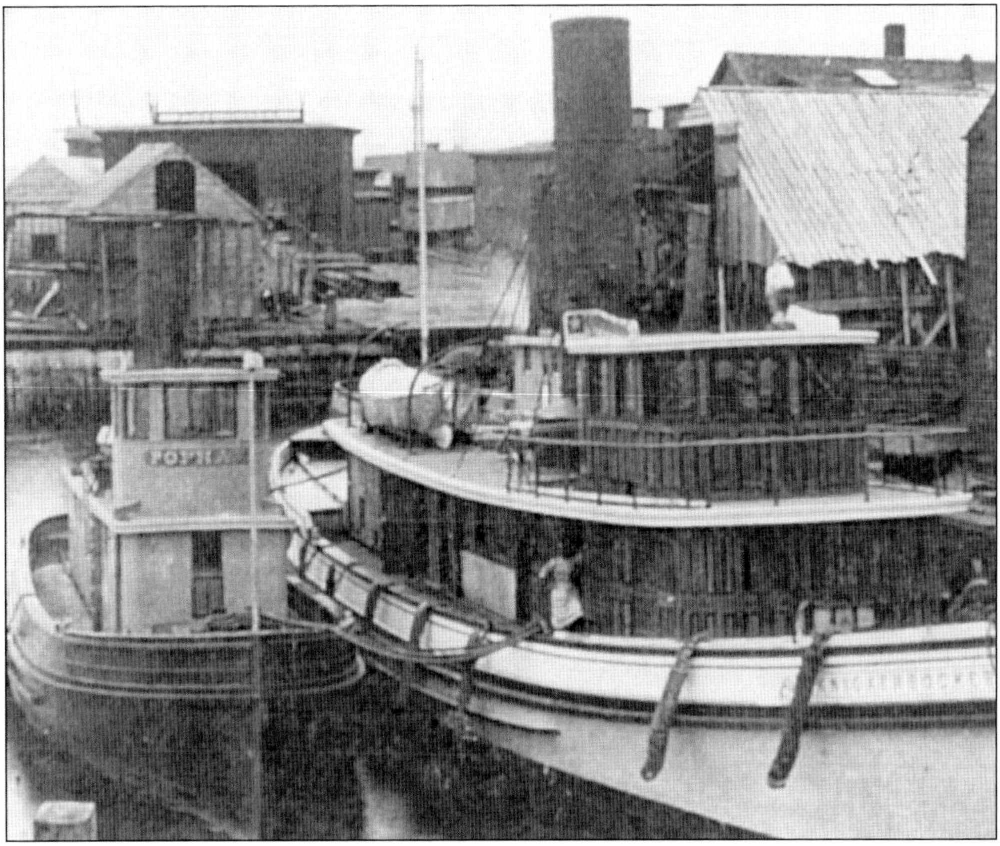

Tugboats. Most of the river ferries and harbor tugs were also built in Bath. The *Popham* and the *Knickerbocker* were part of Captain Benjamin Morse's Knickerbocker Towage Co., operating on the river from its mouth to the fall line.

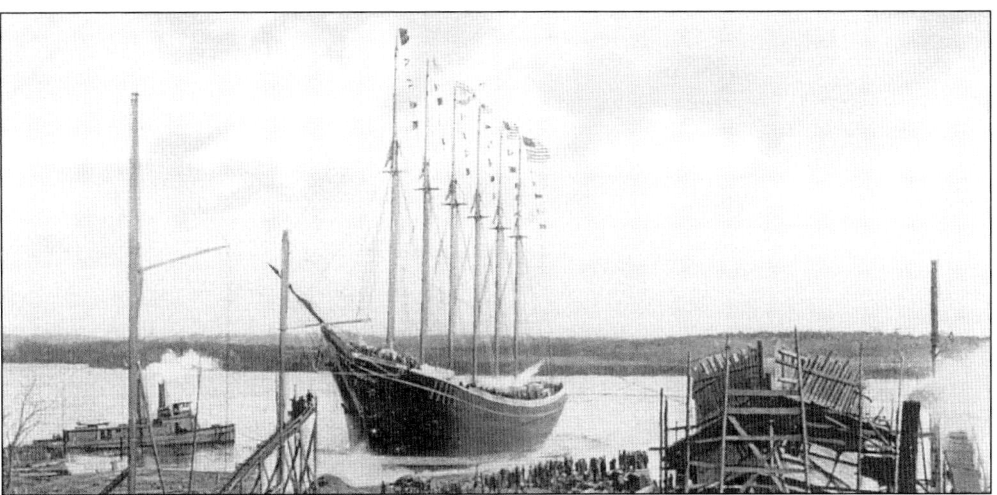

A six-masted schooner. Builders greatly increased the sizes of their vessels in the 1880s and '90s, when four and five masts were common. The *Ruth E. Merrill*, shown here at her 1904 launching, was the third of seven six-masters constructed by the firm of Percy and Small. She became part of Portland's huge J.S. Winslow fleet.

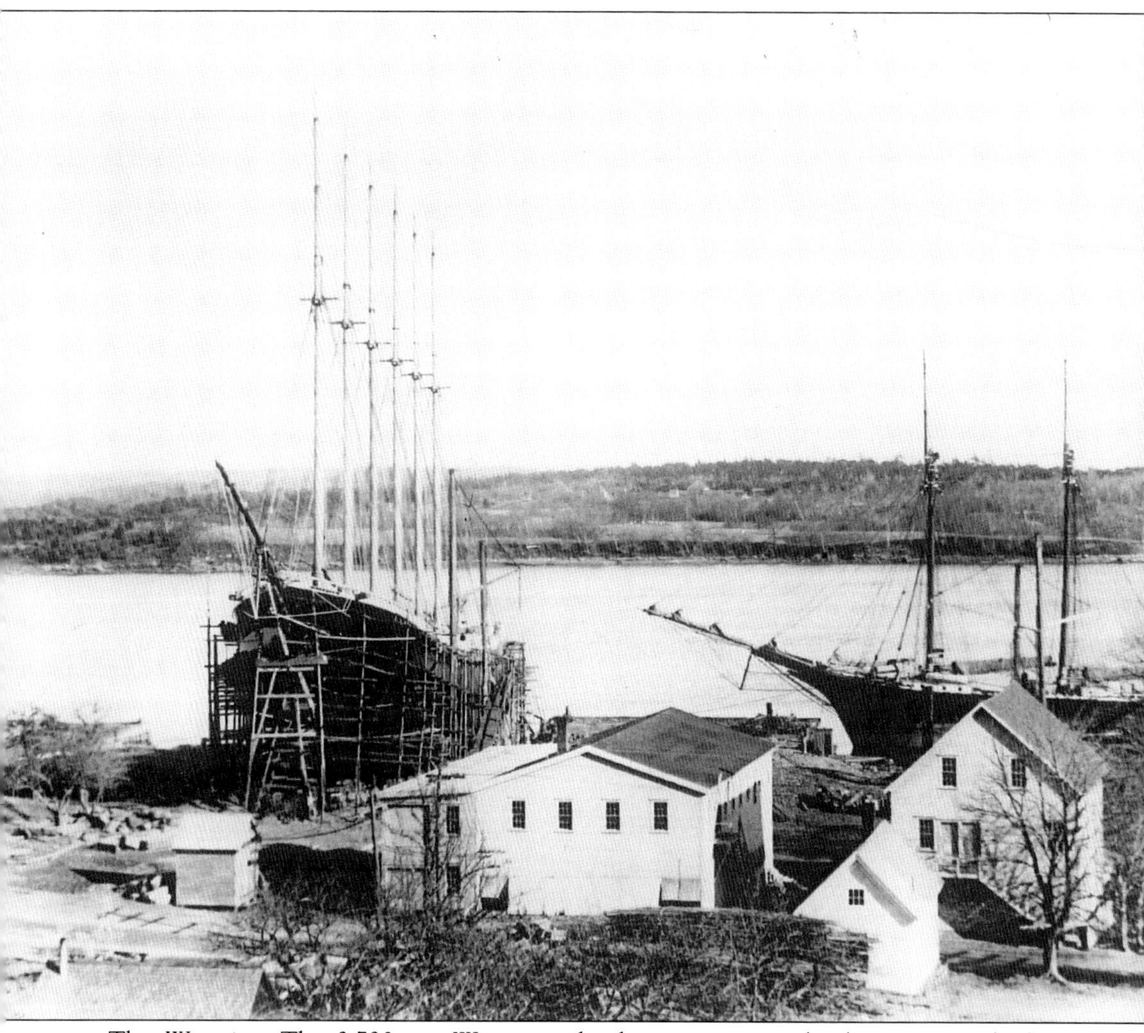

The *Wyoming*. The 3,730-ton *Wyoming*, the largest six-masted schooner ever built, was launched in 1909; and neighborhood boys later told of sneaking aboard early to be "stowaways" for the thrill of the slide down the ways. Also constructed by Percy and Small, the huge vessel was managed by them until it was sold just prior to World War I. The firm completed its last schooner in 1920; but whereas most of the other wooden-ship yards have disappeared, many of the buildings shown here remain, having become part of the Maine Maritime Museum in the mid-1970s.

A figurehead for the *Belle of Bath*. Among the skilled men who contributed the elaborate carvings found on many wooden vessels was Civil War veteran Colonel Charles A.L. Sampson. Sampson's shop on Front Street produced figureheads for ships constructed in other towns, in addition to many built locally. This furbelowed woman was prepared for the *Belle of Bath*, a ship built in 1877 by the firm of Goss and Sawyer and used in the Far Eastern trade. Sampson did similar "Belles" for at least two other ships. Reportedly, the outstretched arms could be removed when at sea and returned to position in harbors, when the ship would be seen up close.

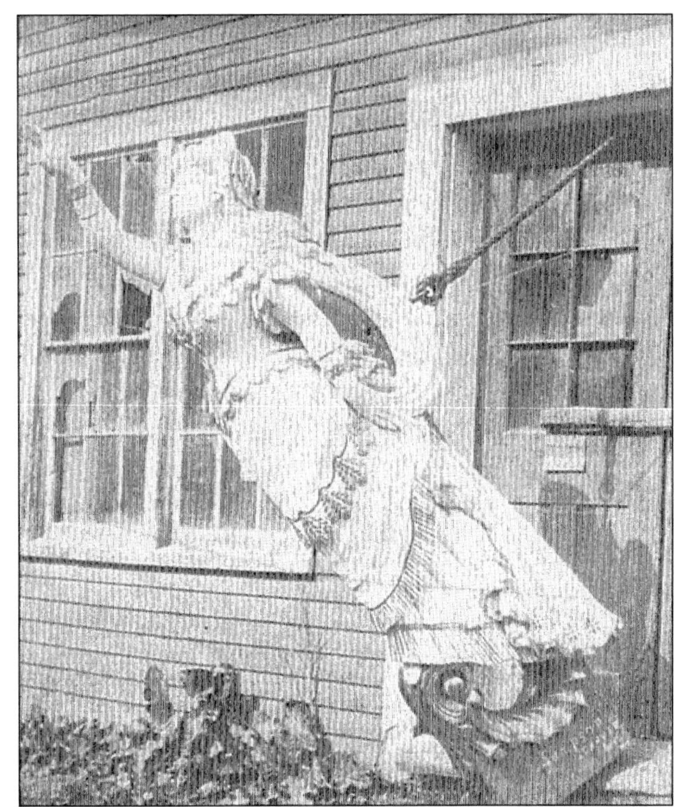

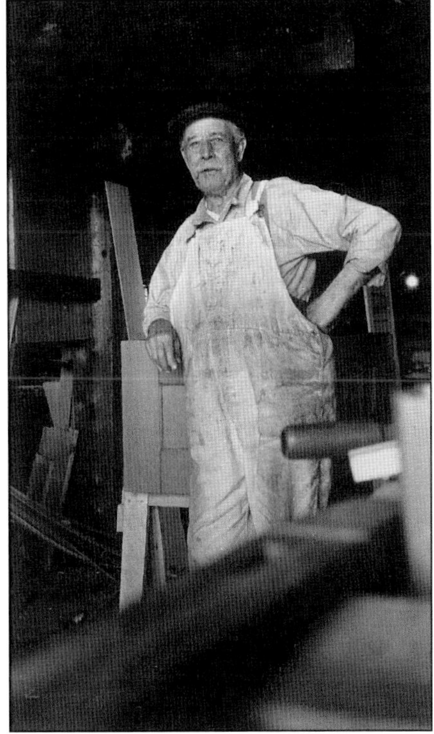

Edwin Trott, painter. Skillful painting was also in demand. Edwin Trott was at the Percy and Small yard when his picture was taken. His specialty was painting decorative gold leaf details on vessels, and he worked at the Deering yard as well. Trott was skilled at many occupations, and when demand for one skill ceased, he moved on to another (see p. 105).

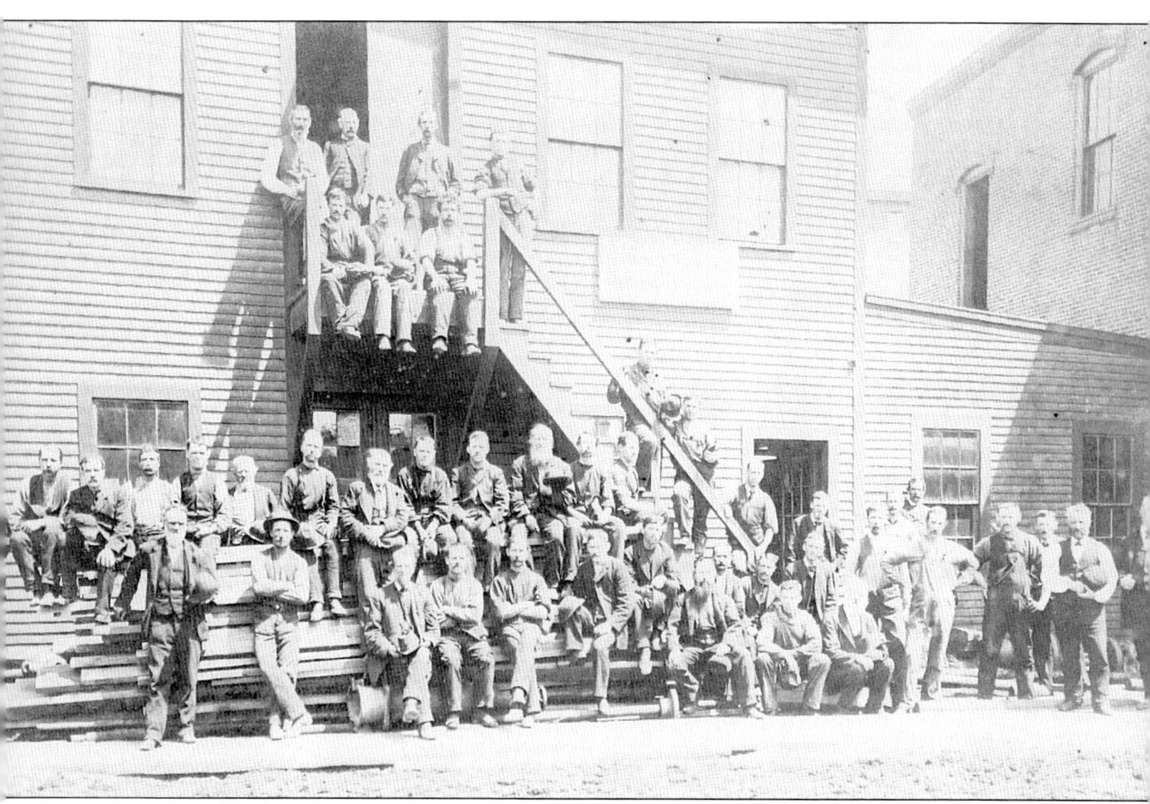

Bath Iron Works: where it began. After General Thomas Worcester Hyde returned home from the Civil War, he went into the foundry business in this location on Water and Front Streets, where what was soon known as "Bath Iron Works" operated for about twenty years. The sign, reading "Turning and Pattern Making," as well as the lumber on which the men are sitting, shows that the business involved wood, as well as iron and brass. The size of the crew suggests that even then the concern was contributing to employment in the town. In 1885, Hyde's firm purchased the recently-failed Goss Marine Iron Works and set up an additional business on the river.

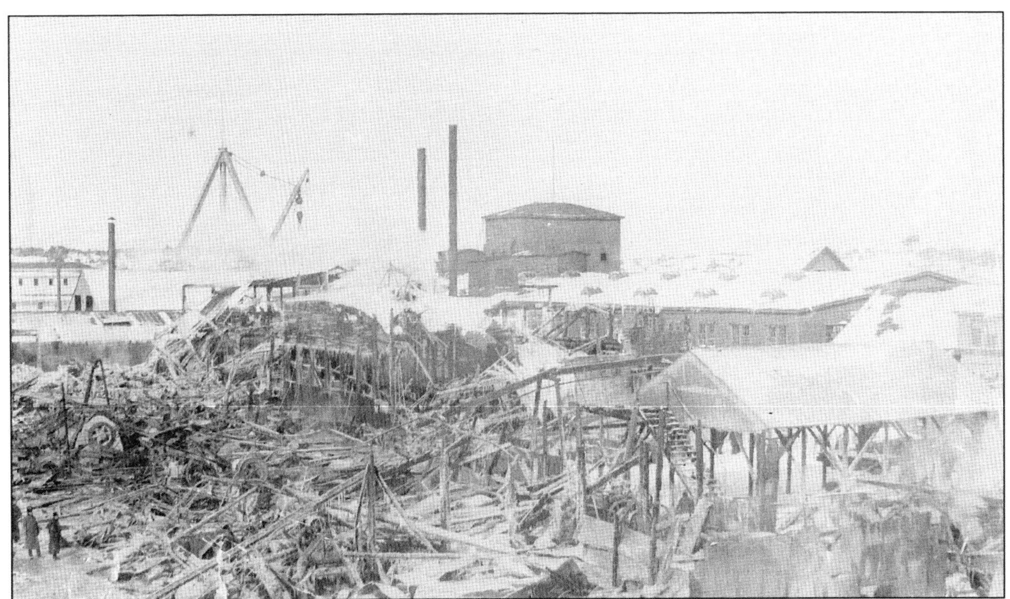

Disaster, 1894. General Hyde was able to obtain a few contracts from the new U.S. Navy in the 1890s—but the business was badly damaged by fire in February 1894, during a major snowstorm which contributed ice and a layer of snow to the scene. In spite of threats to the contrary (the damage was extensive because of problems with the city water supply, and Hyde blamed city officials for ignoring his earlier recommendations), the yard was rebuilt.

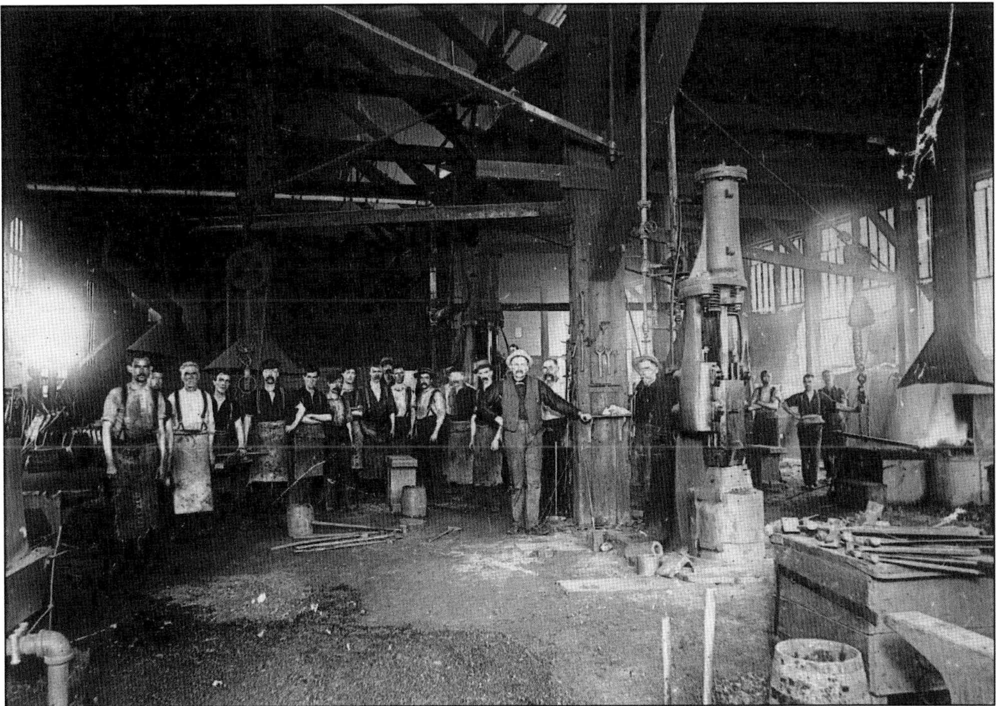

The BIW blacksmith shop, about 1900. Blacksmiths wore leather aprons for protection; and everyone, except perhaps the foreman, got dirty. The man on the left has been identified as Charles Plant.

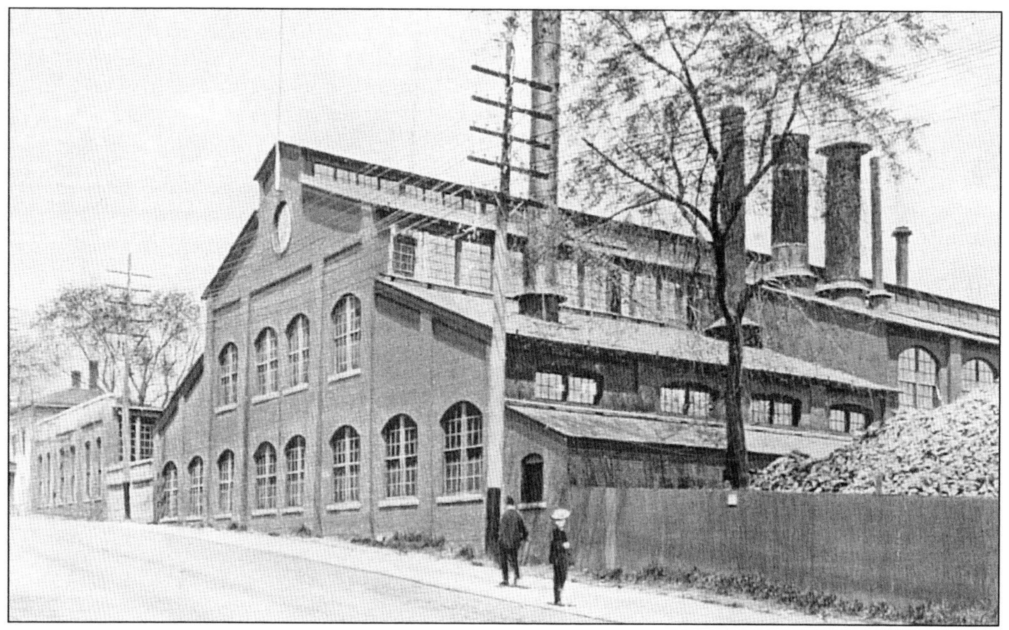

The Hyde Windlass Company. Hyde also organized a separate company to manufacture a machine he patented for easier handling of large anchors. Originally located on Water Street, the concern was moved in 1897 to this building at Federal and Washington Streets. In 1940 it was moved again, this time to East Brunswick. Hyde Windlass would produce different parts for the shipyard, but remained a separate corporation until 1961.

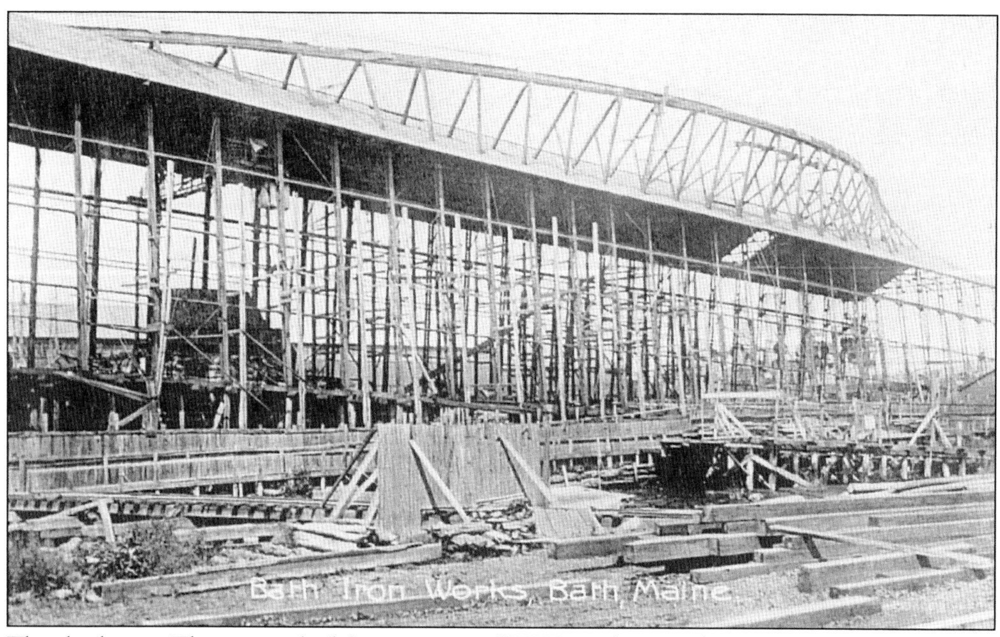

The shiphouse. This unusual edifice was one of BIW's early contributions to the city's skyline. From the late 1890s into the 1910s, the waterfront was dominated by this huge structure, topped by a monorail for carrying metal plates to ships on the ways beside it.

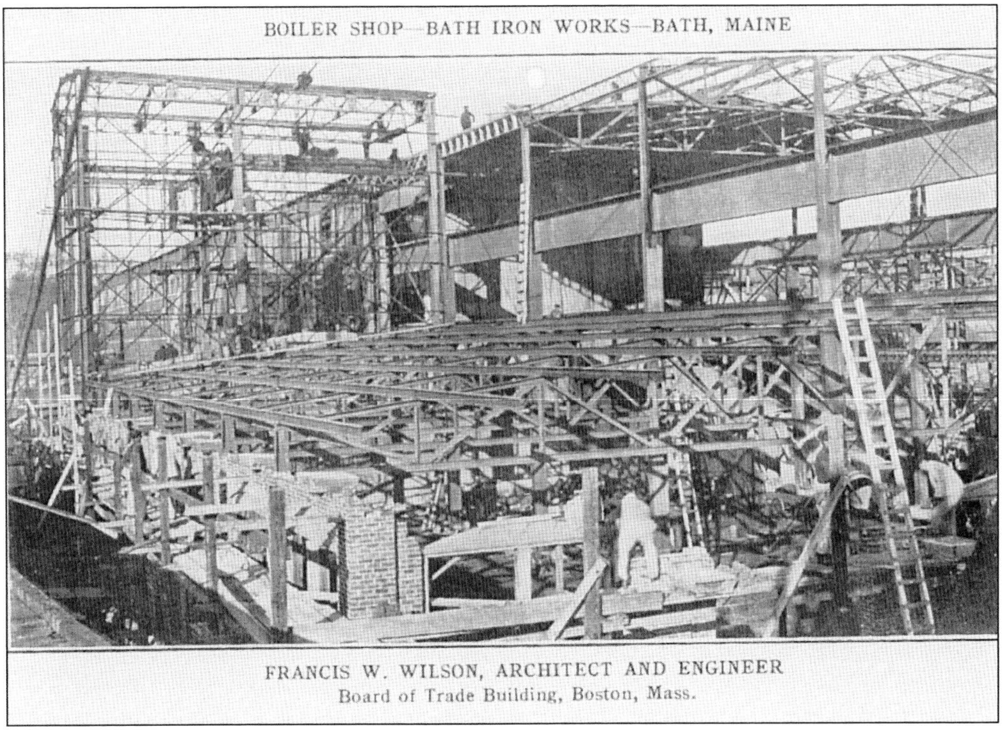

BOILER SHOP—BATH IRON WORKS—BATH, MAINE

FRANCIS W. WILSON, ARCHITECT AND ENGINEER
Board of Trade Building, Boston, Mass.

Building a new boiler shop. A fire in the summer of 1908 damaged the firm's boiler shop and led to its rebuilding and expansion. Apparently the architect felt the work was important enough to warrant an advertising postcard.

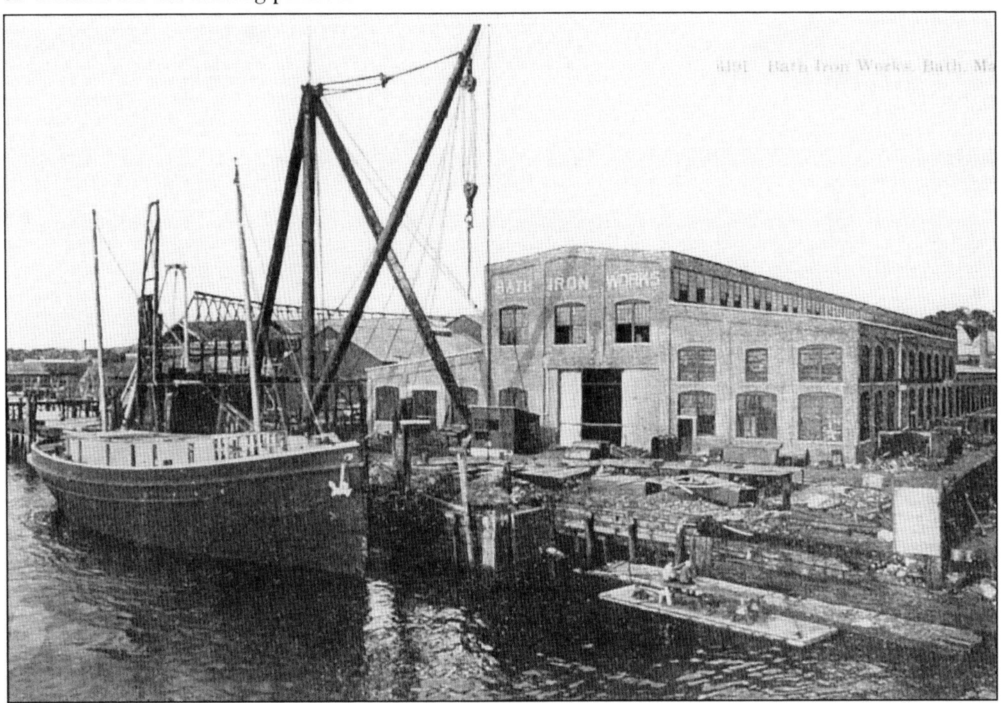

A view of BIW, *c*. 1909. The completed shop stood slightly to the north of the shiphouse.

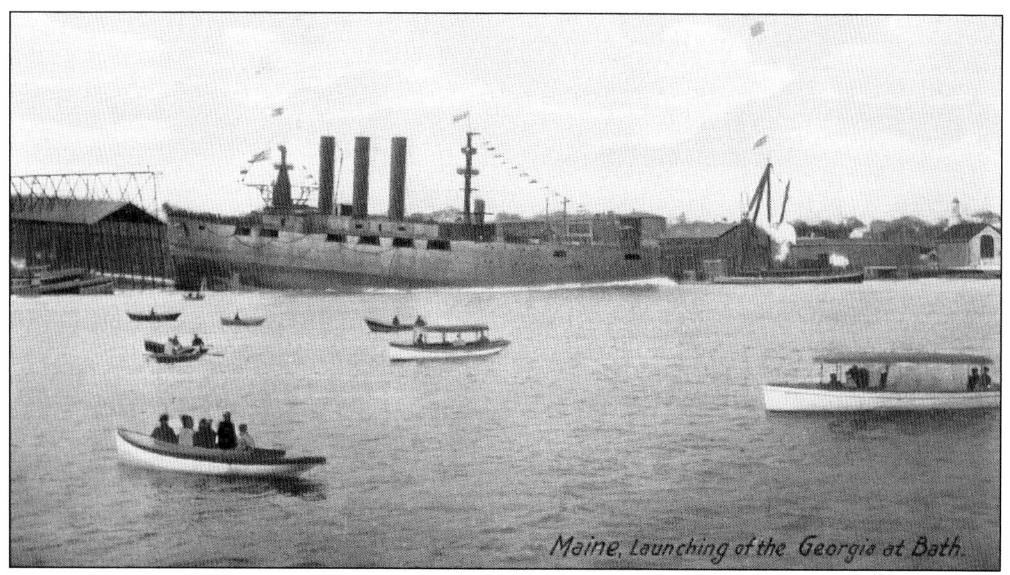

The *Georgia*, 1904. At the turn of the century, BIW's output varied from luxury yachts to commercial steamships and a range of naval vessels. The *Georgia* was the yard's first and only battleship. Reportedly, her draft occasioned concern about navigating the channels downriver, but her captain managed the trip without mishap. Although she was the fastest battleship in the fleet when built, more than a decade would pass before the next war, and the vessel's fighting record appears limited. However, local people took pride in the fact she transported 50,000 men to Europe to serve in World War I.

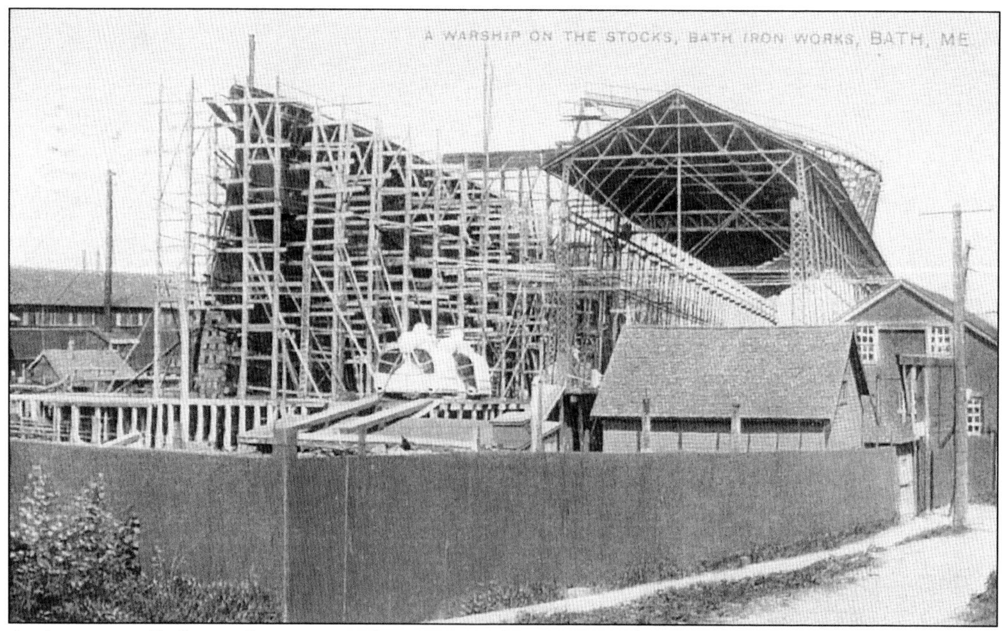

A destroyer. Early in the twentieth century, the Navy realized a need for smaller craft: this unnamed warship is one of the eleven destroyers launched during the period between 1909 and 1913.

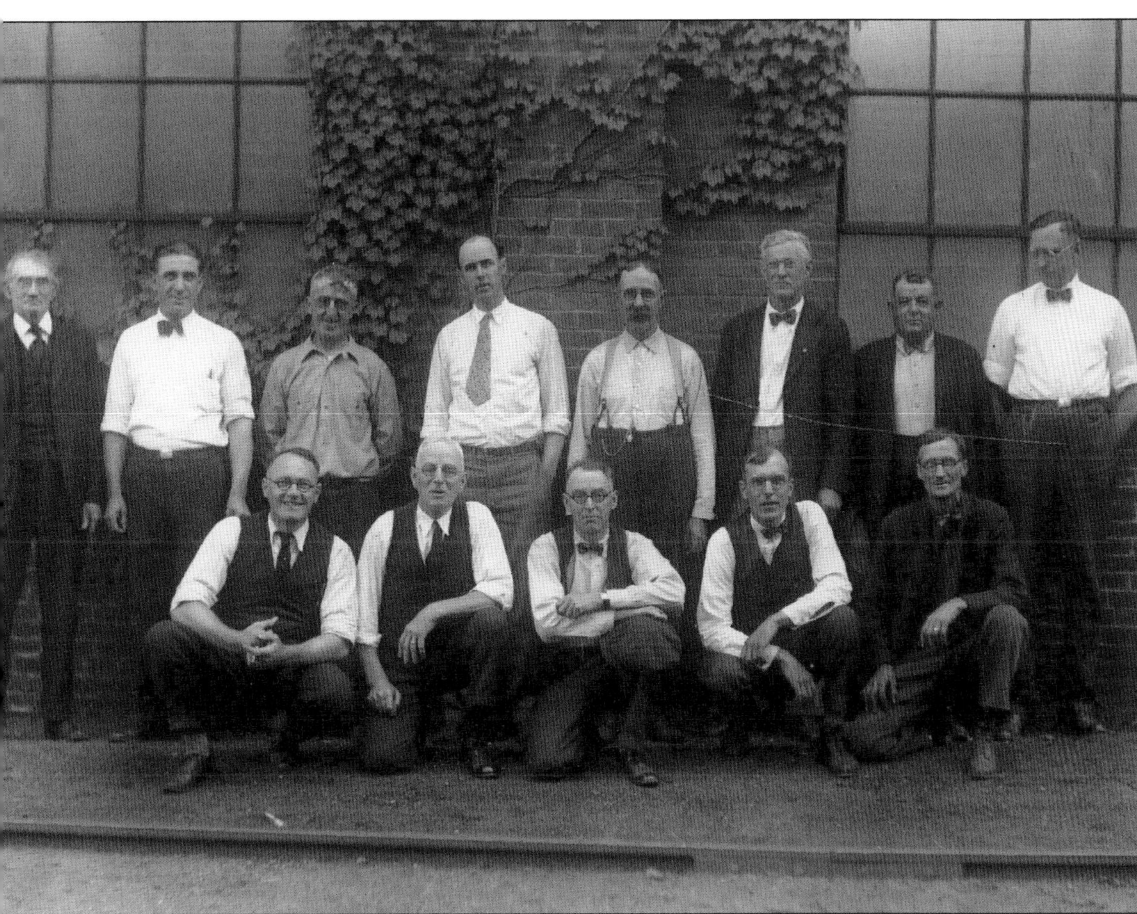

Foremen in 1928. BIW's history is far from even, and the business has undergone considerable reorganization. In the mid-1920s the yard was closed and much of the machinery sold off, but new leadership brought a new beginning in 1927–28. The men serving as foremen posed for a photograph in September 1928, and their areas of expertise give some idea of how varied work in a modern shipyard can be. From left to right are: (front row) Harry Wallace, electrics; Bert Dickinson, plate shop; Howard Nash, mold loft; Arthur King, shipyard; and Omar Fullerton, shipfitting; (back row) Richard Winchenbach, machinist; Mr. McCabe, paint shop; Jim Biggins, blacksmith; Stanley Brown, shipyard; Harry Richardson, pipe shop; Moulton Baker, joiner shop; Frank Bowker, carpenter; and Henry Shaw, patternmaker.

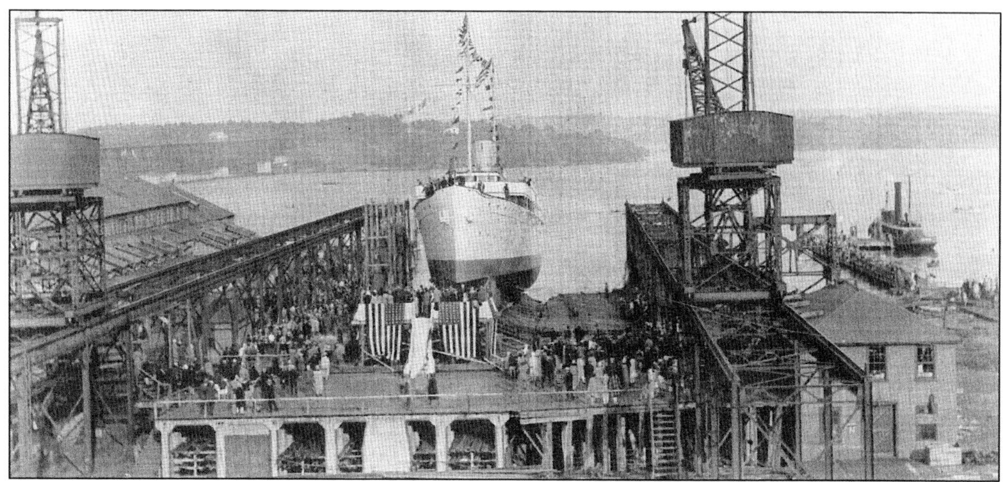

A launching, 1928. The *Vanda* was the first contract of the revamped Bath Iron Works Corporation and the first of nineteen luxury yachts produced by late 1931. She later served as a naval gunboat, the *U.S.S. San Bernadino*, in the Pacific.

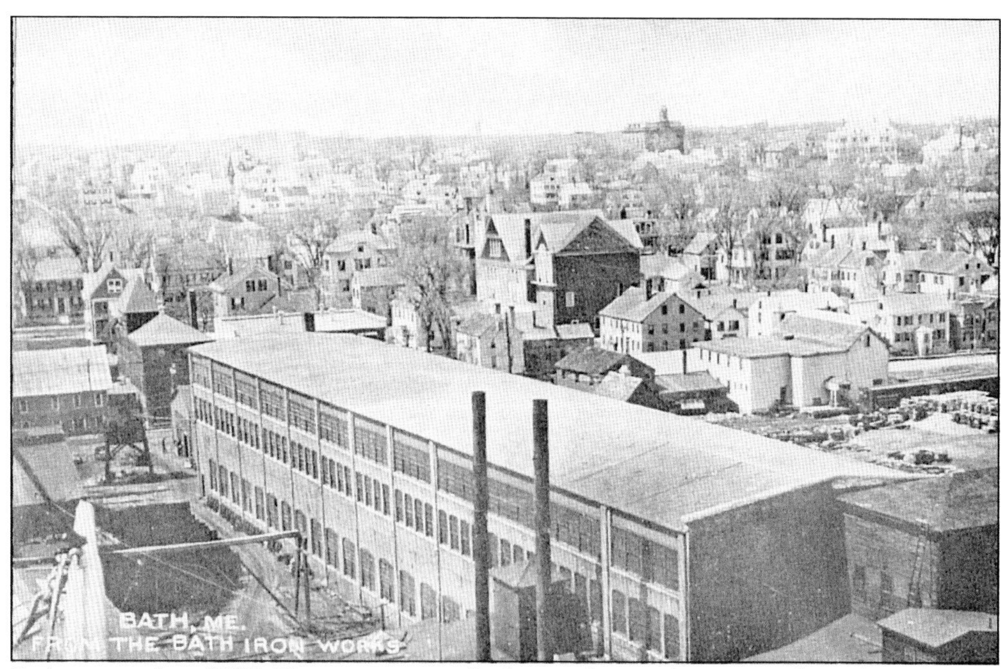

Bath as seen from BIW. This view is actually from a ship in the river, judging from the spar in the lower left corner of the photograph, and indicates the integration of yard and city. The Hotel Sedgewick is to the right of the courthouse on the skyline. The large building in between, the People's Church, was eventually razed to make way for a BIW parking lot.

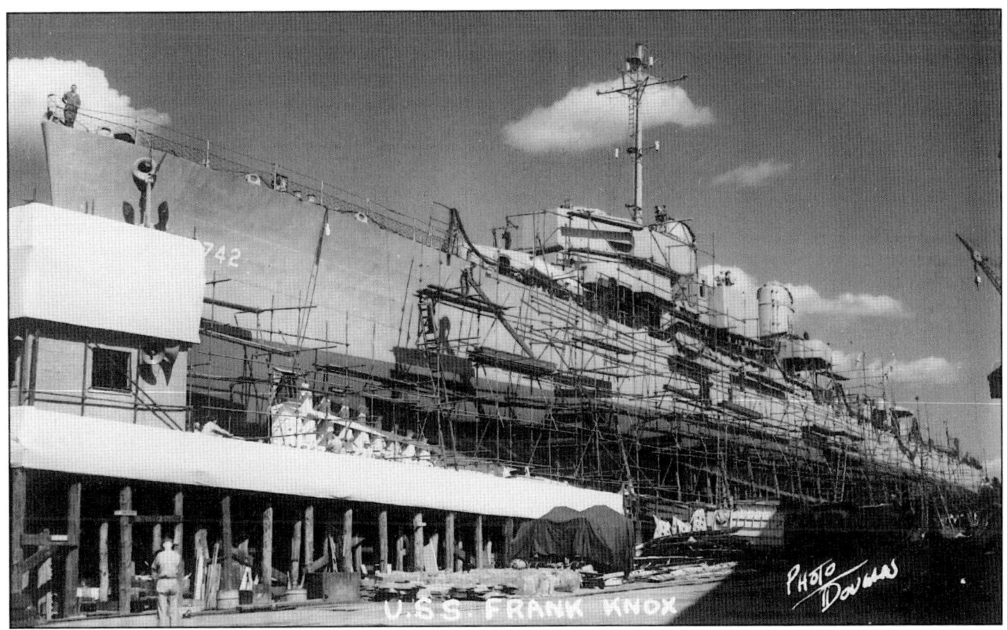

Helping win World War II. The depression cut off the demand for the luxury yachts; but Bath Iron Works was able to capitalize on the naval buildup before and during the World War II, when the company boasted having produced a quarter of all destroyers built in the country for the U.S. Navy. The *Frank Knox*, named for F.D. Roosevelt's third Secretary of the Navy, was among them.

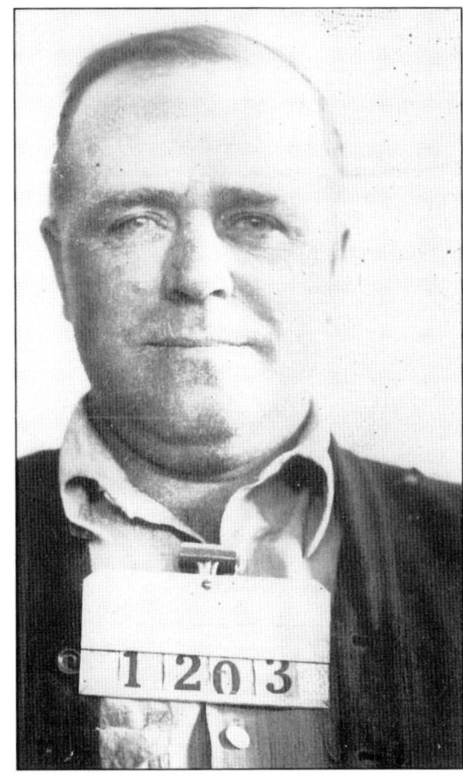

An I.D. card. Government contracts demanded security; and all employees were provided with photographic identification cards, later replaced by badges. This one belonged to Raymond Clark.

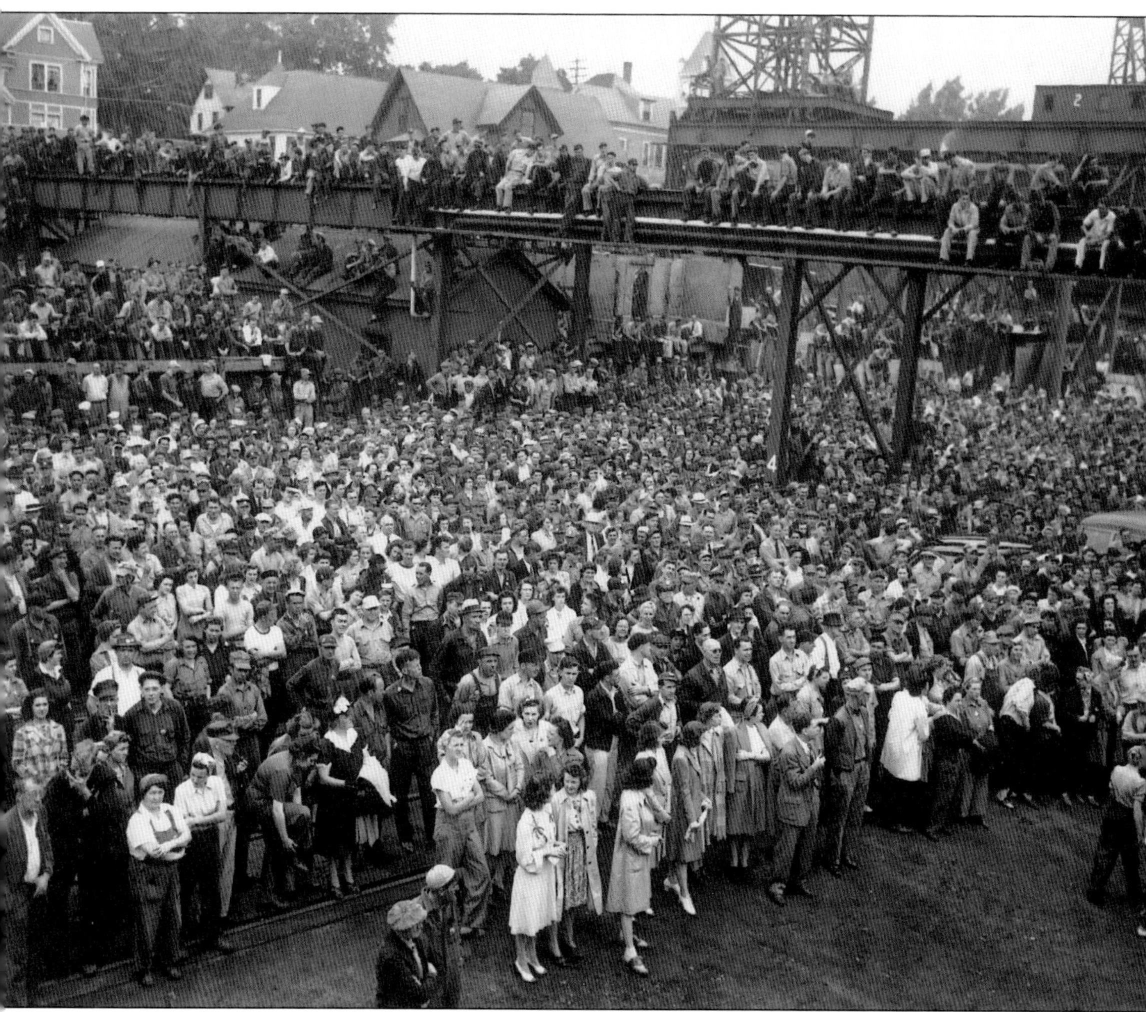

Observing a launching, 1943. At every launching, the yard was filled, and the nearby bridge was often lined with observers. The women in heels in the foreground were probably office workers, but near them are others—wearing slacks and with their hair tied up—who were prepared for heavy work. At BIW, as in other war plants, women were given what had always been considered men's jobs; and they did them well.

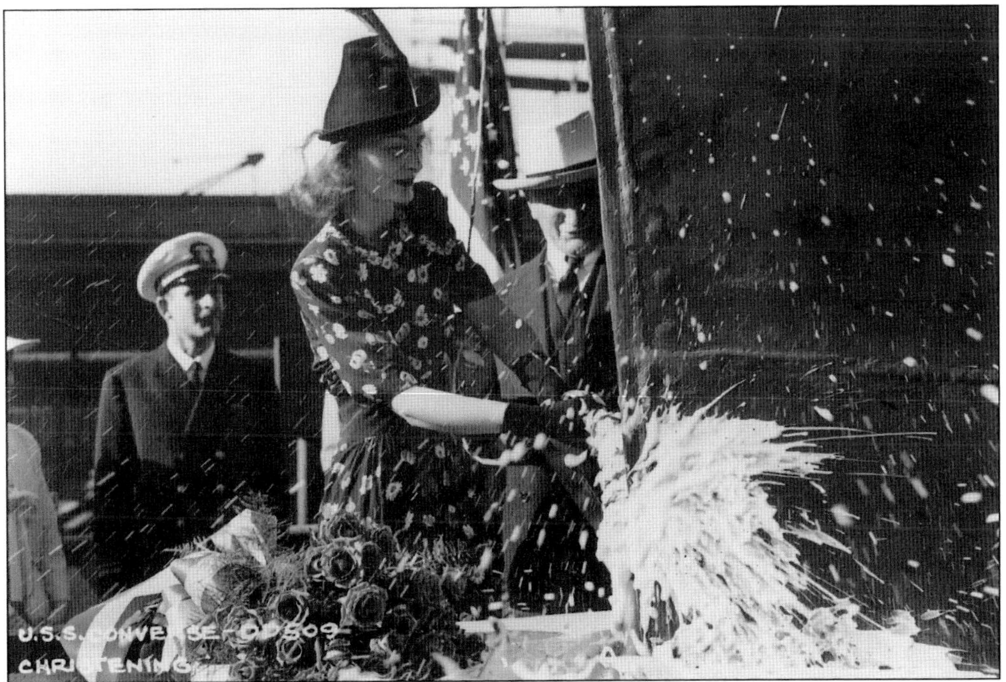

Launching a destroyer: at the bow. Even when launchings occurred as often as twice in a month, they were considered real events. Photographers were always on hand, often catching vessel slipping down the ways (as on p. 64) and trying to capture the splash of the champagne at the bow. In the summer of 1942, Audrey V. Jackson christened the *Converse*. Her headgear serves to remind a more casual generation of the importance of hats for the well-dressed women of the 1940s.

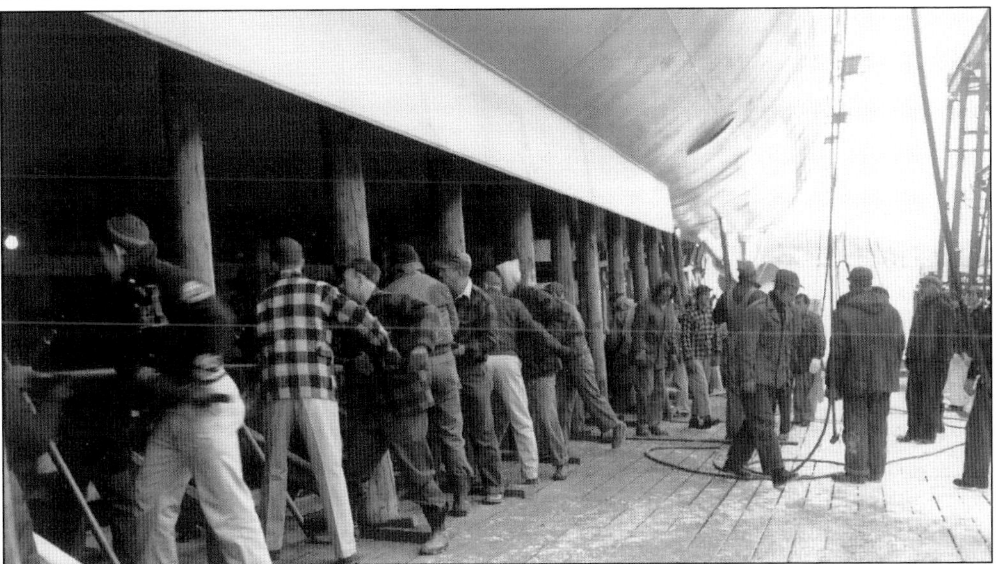

Launching a destroyer: by the ways. The smashing bottle was dramatic, but the *real* reason the vessel moved was found below, where hundreds of workers, less stylishly garbed, drove wedges to lift the keel and facilitate its slide down the ways. This crew launched the destroyer *Edson* on January 4, 1959. (The yard was also busy during the Cold War.)

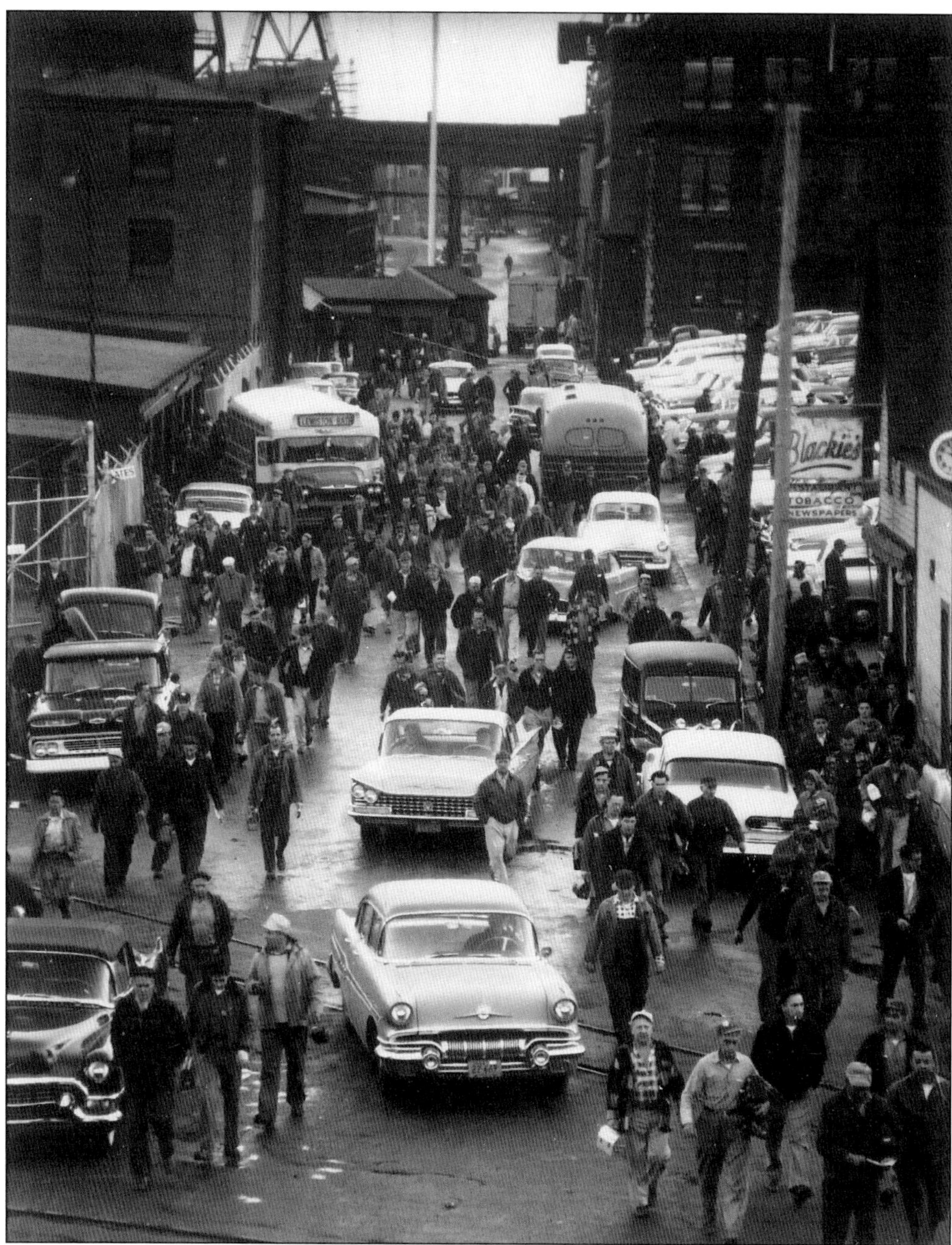

Quitting time. BIW was always important in providing job opportunities for Bath men, and during World War II the firm became a major contributor to employment in a larger area, as workers traveled from fair distances away to get to the yard. The situation continued, as can be attested by anyone who has tried to drive through Bath or anywhere along nearby Route One at a time when shifts at the yard were changing. This outrush of men near the main gate in the late 1950s would be only a small part of the work force. Note that the bus was from Lewiston.

Five

SCHOOLS

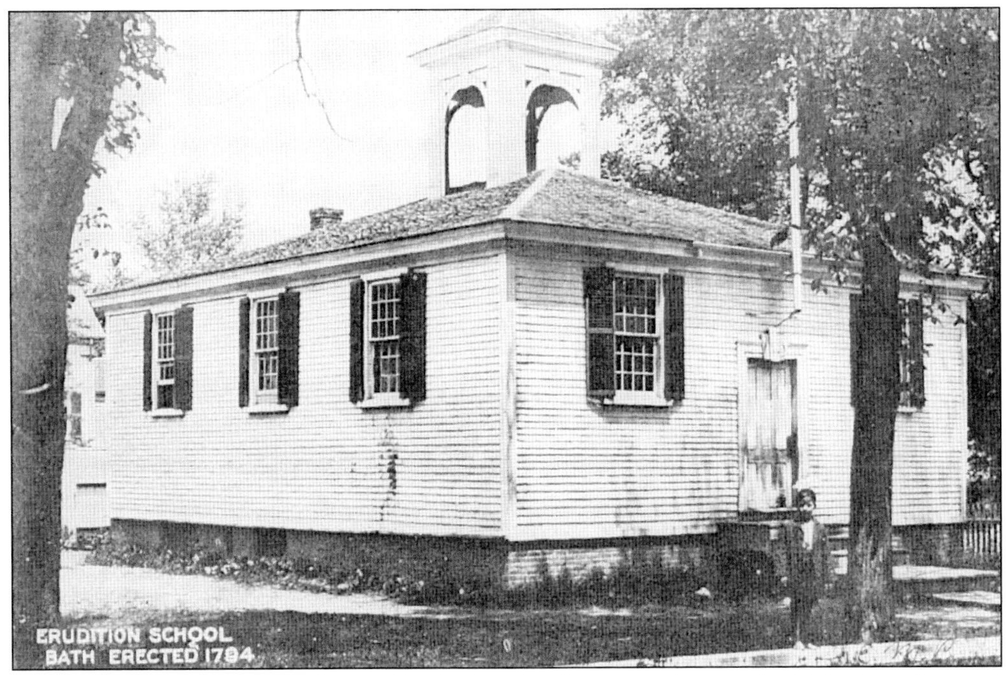

The Erudition School. The first public-built schoolhouse in the city had "Erudition" carved above its door. It stood on High Street, near Center Street, from 1794 until 1900, but was unused for many years because its single room was much too small for an urban population. When the lot was developed, the old structure was saved and moved to a spot near the high school, but then allowed to deteriorate.

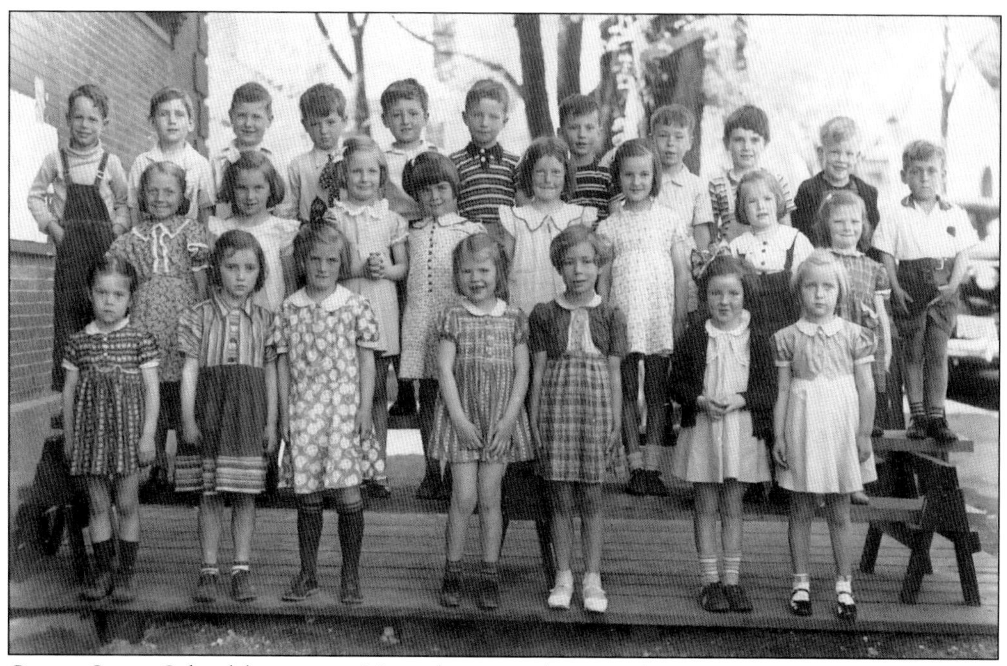

Center Street School beginners. More than two dozen multi-room elementary schools were built in the nineteenth-century city. This eager sub-primary class began their educational lives in the fall of 1939 at the Center Street School—a brick structure which had been a fire station for over two decades before being "recycled" as a schoolhouse in 1889. It served well, but in 1950 was declared "a disgrace," closed, and razed to make a parking lot.

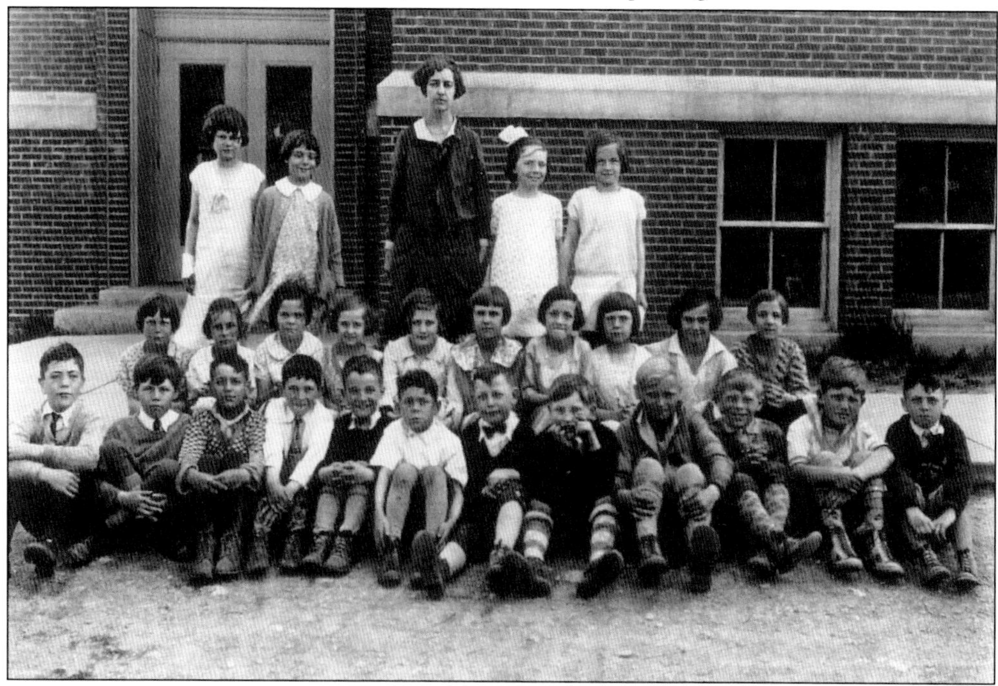

A Mitchell School grammar class. A few years earlier, a more advanced class was photographed at the newer Mitchell School, which served the South End from 1915 to 1977.

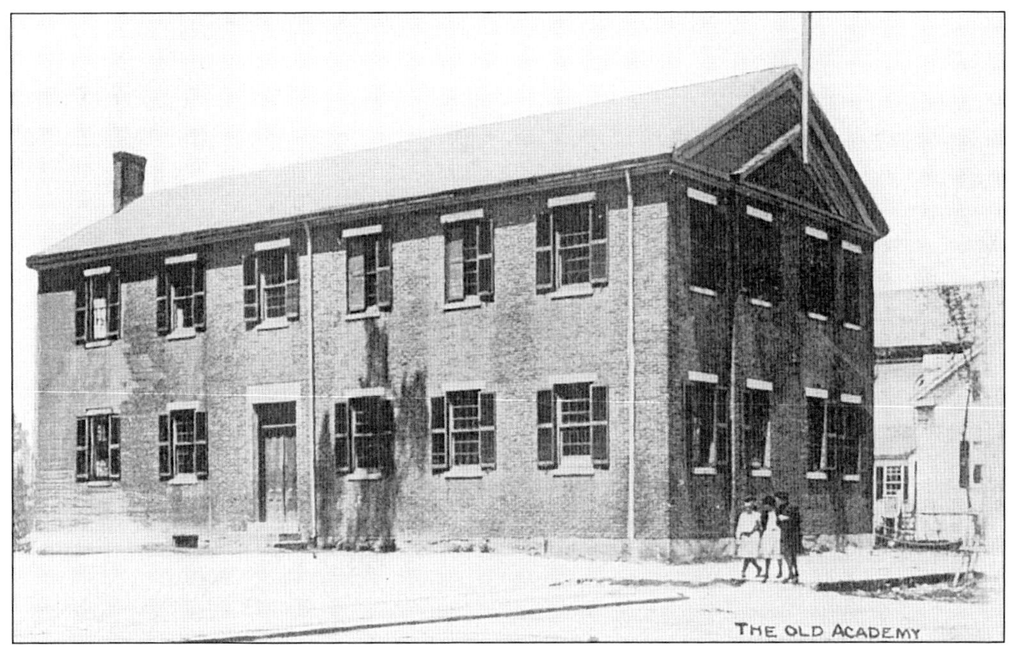

Bath Academy. Secondary schooling began with private academies. Bath Academy, built in 1828 on Academy Street, became a city-owned high school and served as such until 1860.

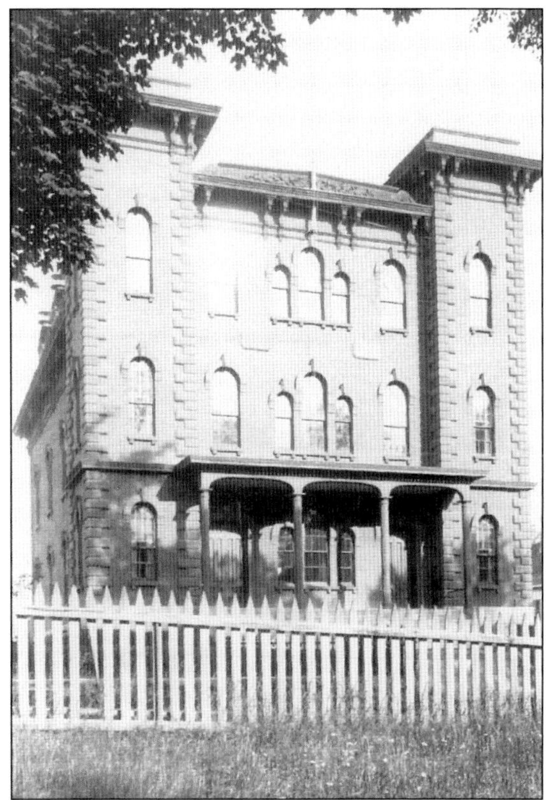

Bath High School. In 1859, Bath architect Francis Fassett was commissioned to design the new Bath High School building. Located on High Street, the twin-towered building later became Central Grammar School.

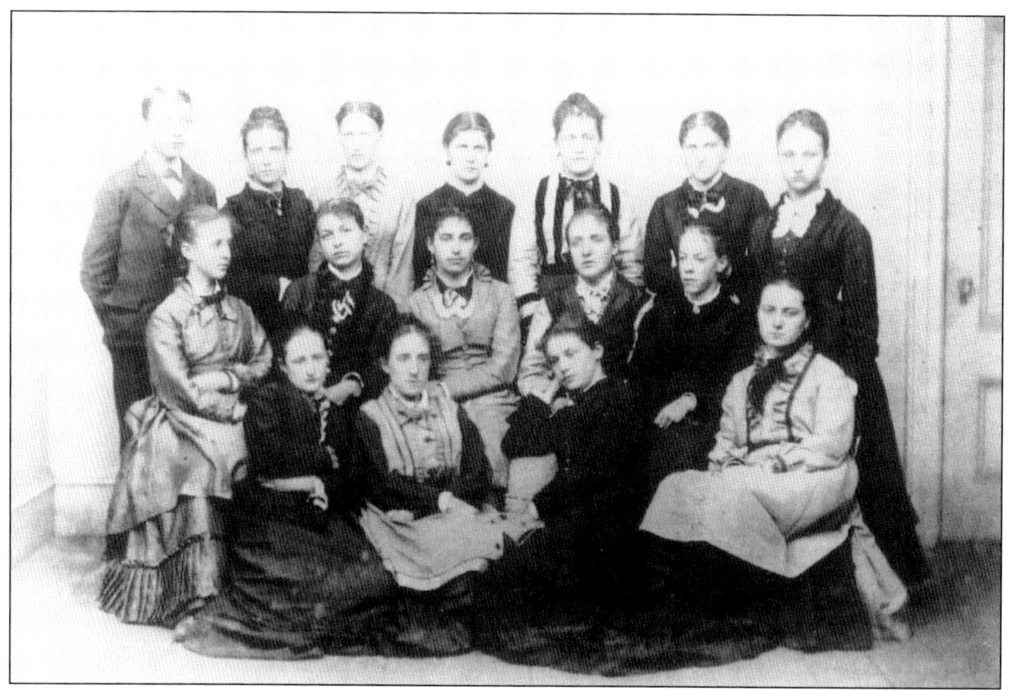

The Bath High School Class of 1875. This group includes Mr. Joseph Finley, Miss Baker, Isabelle Crowell, H. Jenks, M. Jenks, Emma Magoun, Lizzie Moses, A.L. Palmer, A.M. Palmer, ? Purington, Abbie Rairden, Alice Skillings, Alice Swett, and Julia Watson; but with no note given as to which was which, only the lone male can be identified.

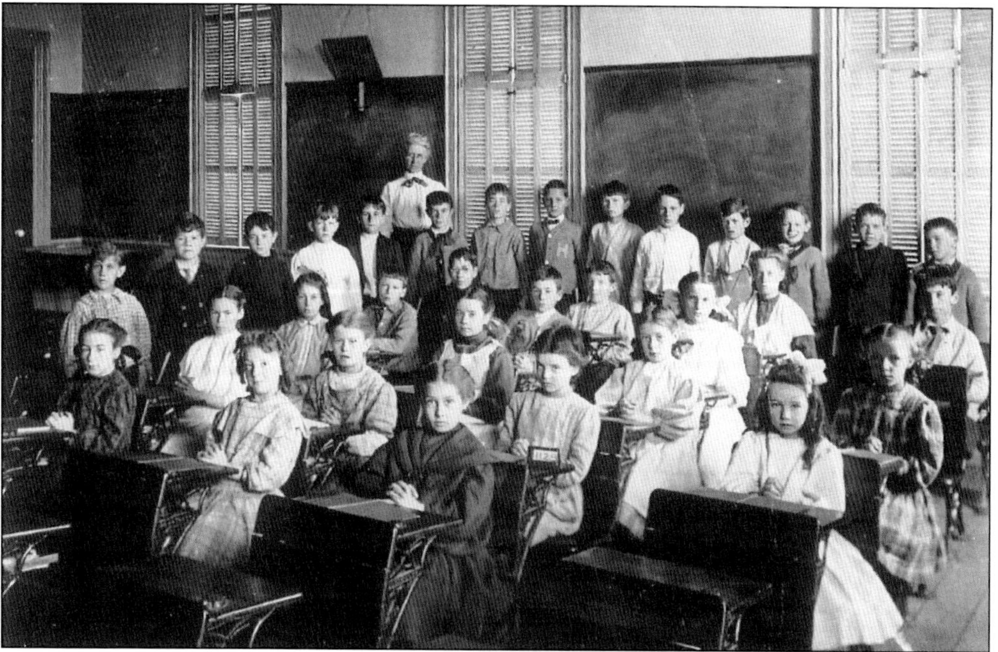

A ninth grade classroom, 1915. This is a rare look at the interior of the old Bath High School. The teacher was Miss Magoun (probably Alice, who worked at the high school, rather than Emma [in the top photograph], whose teaching career was at the grammar school level).

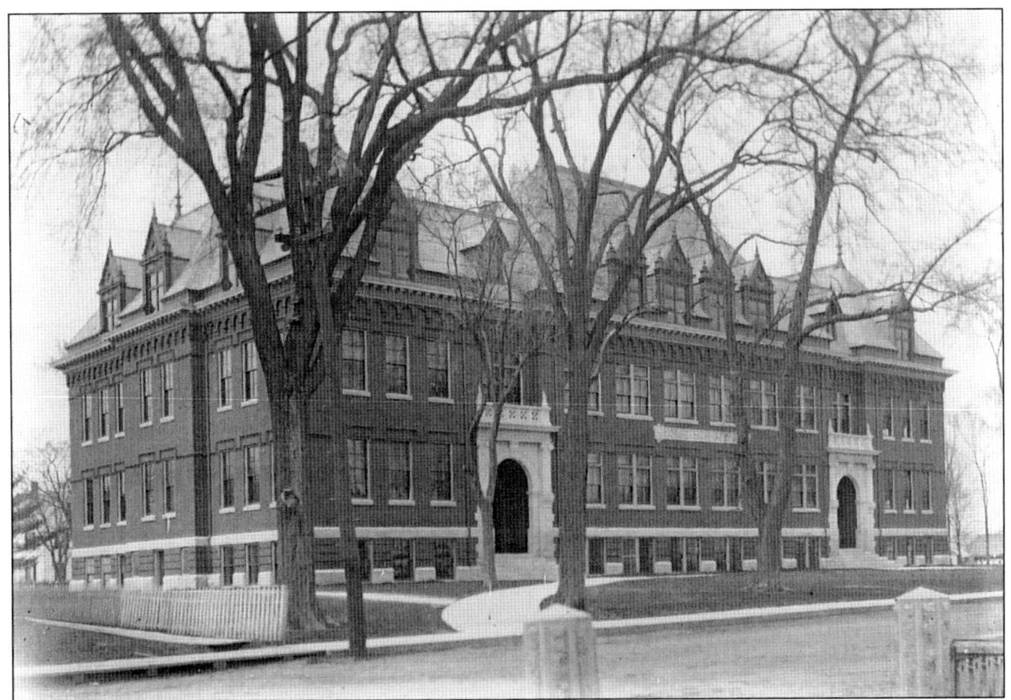

Morse High School, 1903. The need for a larger building was met when financier and entrepreneur Charles W. Morse donated money for a new high school to be named in honor of his mother. It was constructed at High and Academy Streets.

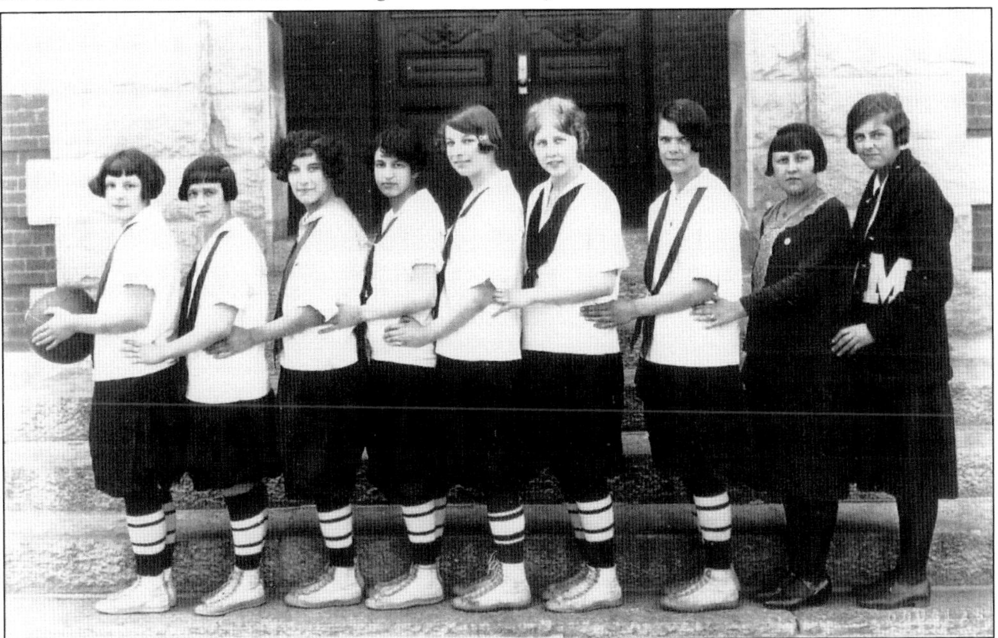

The girls' basketball team, 1926–27. Posing on the school steps in their middies, bloomers, and high sneakers are, from left to right: Ola Ward, Beatrice Burgess, Gladys Commeau, Shirley Mank, Ellen Dollof, Helen Decker, and Marie Scott. Eleanor Blake and Eleanor Webster are in street clothes, although the latter sports a letter sweater.

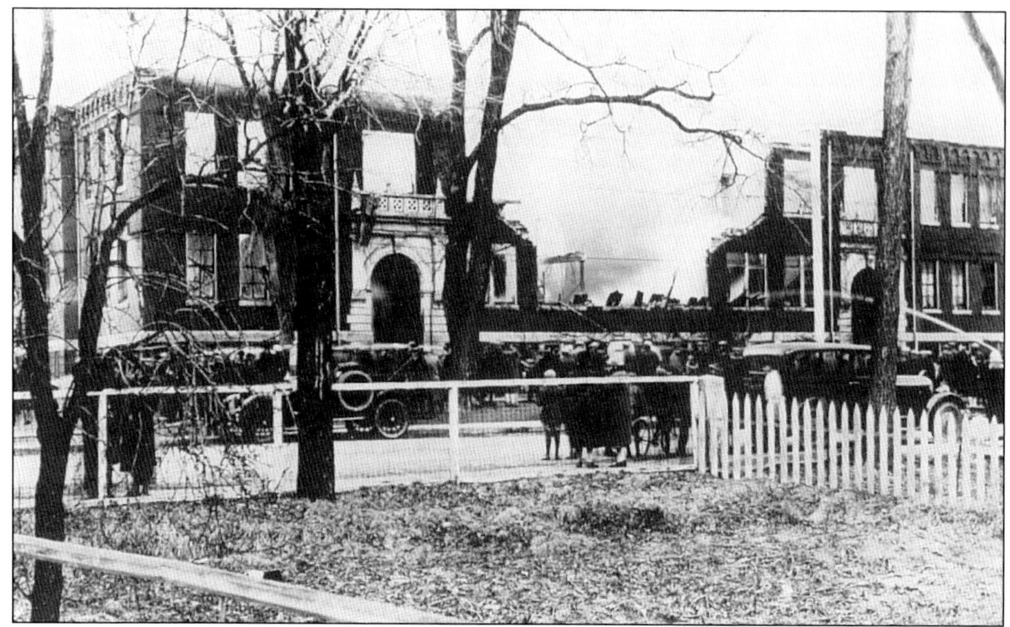

After the fire. A fire demolished the high school in the early morning hours of March 23, 1928. A student recalls attending an operetta there the previous evening.

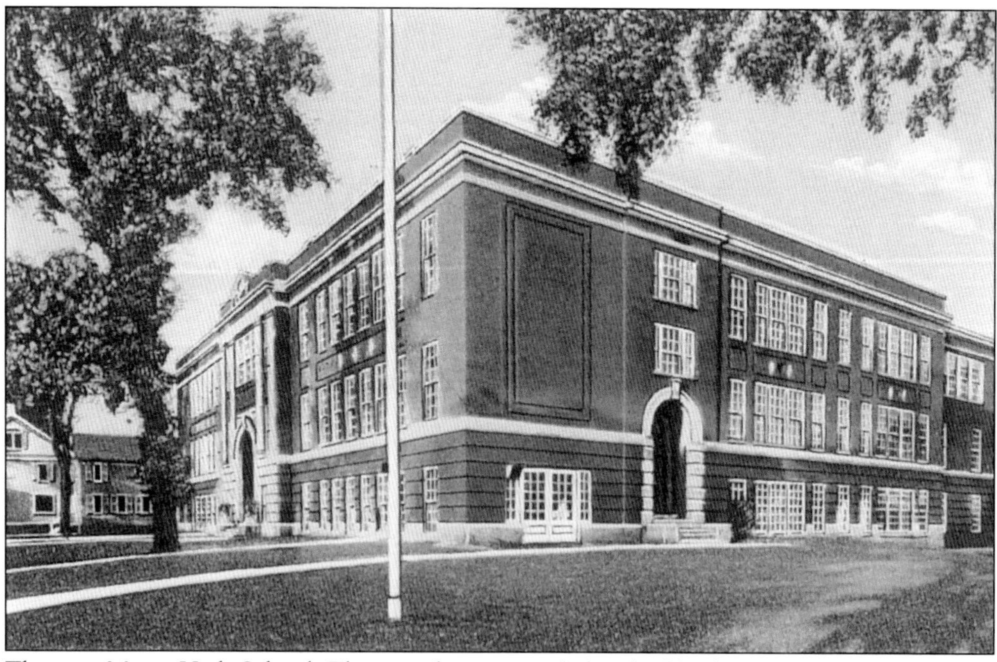

The new Morse High School. The city then proceeded to build a larger structure, which has since been expanded considerably.

Coaches, 1947. The excitement of a basketball game between Morse and Cheverus High Schools is reflected in the "body language" of coaches Duncan Farrell and Dennis Murphy.

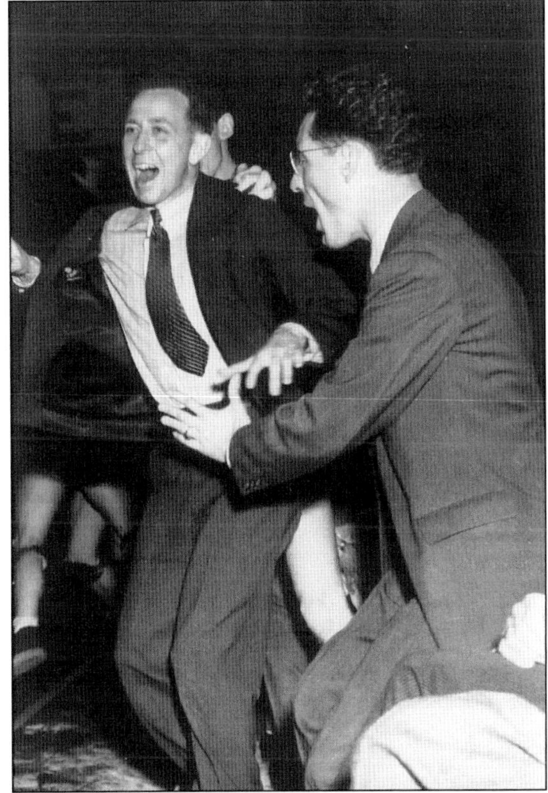

Regional champions, 1947. The team went on to bring home their first regional trophy that year. Flushed with victory are, from left to right: Bob Smith, Ken Coombs, Squeak Irish, Blaine Trafton, Paul Ouellette, Coach Farrell, Ace Burgess, Knute Holmsen, Everett Parker, Charlie Andre, and Ted Sturtevant.

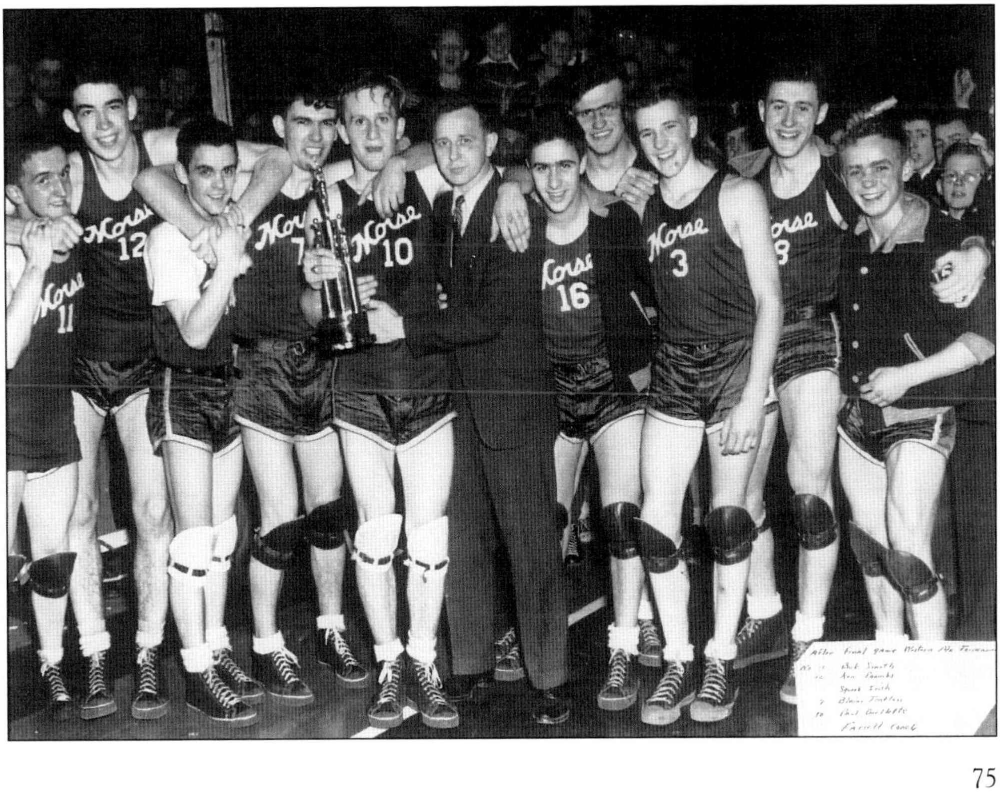

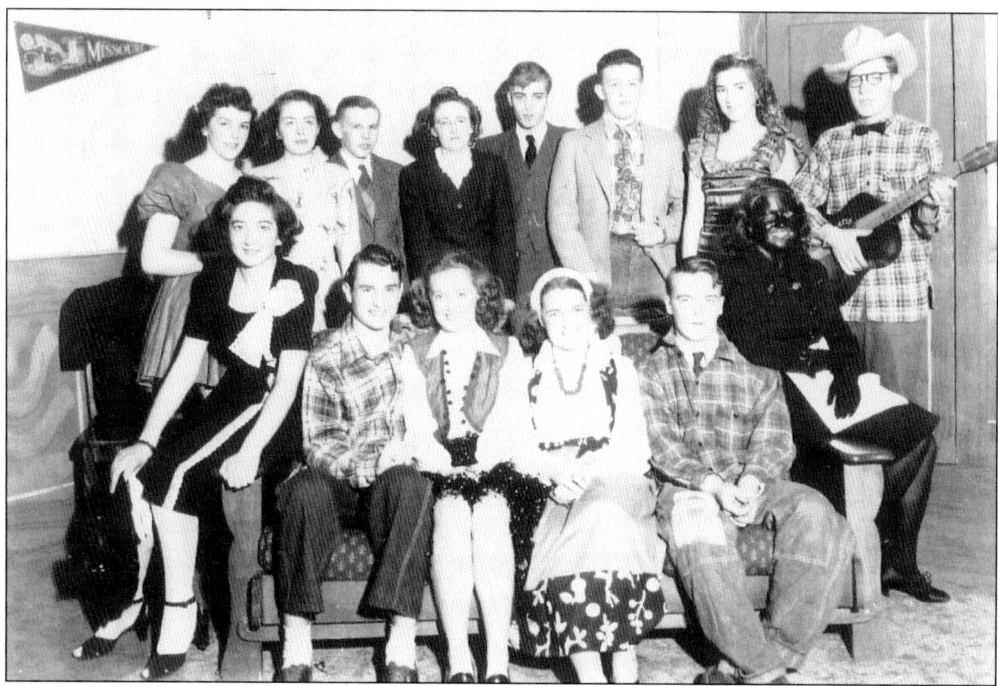

A class play, 1946. Drama has also flourished at Morse High School, and various productions have won prizes. The cast of one play included: Edward Morse, William Barber, Rita Collins, Horace Morse, Barbara Preney, Valerie Nickerson, John Wishart, Ruth Small, Sarah Silverman, Riva Greenblatt, Jean Small, Charles Godfrey, and Gerald Gogan. The play was directed by Miss Irish. This was, of course, before the days of "political correctness."

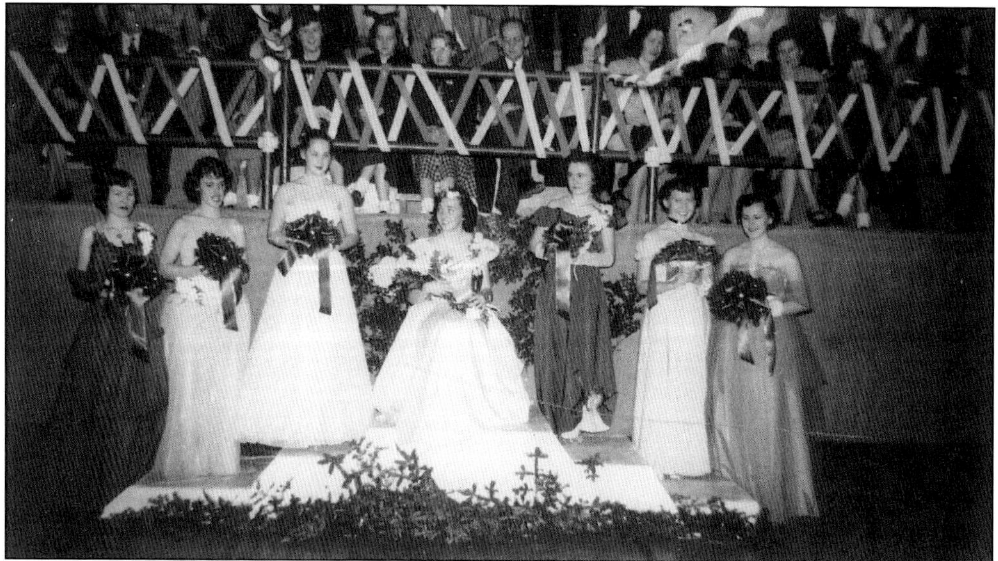

The Mohiba queen and court in December 1950. The annual Morse High Bazaar, a tradition which began in 1927, came to include variety or talent shows and a grand ball, both for enjoyment and as a way of raising money for school activities. In 1950 the queen was Connie Carlisle, and her court included, from left to right: Betty Adams, Sally Footer, Barbara Green, Nancy Pratt, Nancy Brown, and Sue Stover.

Six

Public Buildings

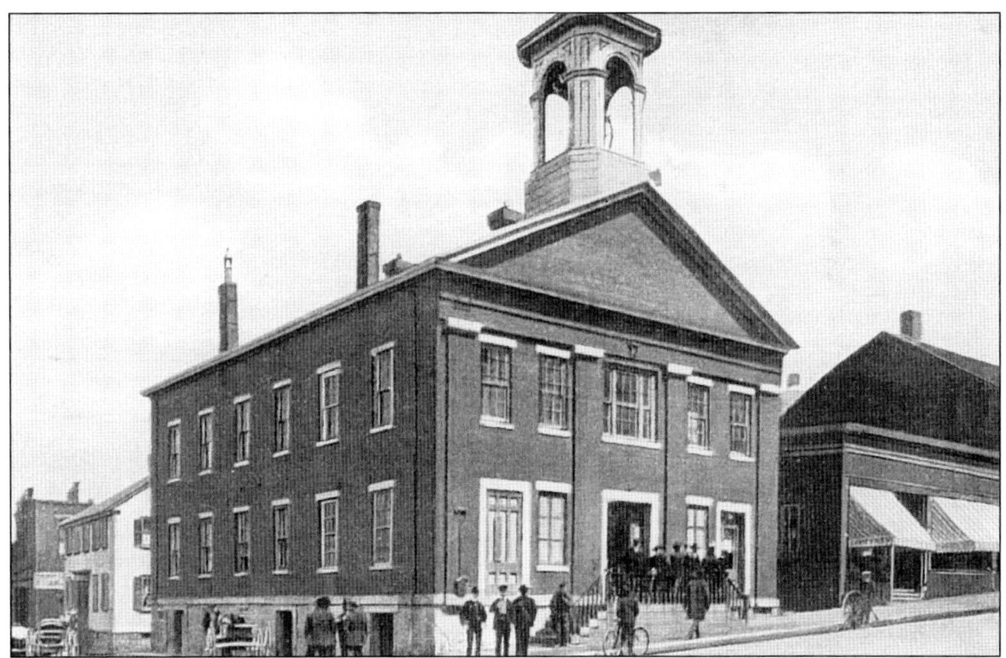

The first City Hall. Incorporated as a town in 1791, Bath erected a town hall on Center Street in 1835. When the government was reorganized as a city in 1854, the building began seven decades of service as City Hall. The belfry was added in 1861 to house a Revere bell previously used in the old Universalist church.

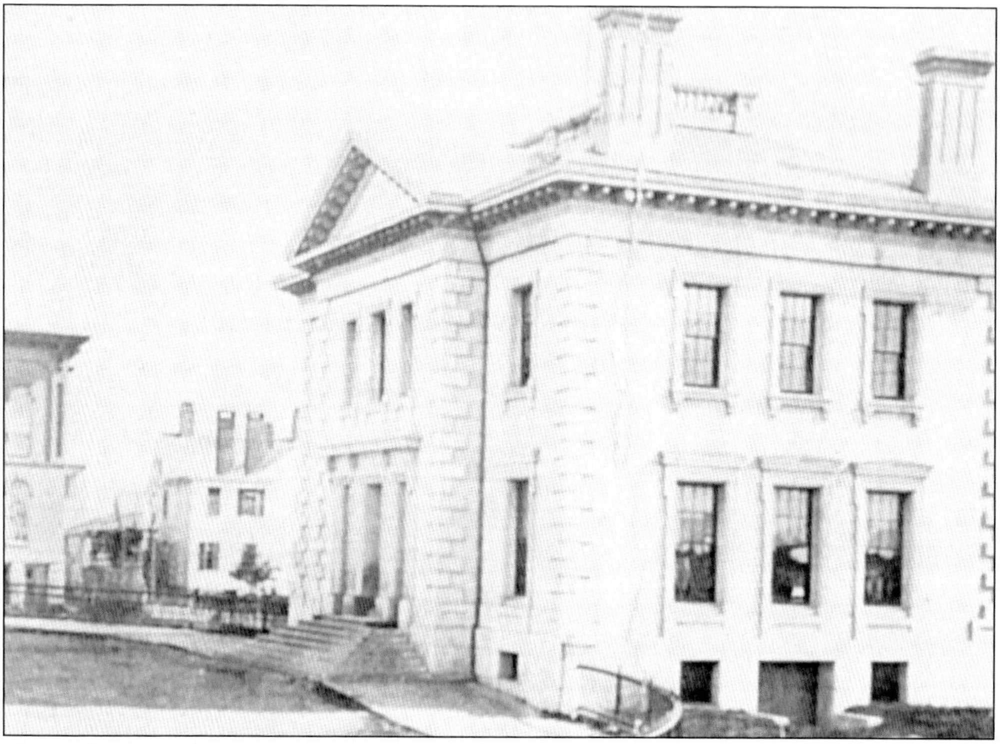

The Federal Building. This formal custom house, designed by government architect Ammi Young to use Maine granite, was located near the harbor in the late 1850s, on some of the property that had once belonged to Maine's first governor, William King. King's former house was moved to make way for the new building. Note the other large old residence that still stood in the 1870s between the commercial building next door and the wharves.

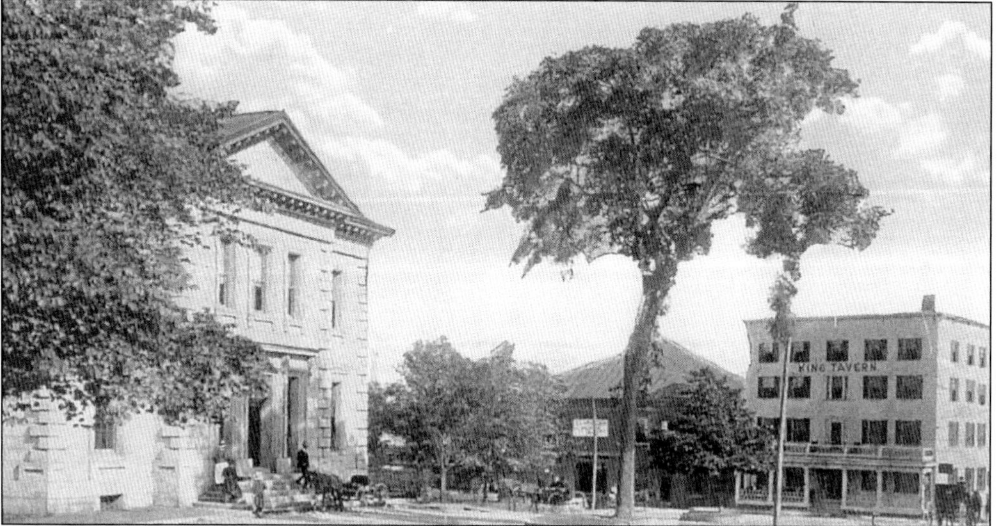

The custom house neighborhood. This postcard—printed after the Federal Buildings' iron fence was removed in 1911, but before the semicircular drive was replaced by lawn twelve years later—shows the spatial relationship between the custom house and the new location of King's former house.

The Sagadahoc County Courthouse. For over a decade after Bath became the seat of the new Sagadahoc County in 1854, county offices occupied space in City Hall. They moved into the new brick courthouse on the hill at Center and High Streets in 1868.

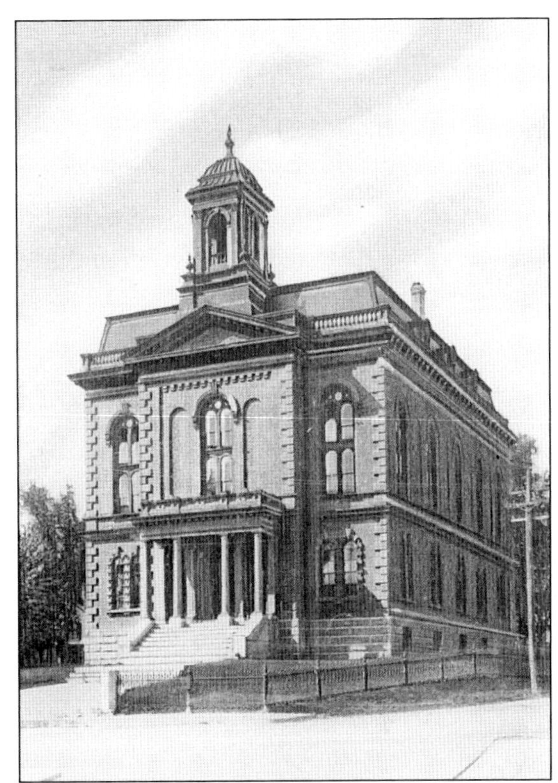

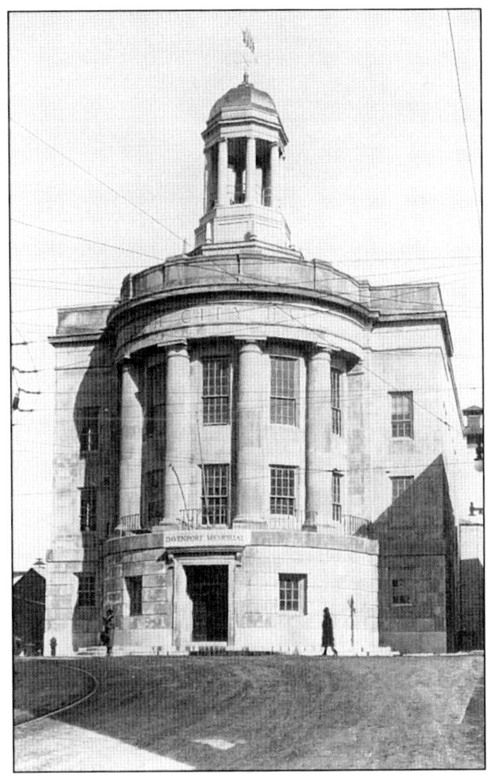

The Davenport Memorial. The new City Hall was built in 1928–29. The lot and money for the granite structure were donated to the city, and the building was named in honor of the donor's father, Charles Davenport. The town purchased more land on Front Street to place the building at the head of Center Street. (For the buildings removed, see p. 89.)

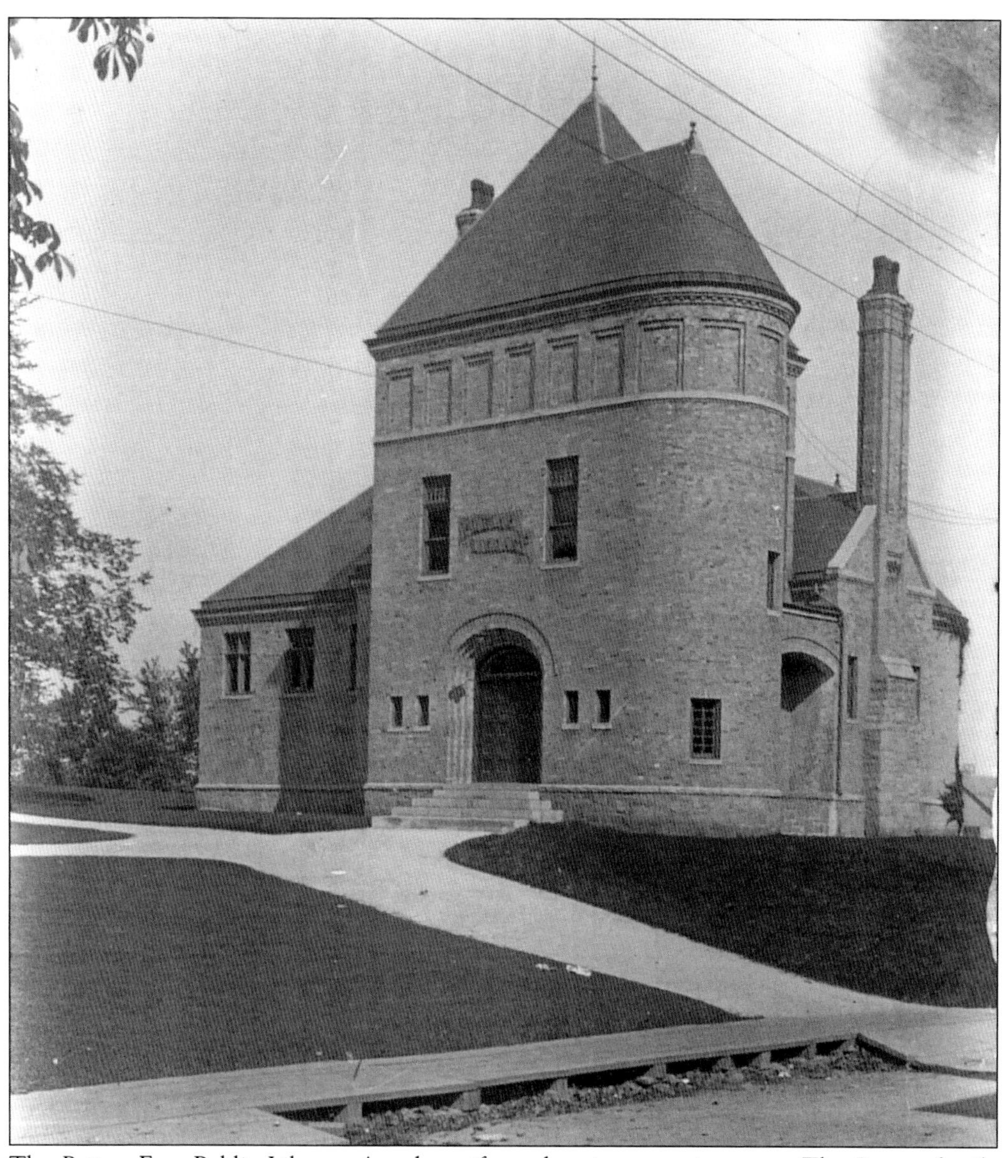

The Patten Free Public Library. Another gift to the city came in stages. The Patten family purchased the library books once belonging to William King in about 1854 and donated them to the Patten Library Association. Many years later Galen Morse provided the money to erect a new building next to the park. The Patten Free Library, designed by Bath-born George M. Harding, opened on the first day of 1891 at Summer and Front Streets.

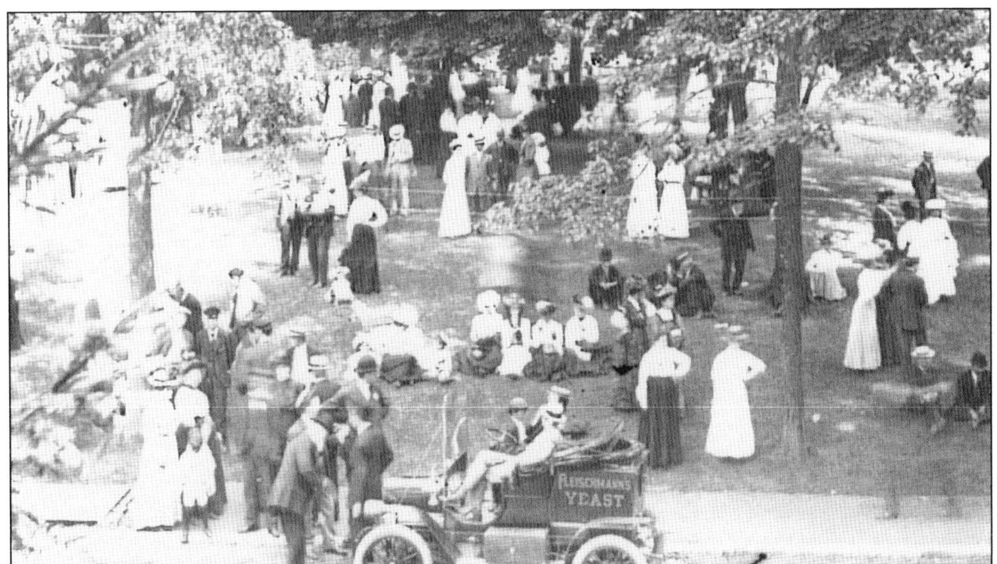

The city park. The park itself represents both civic and private contributions and is set on land purchased in the 1850s and '60s. It was landscaped and given its bandstand in the 1880s. This relaxed group, from the early twentieth century, is taking advantage of the space the park provided for summertime fetes.

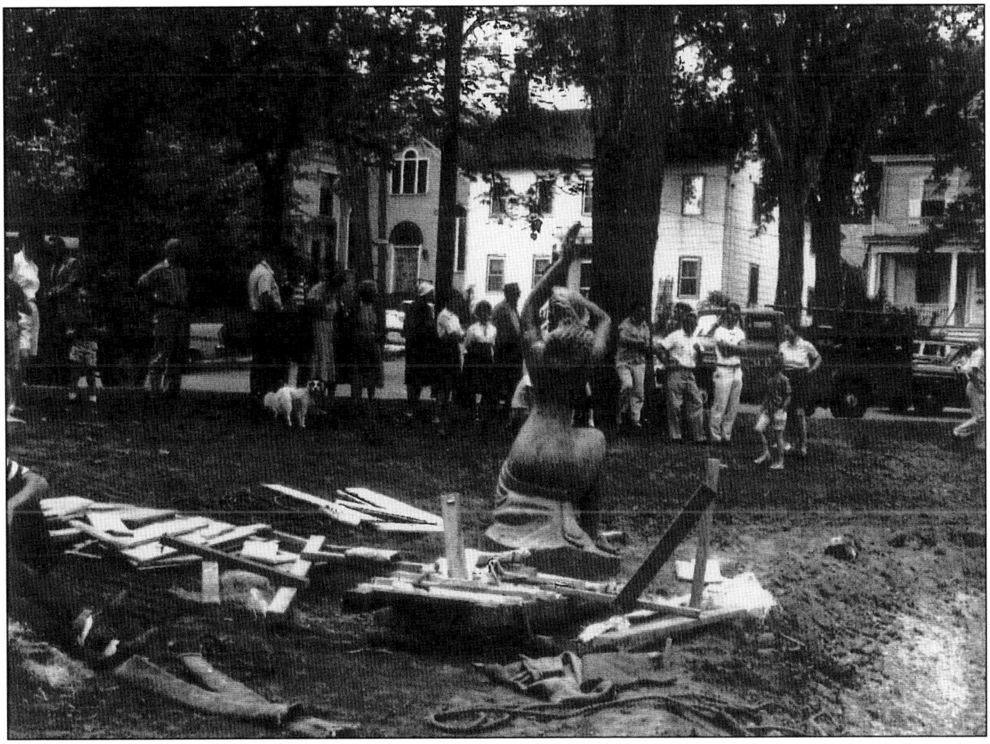

Installing a new fountain, 1962. By the 1940s, the park's pool and fountain badly needed attention; and sculptor William Zorach agreed to design a new fountain. The Bath Garden Club raised funds for the bronze casting of the *Spirit of the Sea*, which—in spite of controversy—was in place by August 1962.

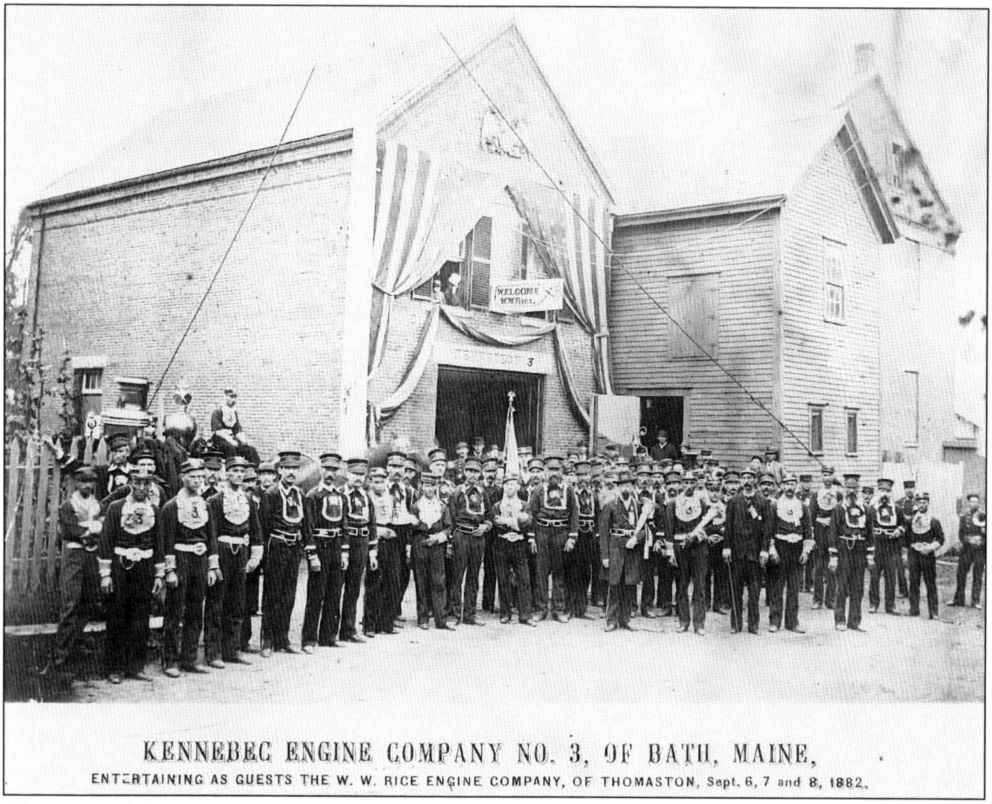

KENNEBEC ENGINE COMPANY NO. 3, OF BATH, MAINE,

ENTERTAINING AS GUESTS THE W. W. RICE ENGINE COMPANY, OF THOMASTON, Sept. 6, 7 and 8, 1882.

The Central fire station. The city of Bath maintained up to four fire stations. The Kennebec Engine Company No. 3 had a brick building, built in 1853 partly on the "flats" of the tidal inlet beside Water Street, near the downtown area. It stood for over a century until condemned in 1957.

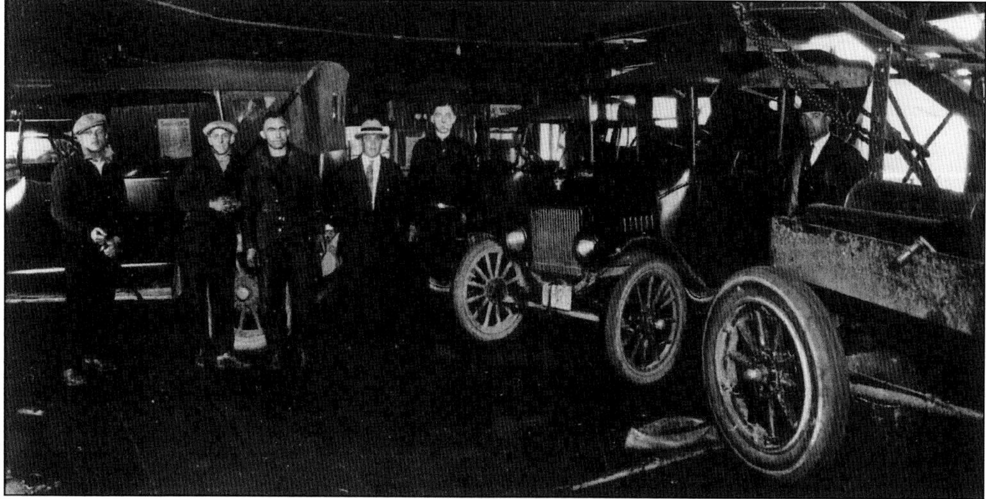

The city garage. The city also had to maintain facilities for its vehicles; this included, in the 1930s, a garage for the upkeep of road trucks and city cars. Shown inside the city garage on Commercial Street are workers and a couple of visitors. From left to right are Zach Eramo, Clarence "Blue" Merrill, Bob Linekin, unknown, Carl Linekin, and Julius Gediman.

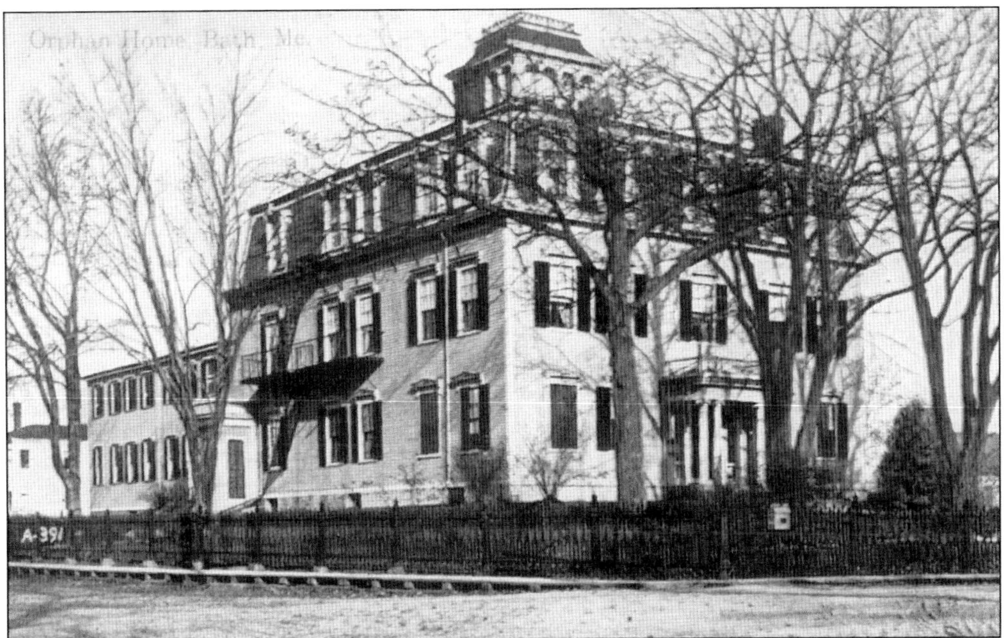

The Bath Military and Naval Orphan Asylum. Donations from the city's religious societies helped form, in 1866, an institution with the stated intention of caring for needy children of men who had served the Union. It became a state institution by 1870, and was housed in an 1800-era house that had been remodeled and enlarged to suit. Being open to "half-orphans," the Home could assist families in difficulty.

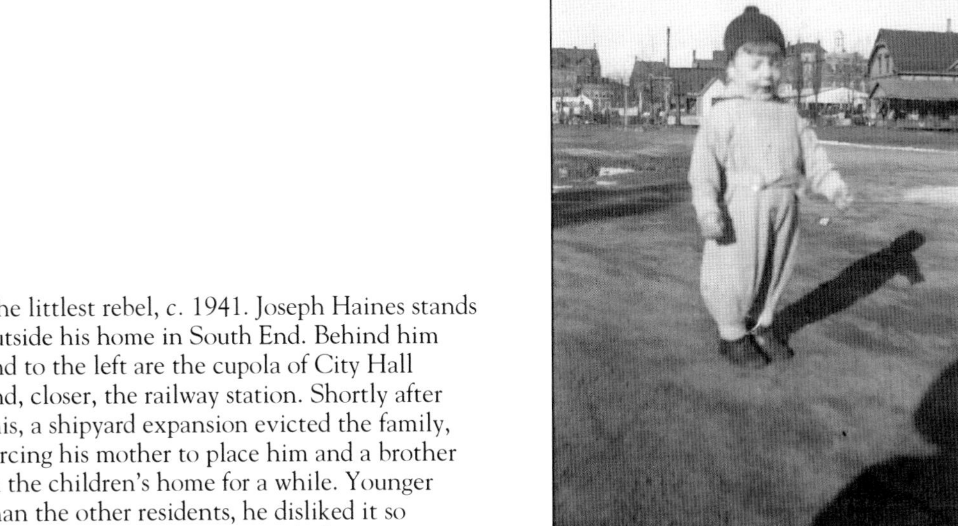

The littlest rebel, c. 1941. Joseph Haines stands outside his home in South End. Behind him and to the left are the cupola of City Hall and, closer, the railway station. Shortly after this, a shipyard expansion evicted the family, forcing his mother to place him and a brother in the children's home for a while. Younger than the other residents, he disliked it so much he tried to run away with the circus!

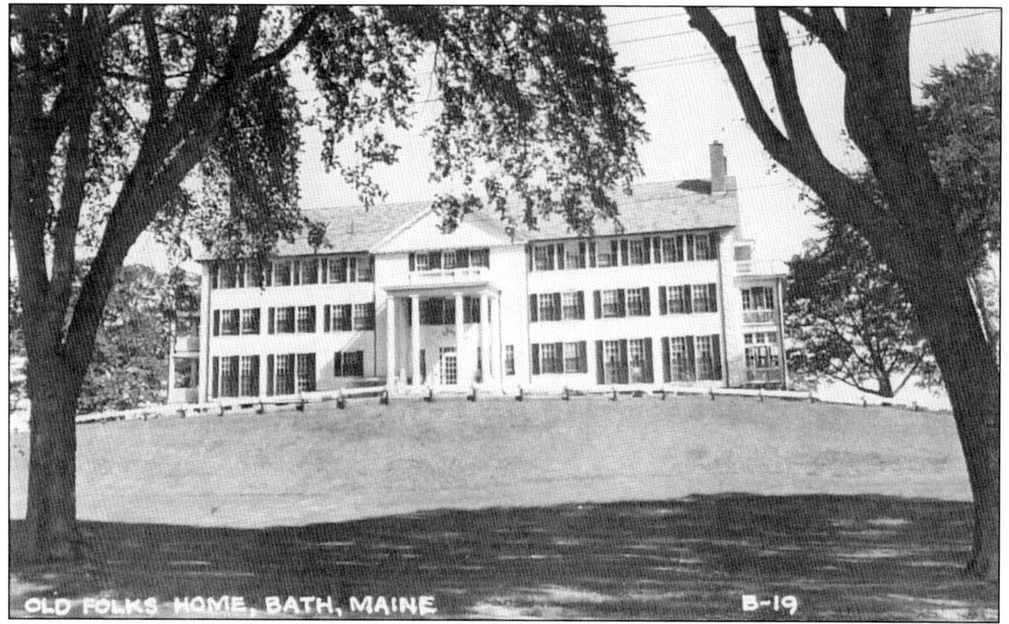

The Plant Home. Older citizens were served through the generosity of another Bath native, shoe manufacturer Thomas Plant. In 1917, the Boston firm of Coolidge and Carlson planned this Neo-Colonial home for the elderly, built in the South End on Hospital Point, the former location of an 1820s marine hospital. It soon absorbed the Aged Couples' Home, established by the King's Daughters in 1893.

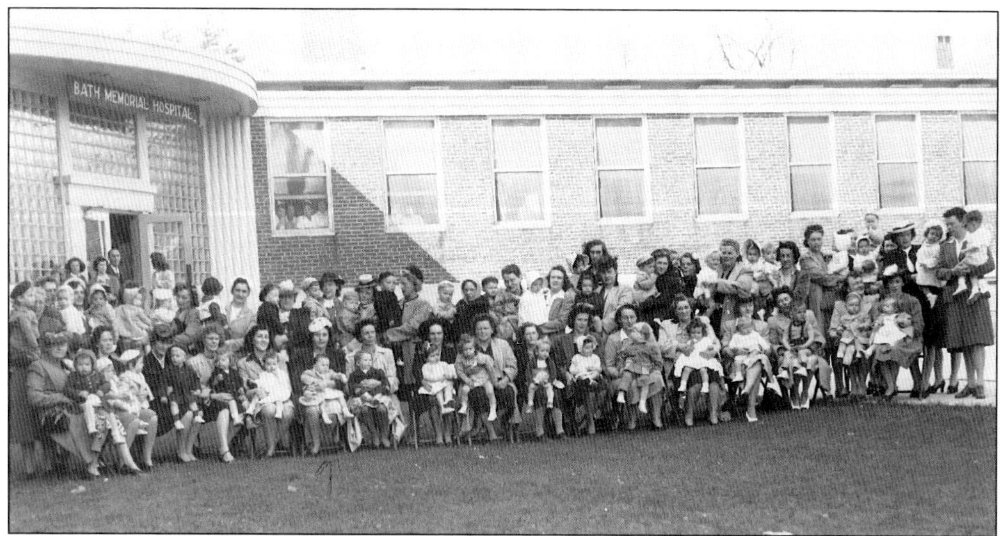

New citizens of 1945. In the fall of 1946, Bath Memorial Hospital, founded in 1907 as Bath City Hospital, celebrated the previous year's large crop of babies by inviting them all back for "Hospital Day." Their mothers posed with them in front of the building while staff watched through windows.

Seven

Getting Around

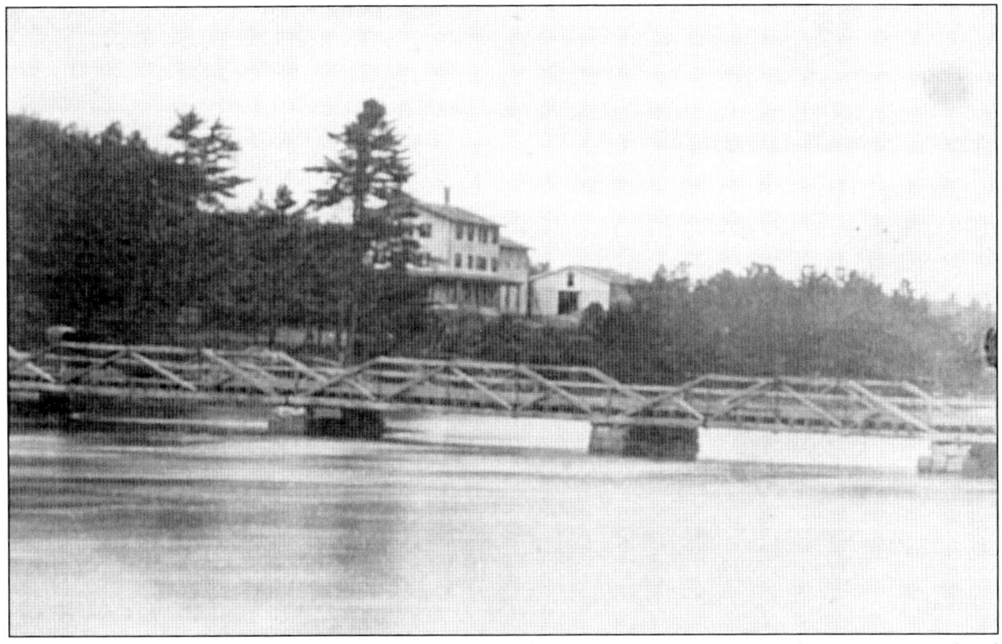

Bull Rock Bridge. Bath was beautifully situated for water transportation; but going overland posed problems, with the Kennebec River on the east, Merrymeeting Bay (where the Androscoggin and Kennebec Rivers join) on the north, and an inlet so long it was named the "New Meadows River" forming most of its western boundary. Most of the southern border was either a tidal inlet or a marsh. Bridges were so important to the citizens that Bath officials accepted financial responsibility for a bridge across the lower Androscoggin between East Brunswick and Topsham, as well as for maintaining Bull Rock Bridge at New Meadows. The latter's Brunswick end is shown above. Bath had to finance its upkeep even after West Bath became a separate municipality.

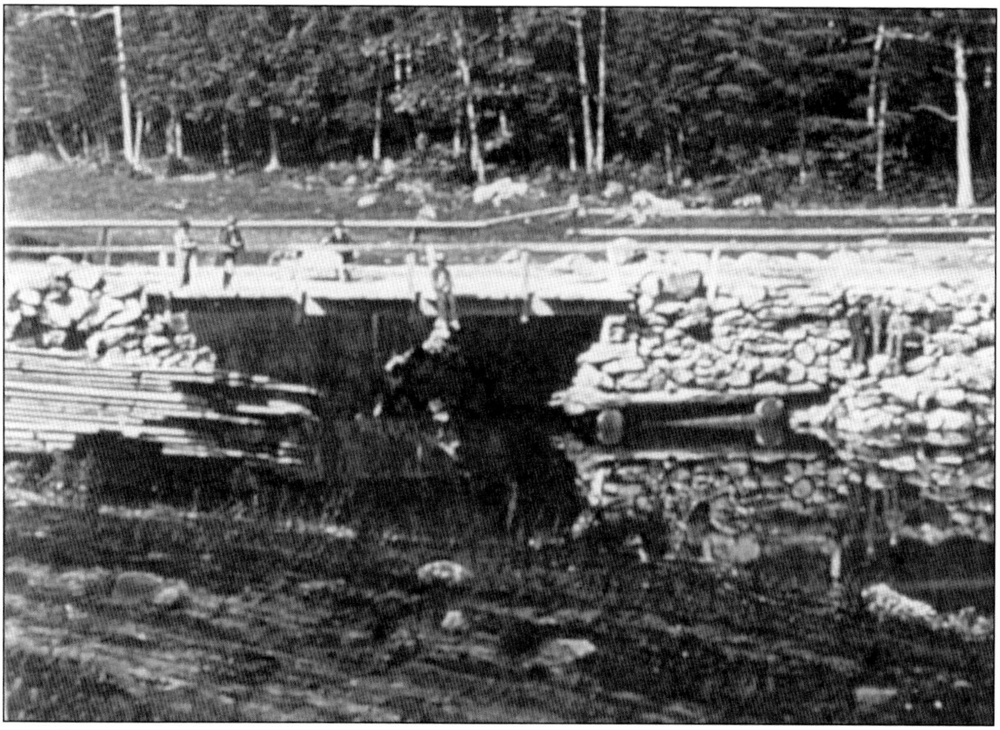

Sewall's Bridge in the 1870s. The short stretch of land between the New Meadows River and Merrymeeting Bay could best be reached by crossing Whiskeag Stream. Sewall's Bridge was located near the dam where Dummer Sewall erected a mill in about 1764. It remained a mill site for over a century. Note the lumber nearby.

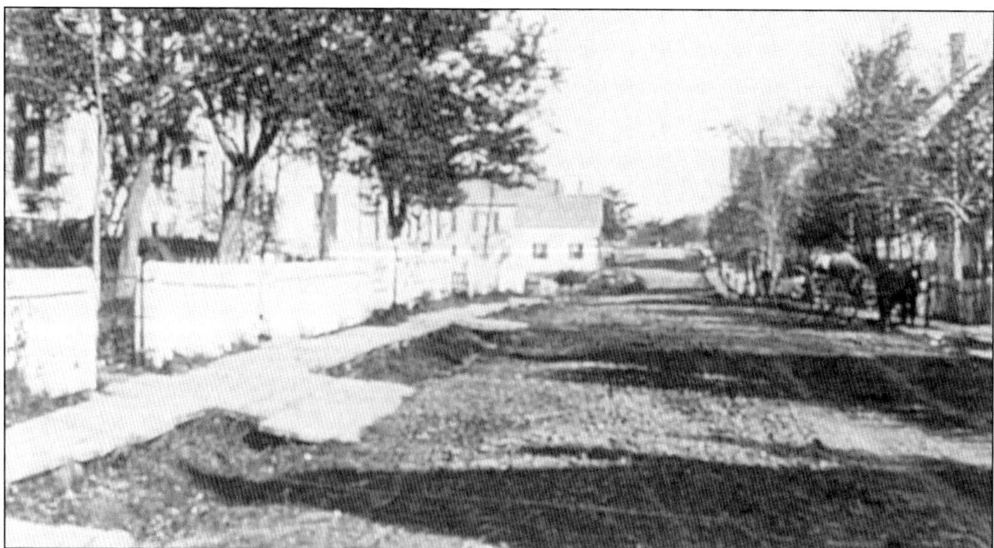

Dummer Street in the 1870s. Roads were unpaved, as were city streets. Not until 1891 was there a move to surface even Front Street, although after the 1894 fire, part of that street was widened and given curbstones and solid sidewalks. In 1904 the city could still only boast 1/4 mile of granite paving (see pp. 89 and 104) and about 4 miles of macadamized streets. Center Street west of Water Street remained dirt until about 1915.

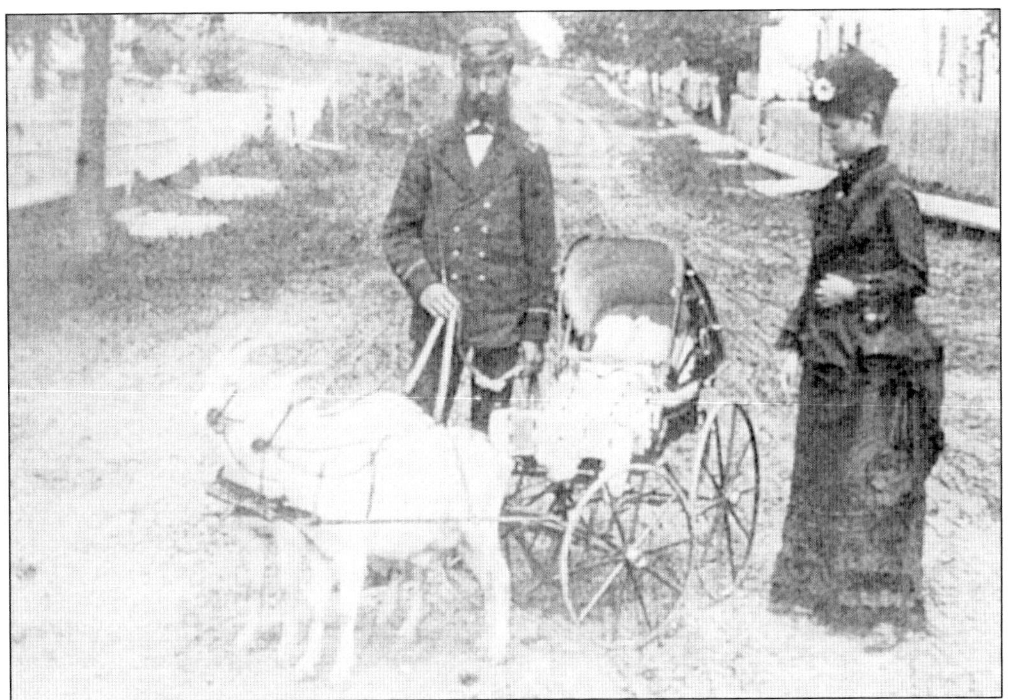

Goat power, 1870s. Before the late nineteenth century, individuals wishing to move themselves or their goods about relied on animal power. Ordinarily this involved horses or oxen, but Mr. and Mrs. Arthur Devreaux employed goats to pull the baby's buggy.

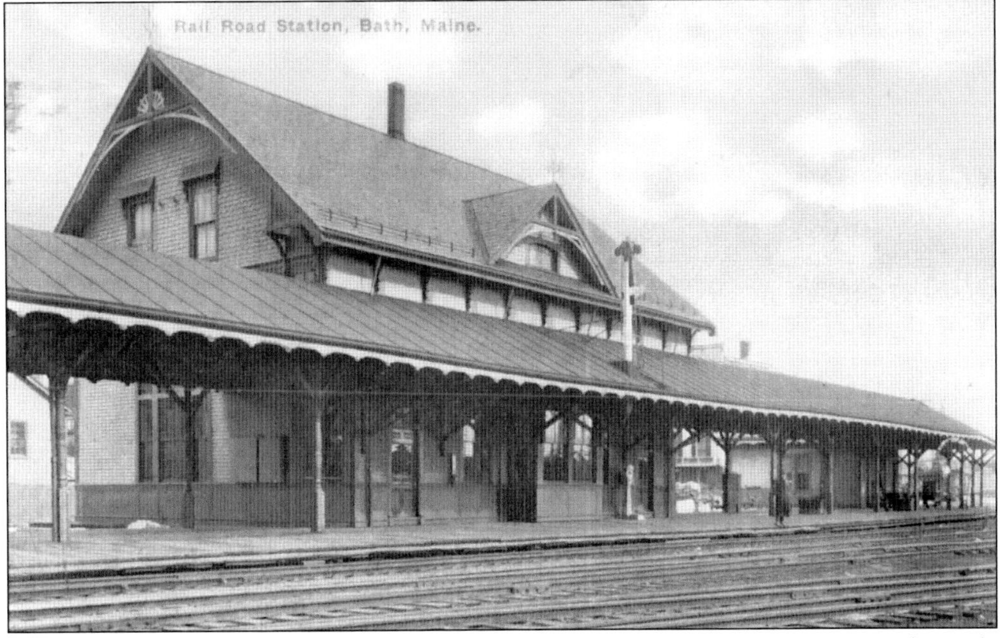

The railway station. Railroads connected Bath to Brunswick and the west in 1849. This early station was replaced in 1941. The city's interest in transportation extended to investments in railroads: a ninety-two-year indebtedness for bonds in the eastern Knox and Lincoln Railroad was not paid off until 1961.

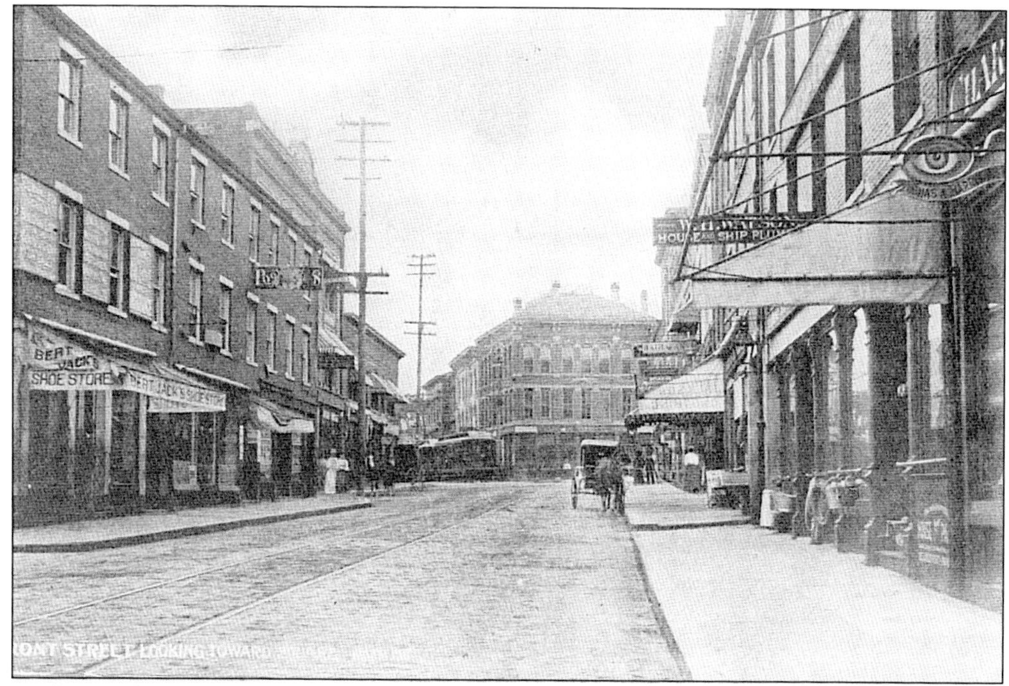

Trolley tracks. Trolleys appeared on Bath city streets by 1893, and connections to Brunswick in 1900 went via New Meadows. The trolleys ran along the centers of business and residential downtown streets, and operated until 1937. This view of Front Street, with trolleys at the curve, should be compared with the view of about a half-century earlier on p. 11.

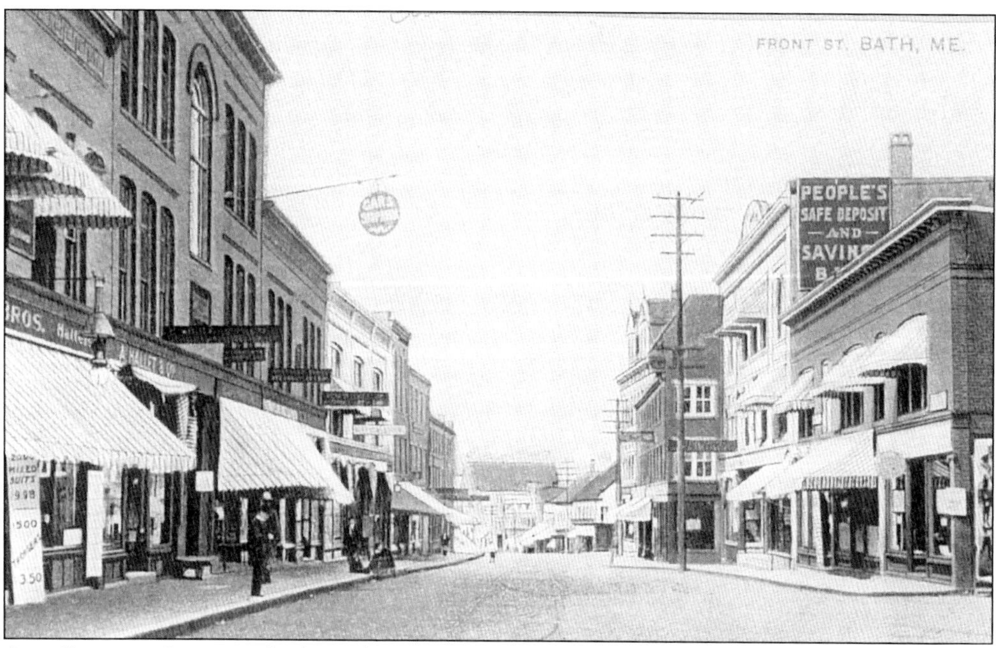

A trolley stop. In a view looking the opposite way along the same stretch of street, the tracks show up less well, but an overhead sign, "CARS STOP HERE," indicates where the trolley could be boarded.

A horse and buggy in the 1870s. The importance of horses can be realized not only by noting how many appear in street pictures, but by the fact that they were often brought out, along with all adults and children, when a home was being photographed. Judge Arthur Dunton lived here on Washington Street.

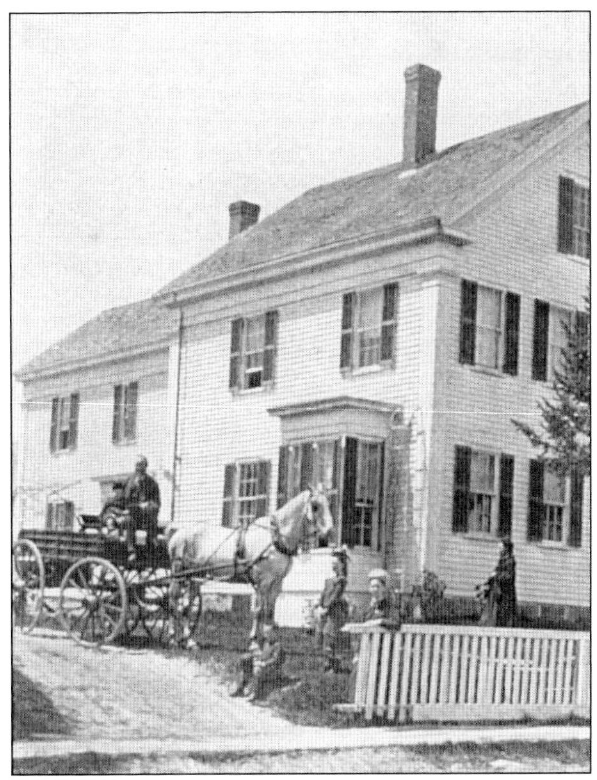

Anti-horse protection. Horses continued to be used for many years: the city highway department did not sell off its last animals until 1947. The posts installed for telephones and electricity proved useful as hitching posts, but bored animals might take to gnawing on anything handy. This made wrapping wires around the posts advisable (see also p. 23.) The buildings shown here are the three on Front Street that were removed in the 1920s to make room for the new City Hall.

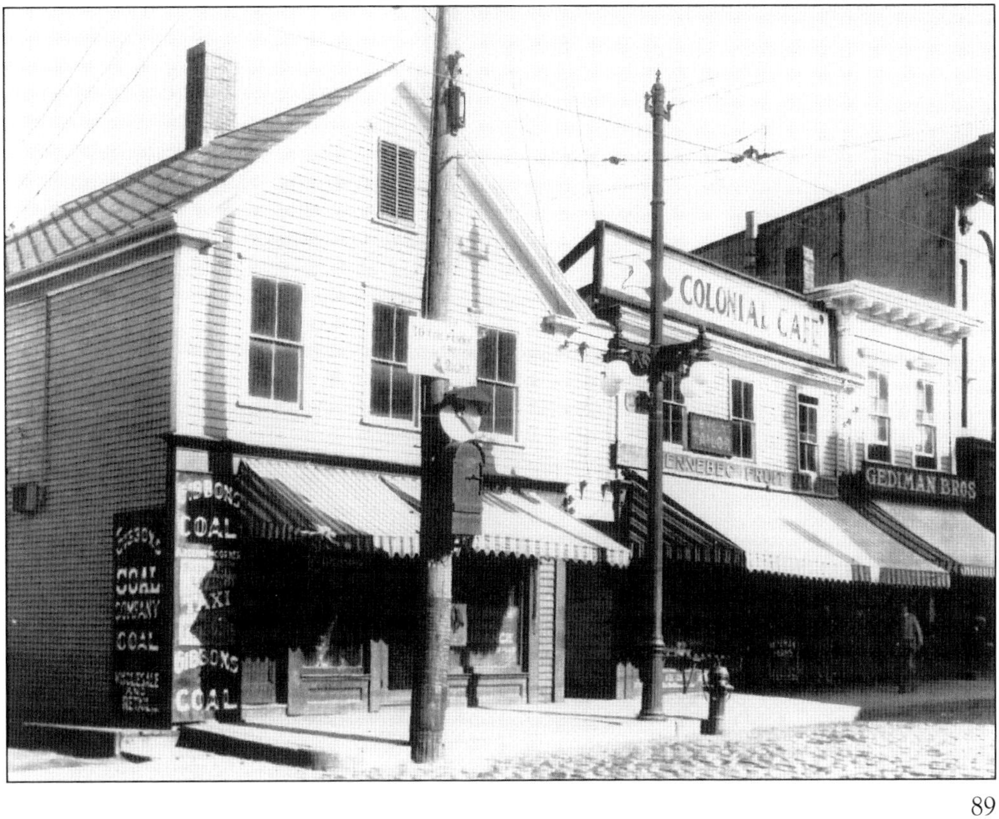

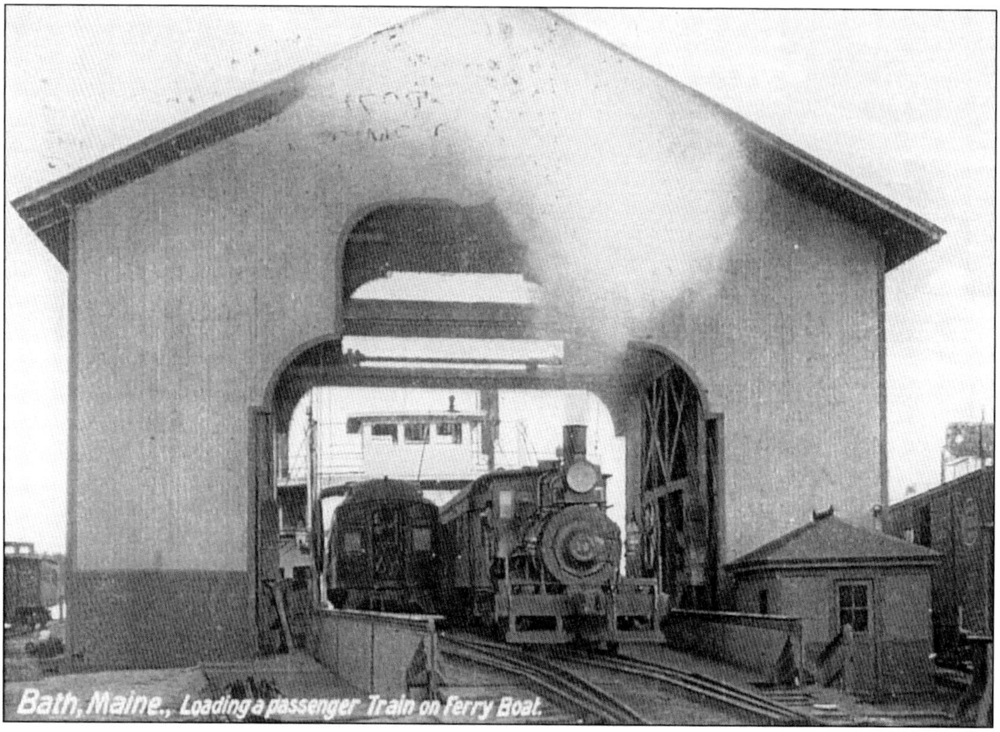

Bath, Maine., Loading a passenger Train on Ferry Boat.

A train ferry loading. Railroads laid toward the east could connect with Bath only by ferry. Until 1927, trains expecting to continue to the east came to the Bath waterfront and were loaded onto ferries to be carried to the other side of the river.

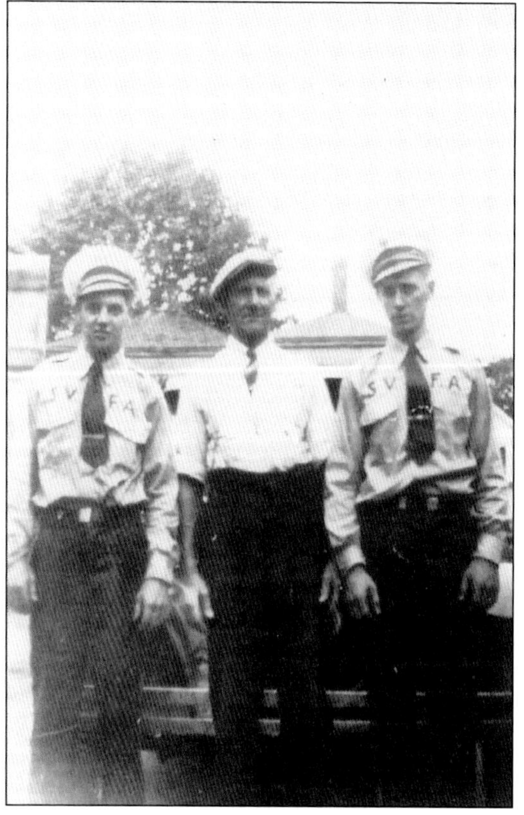

Lester Munsey Sr., shown here between his sons, was one of the men who put the trains on ferries. Lester Jr. and Russell Munsey are wearing firemen's uniforms.

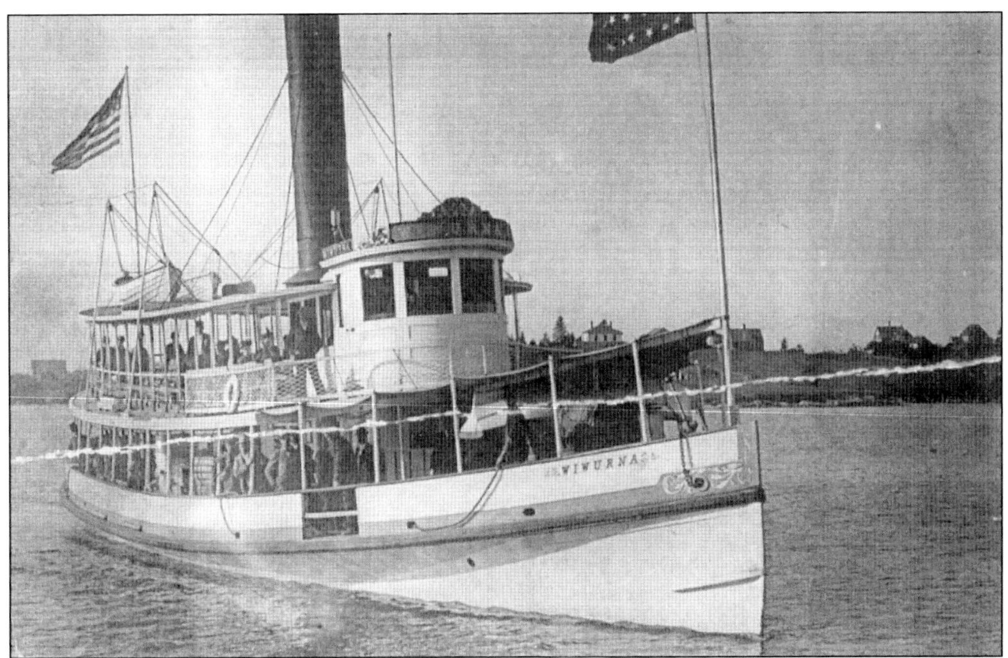

The steamer *Wiwurna* in the 1930s. Small steamboats continued to provide alternate transportation on the river in the pre-World War II years. The *Wiwurna* ran between Bath and Boothbay.

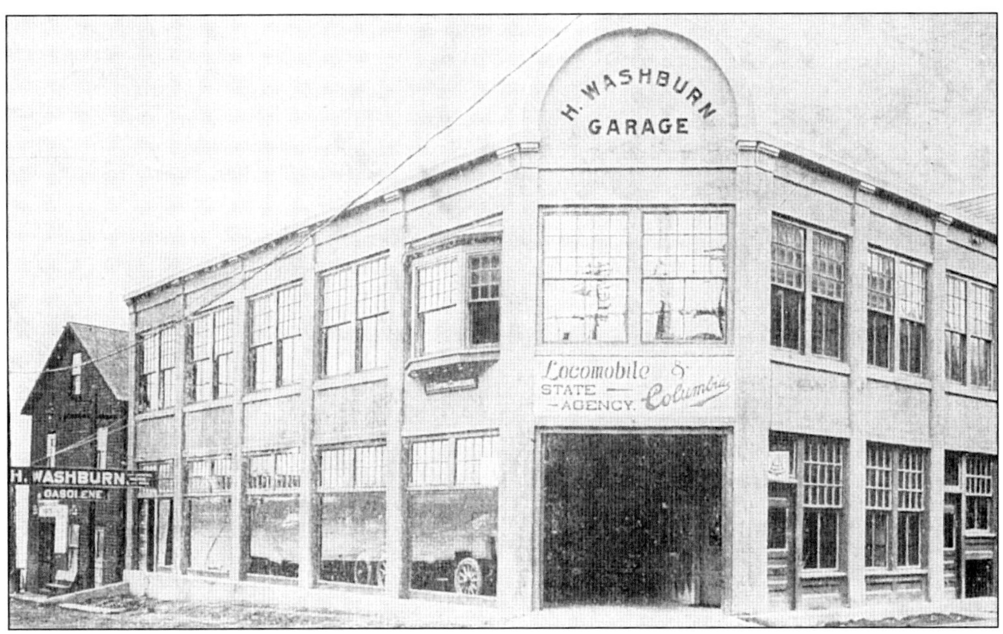

Washburn's Garage. The automobile age arrived with the twentieth century. H. Washburn's Garage, located near the waterfront on Broad Street, was erected in 1908 and was the first poured concrete garage in the state. The upstairs offices included that of a customs official, in the space with the oriel window. (The custom house had not yet been expanded.)

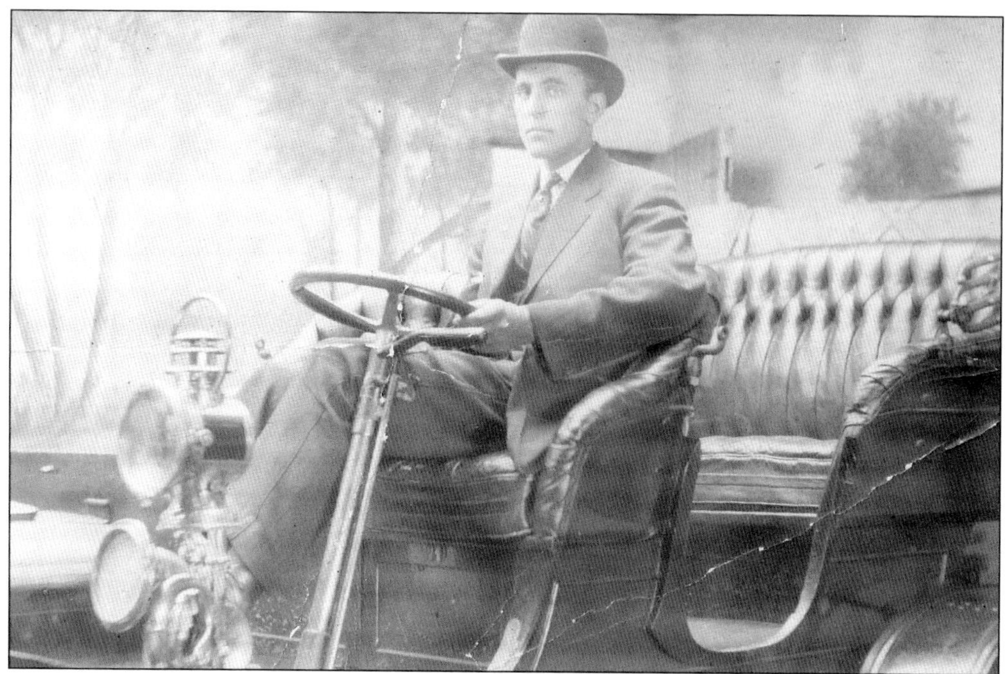

An automobile, *c.* 1908. Joseph White Larrabee is shown posing in a new automobile in front of a painted background. New autos were considered as photogenic as horses had been.

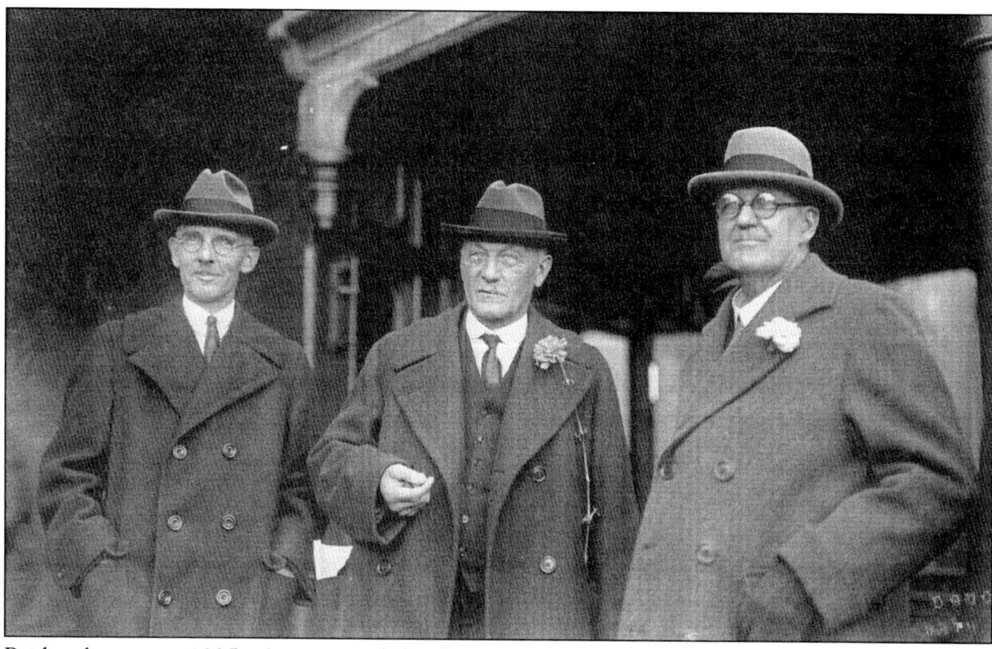

Bridge boosters, 1925. As automobiles became more commonly used, ferries proved less adequate. Lines of cars filled the streets leading to the ferry, making movement in that part of the city difficult. Many voices cried for a bridge at Bath, including those of N. Gratz Jackson, president of Bath's Kennebec Bridge Association; Senator Frank W. Carlton of Woolwich, who worked in the state legislature; and Bath's mayor, George Dean.

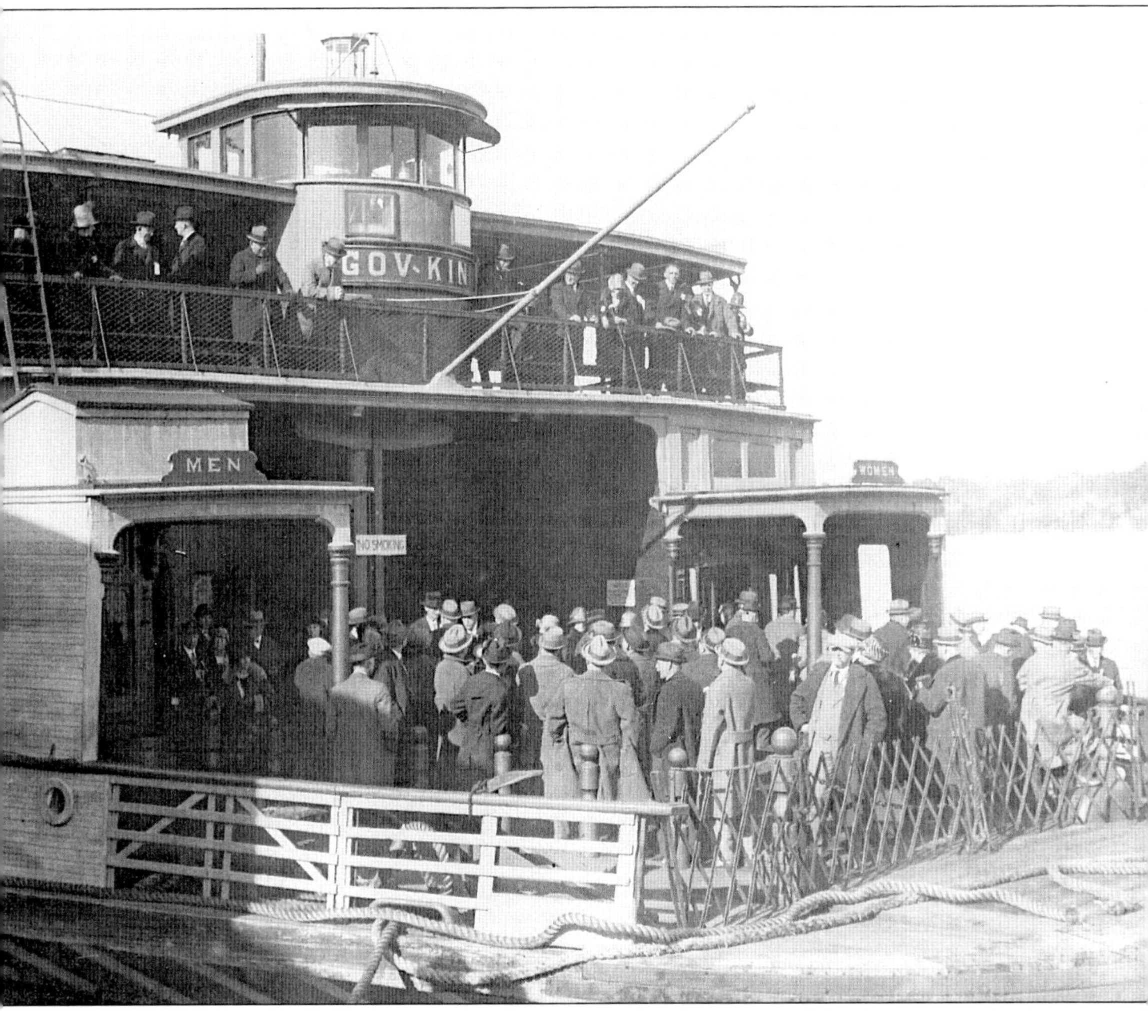

A legislative junket. By 1925 the state legislature agreed to finance a toll bridge, to carry both automobiles and trains. On March 30 of that year the city of Bath hosted the 82nd legislature, offering them a ride on the ferry *Governor King* to look over prospective sites.

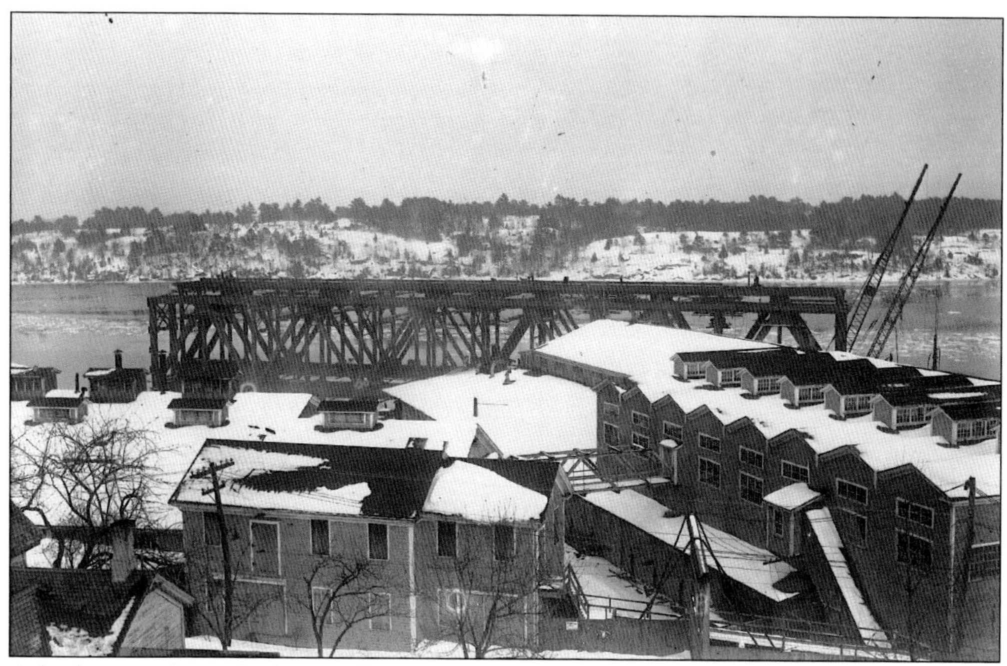

A bridge span being built. Test borings for the bridge piles began in the fall of 1925, and during the next few years the bridge and its approaches were built. Sections of the span were constructed in the North End, upriver from the bridge site, at the old "Texas Yard" (where oil tankers had been built earlier).

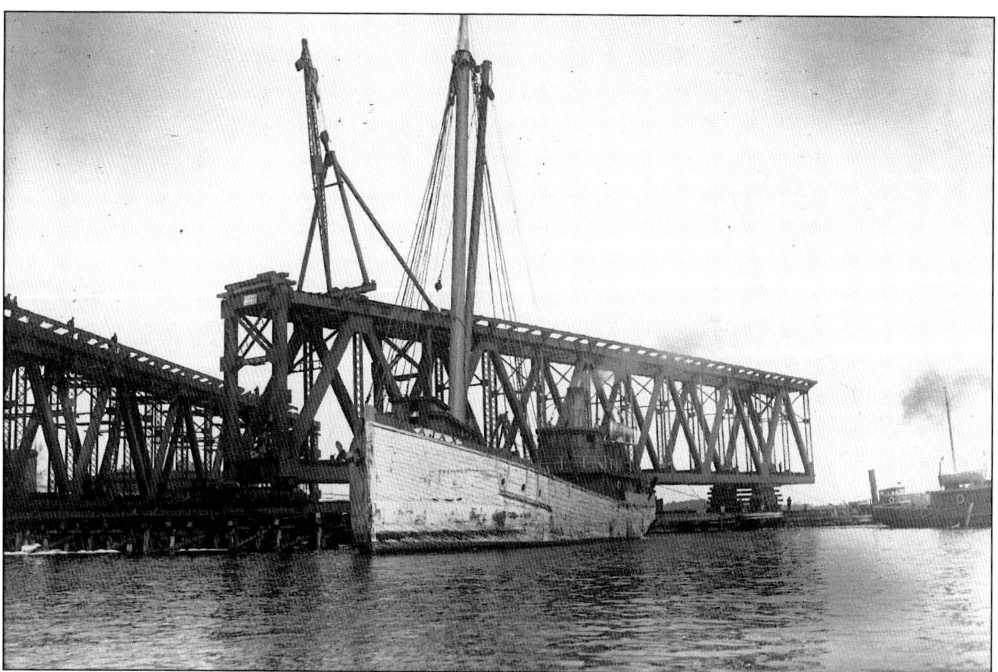

Loading a section. When completed, each individual section was moved onto barges and floated, with the help of tugboats, to its proper location.

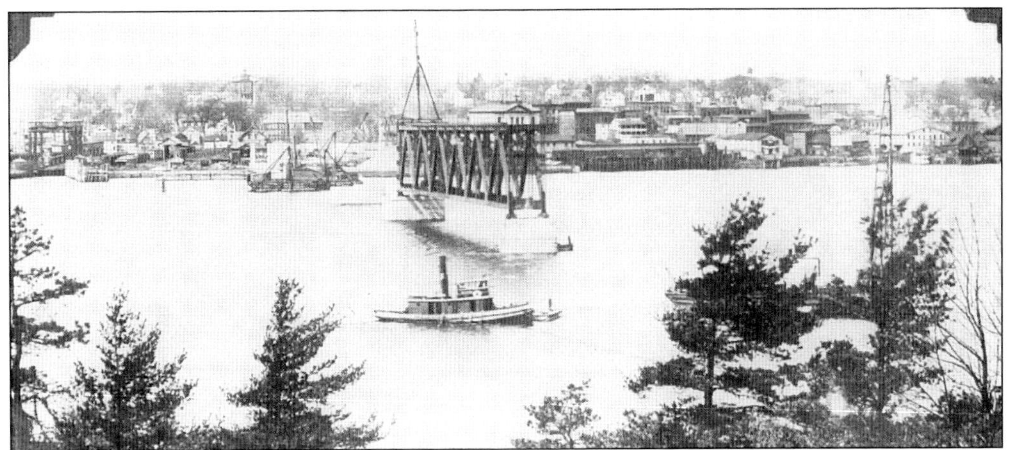

A section in place. The first span was installed between the fourth and fifth piles on March 17, 1927.

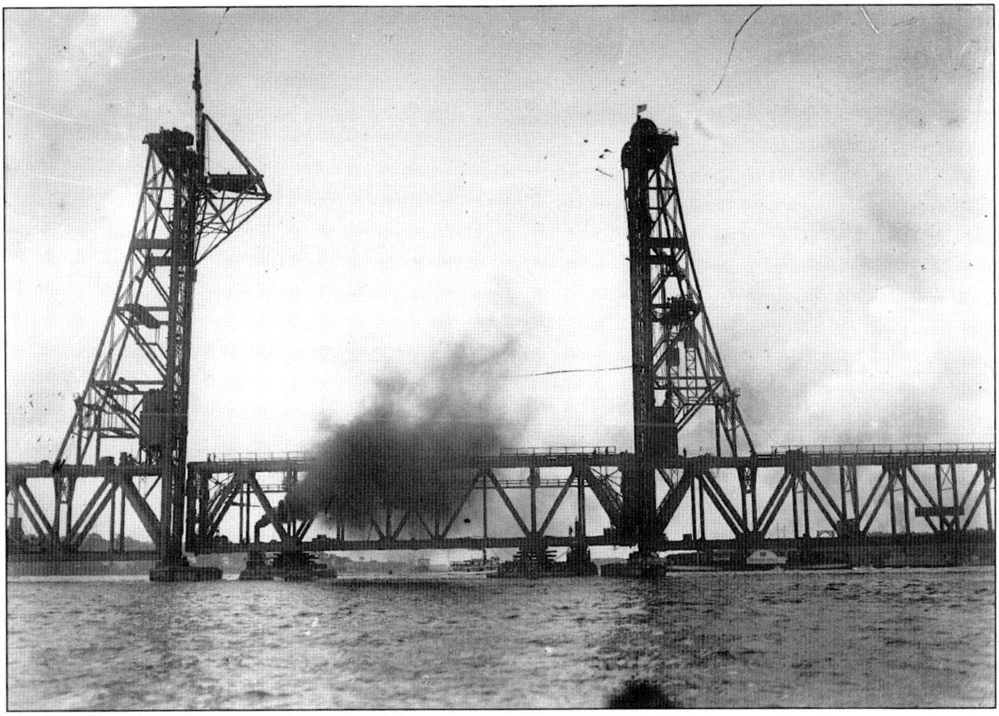

The final span, September 1927. The last span to be put in place was the draw section, the portion which could be raised on towers to allow tall vessels continued use of the river.

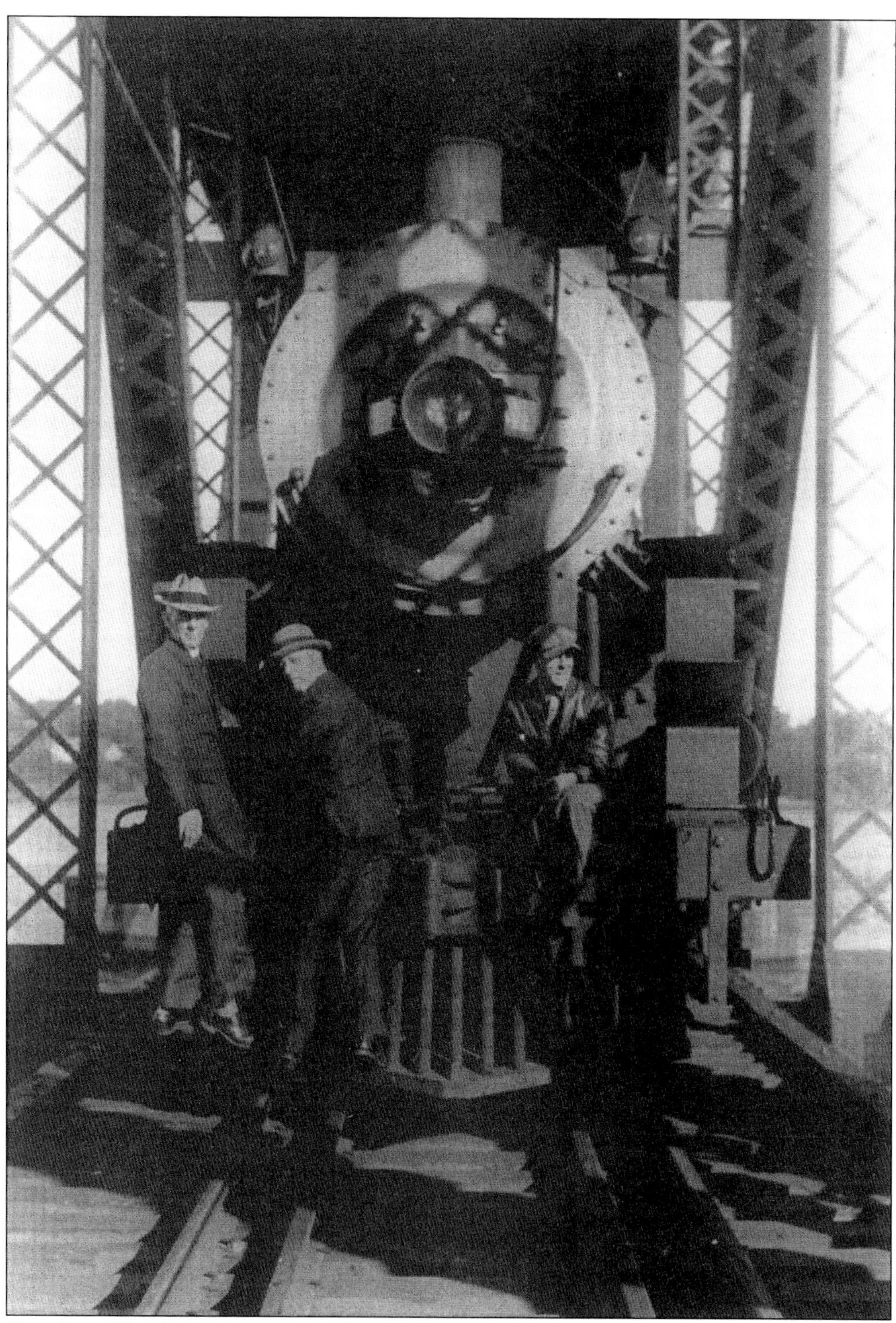

A trial run. The first engine to cross the bridge did so on October 10, 1927. N.G. Jackson, of the Kennebec Bridge Association, is the man on the cowcatcher, to the left. Mr. Jackson also led the way in his auto when the upper deck was opened to traffic about a month later.

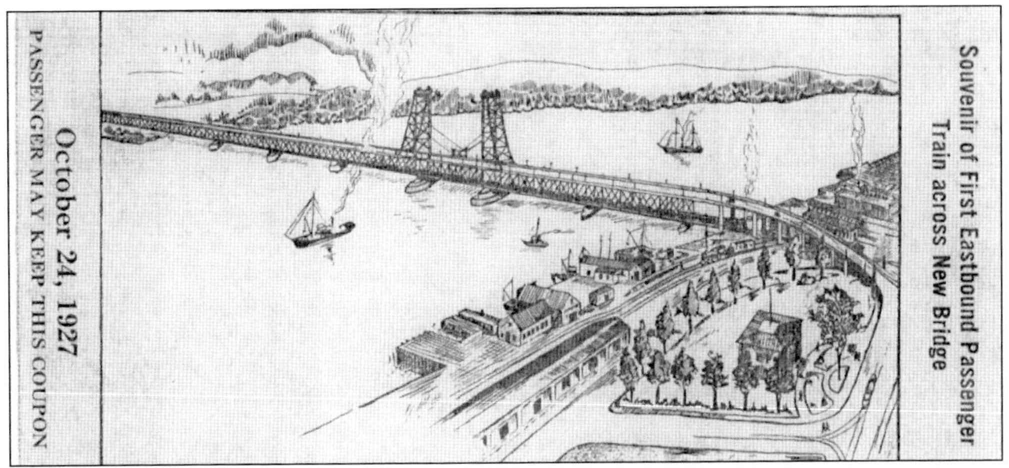

A souvenir ticket, 1927. Special tickets were printed for those taking the first passenger train across the new bridge on October 24. The design includes the custom house at the lower right.

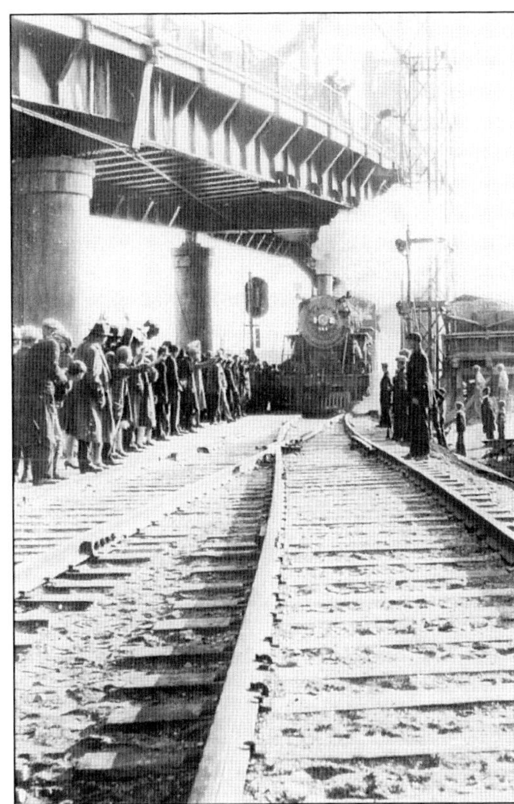

The first train arriving in Bath. A crowd gathered to welcome the first passengers: the bridge opening was truly welcome.

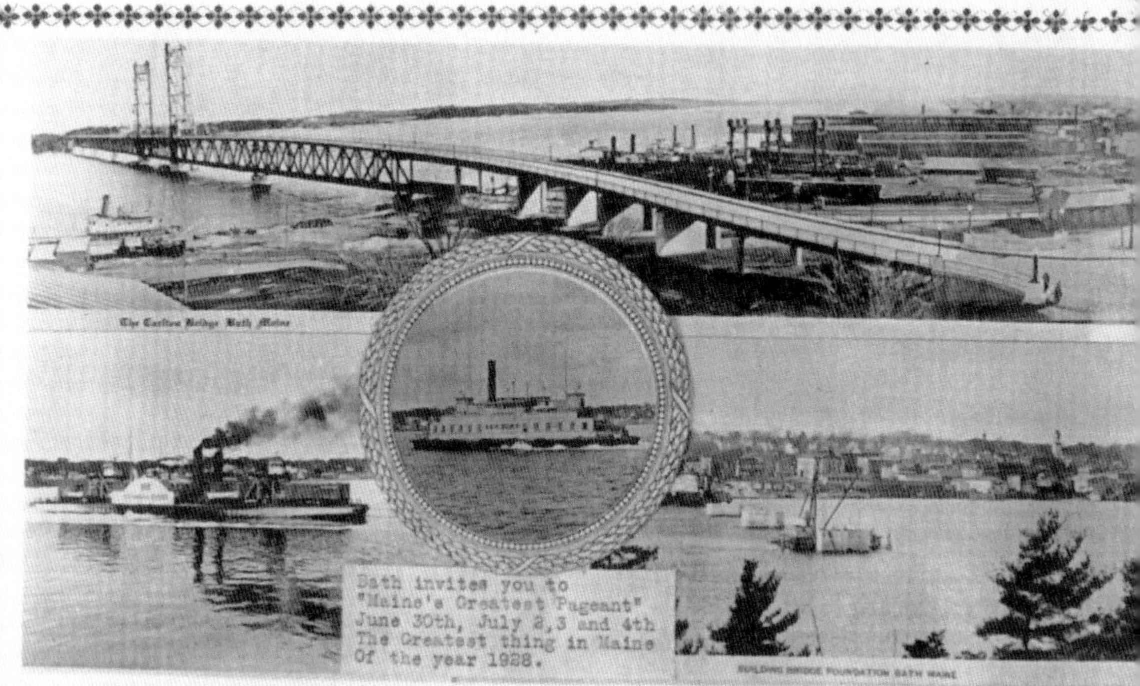

A general invitation. The people of Bath were so pleased with the new bridge that different composite postcards were printed as invitations to its official dedication on June 20, 1928, and to the week of celebration to follow. This example has a photograph of the bridge across the top, with what it was replacing shown below: the BIW-built railroad ferry *Ferdinand Gorges* (lower left) and the auto ferry *Governor King* (center), with pier construction at the lower right. Other "invitation postcards" showed more ferries or many views of the completed bridge.

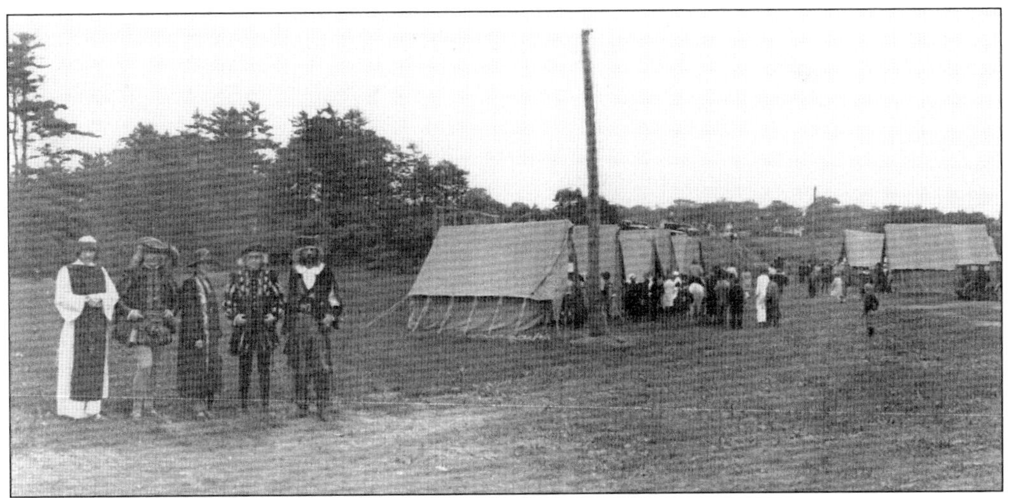

Pageant costumes, 1928. Along with formal ceremonies, the celebration included twice-daily performances of a pageant celebrating the history of the lower Kennebec, presented in a field near Whiskeag Creek. A few participants converse near the tents.

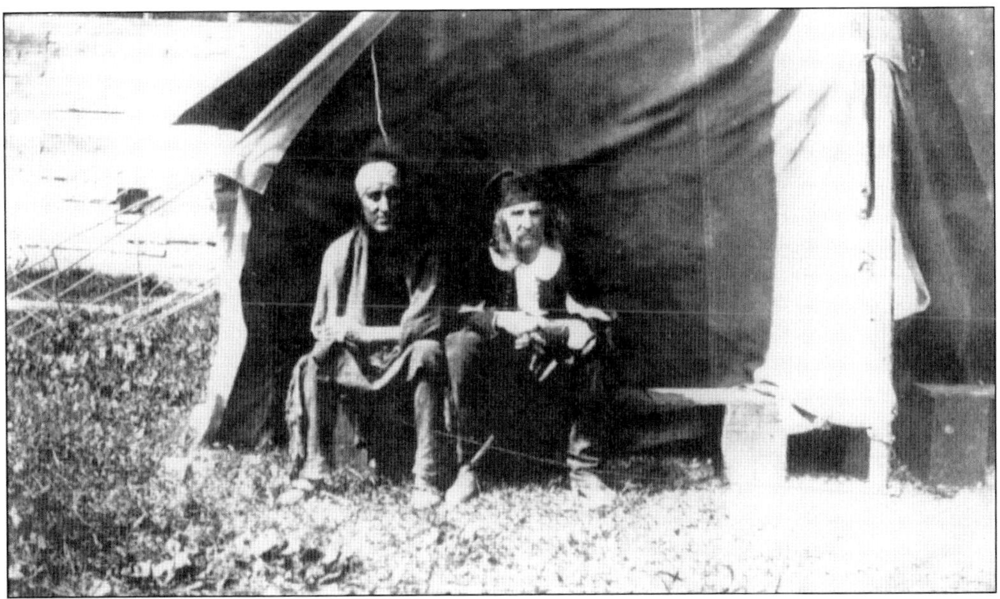

Resting between performances. Here an "Indian" relaxes with "George Weymouth," portrayed by N. Gratz Jackson.

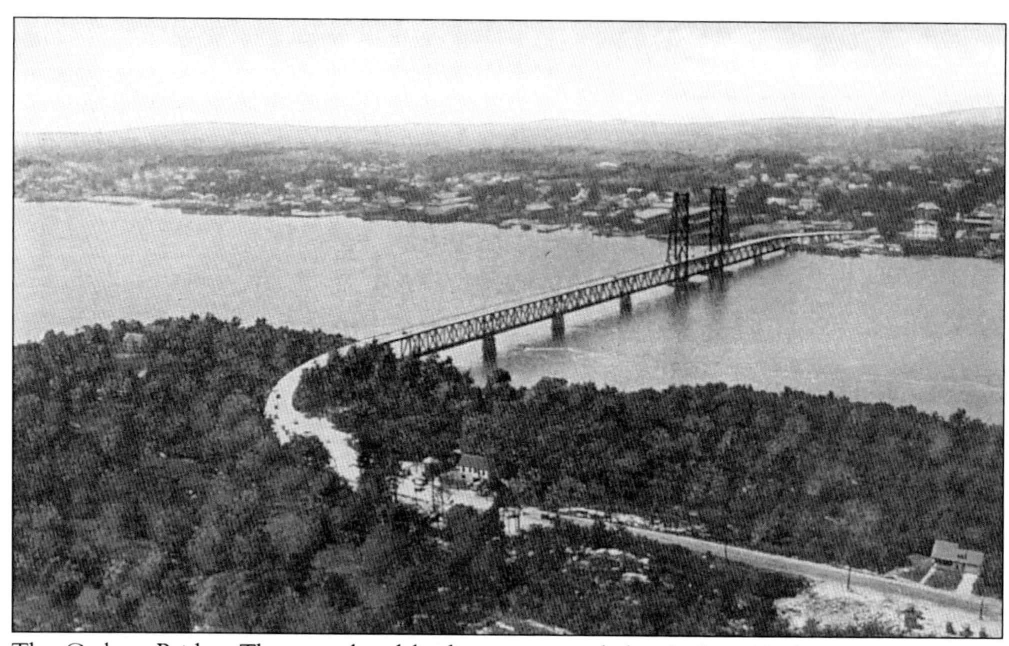

The Carlton Bridge. The completed bridge was named the Carlton Bridge in honor of the Woolwich legislator (p. 92) who had pushed so hard for its construction. This view is from the Woolwich side, where toll booths collected fees until 1948.

STATE OF MAINE

CARLTON BRIDGE

BATH-WOOLWICH

IDENTIFICATION CARD

No. 3357

To the State Highway Commission:

This is to certify that

Kathleen M. Clark

who has signed this card in my presence, is a citizen or bona fide resident of Bath and is entitled to personal use of the Carlton Bridge as provided in order of P. U. C. Feb. 6, 1935.

Effective:

City or Town Clerk

Mar. 14 1935.

Signature of holder

SEE REVERSE SIDE

A bridge pass. Regular users of the new bridge might purchase passes for themselves—or even to use as gifts. This card was a gift to a small girl in 1935.

Eight

WORK AND PLAY

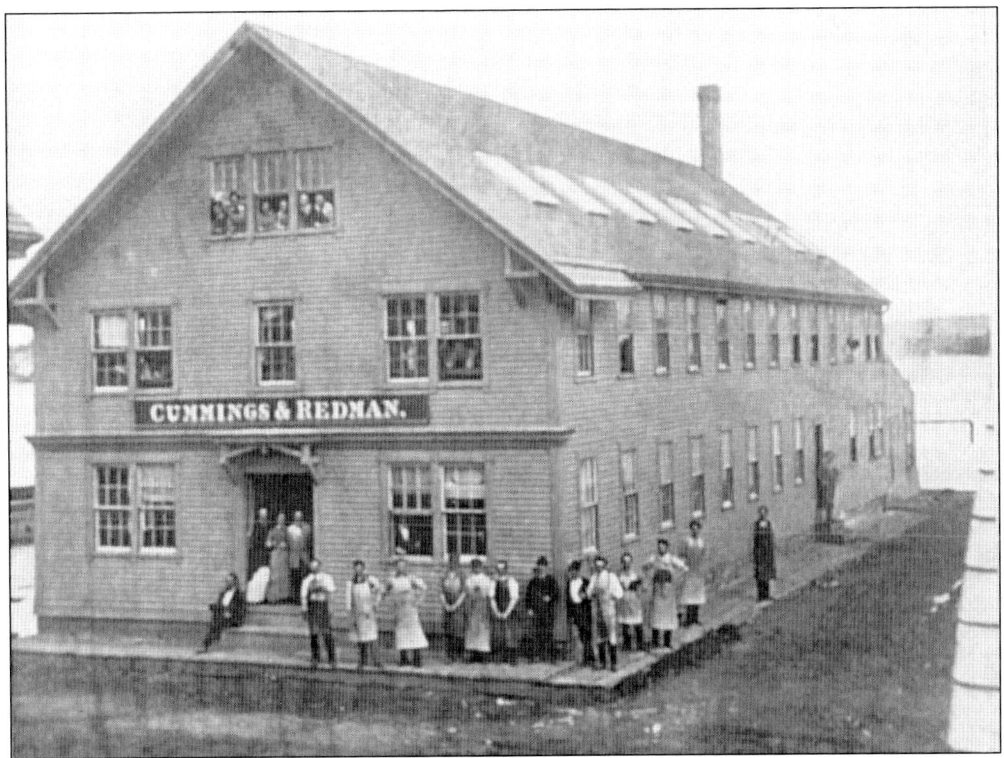

A shoe factory, c. 1874. Even as Bath men produced noteworthy ships, other manufacturing firms were established. The Cummings and Redman Shoe Factory operated in the early 1870s, but had closed by 1876. The aprons on the men in front indicate that leatherwork was not clean employment.

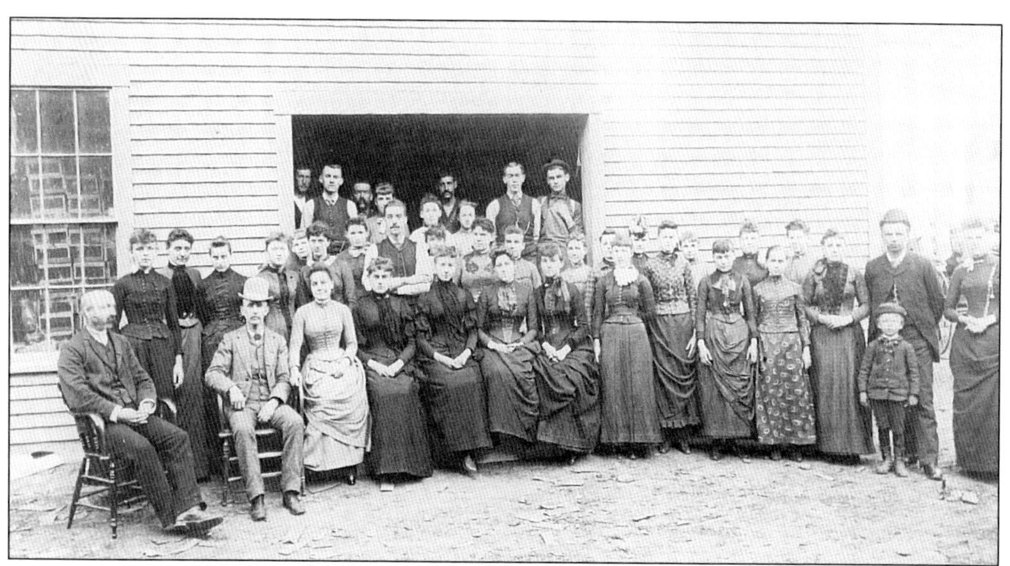

A work crew. Unidentified photographs are seldom good for publication; but this one (labeled only "Bath") is of interest because of the work force pictured here. The ratio of women to men is almost two to one; and they are rather young, even discounting the little boy. Moreover, although a few males are in shirtsleeves, most are better dressed than one would expect to find workers around the crates seen through the window. If the picture represents an outing, why the littered location? The two-faced man on the far left illustrates the time necessary to expose such pictures: turning one's head was *not* recommended.

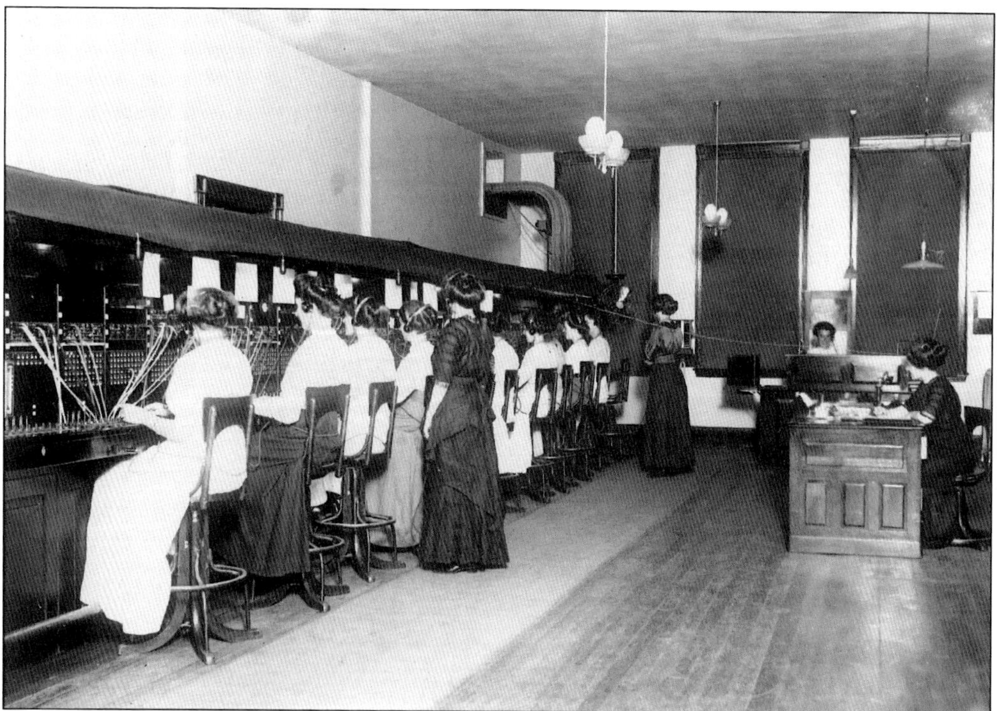

Telephone operators. Bath had a few telephones in the 1880s, and more in the 1890s. As in other regions, the work of operating the exchanges was usually given to women.

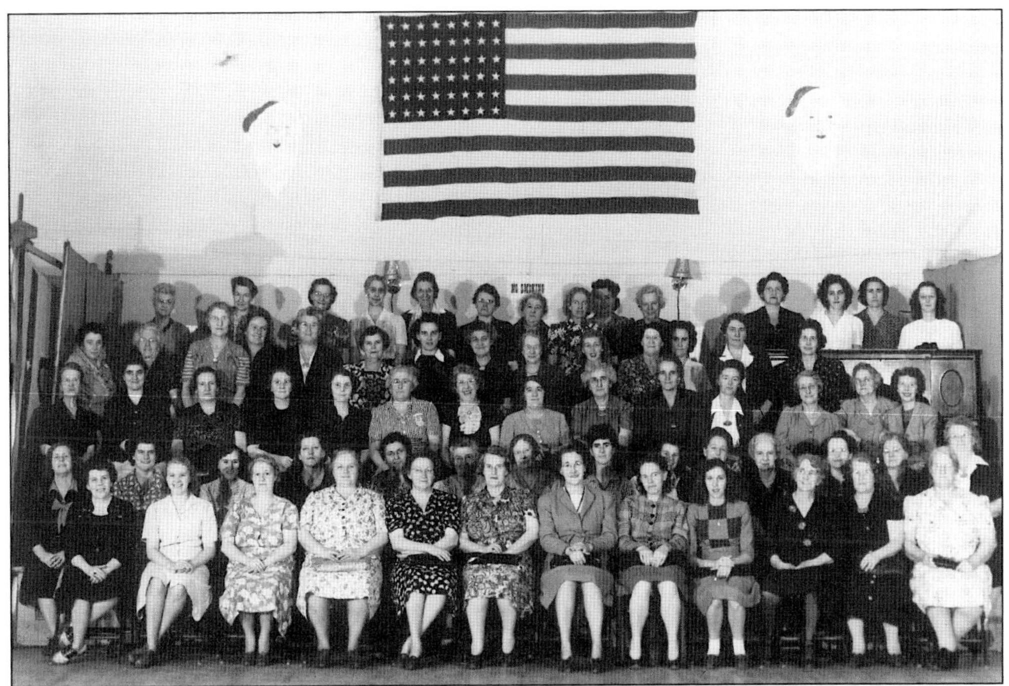

Congress Shirt Company workers, c. 1945. Many women found employment manufacturing shirts and coats. Early Bath firms operated on the putting-out system; but the Middle Street firm which became Congress Shirt, then Congress Sportswear, installed machinery in a large building in 1898. After expanding in 1937 and 1940, the firm had a sizeable work force, about half of whom are shown in this group portrait.

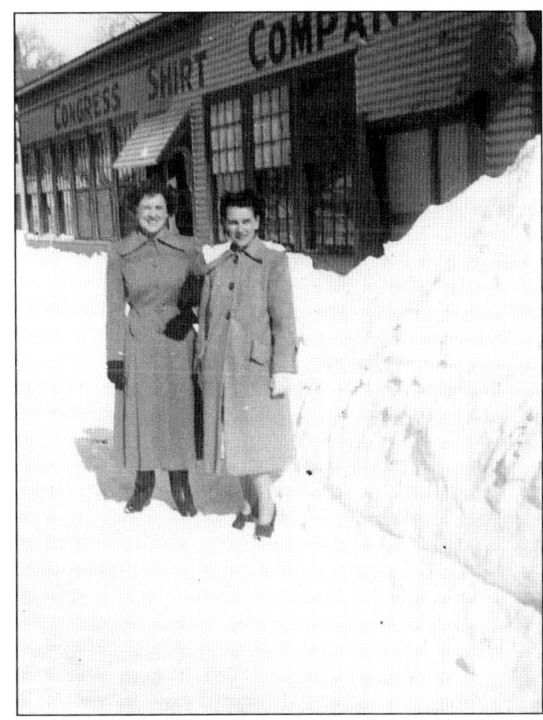

After the blizzard, 1952. Some workers used skis; Grace Waterman had to employ snowshoes on the first leg of her journey to work after a February blizzard. She and a co-worker posed beside a snow pile outside the old Congress Shirt building. The company moved to a modern plant on Congress Street in 1965, and then closed by 1984.

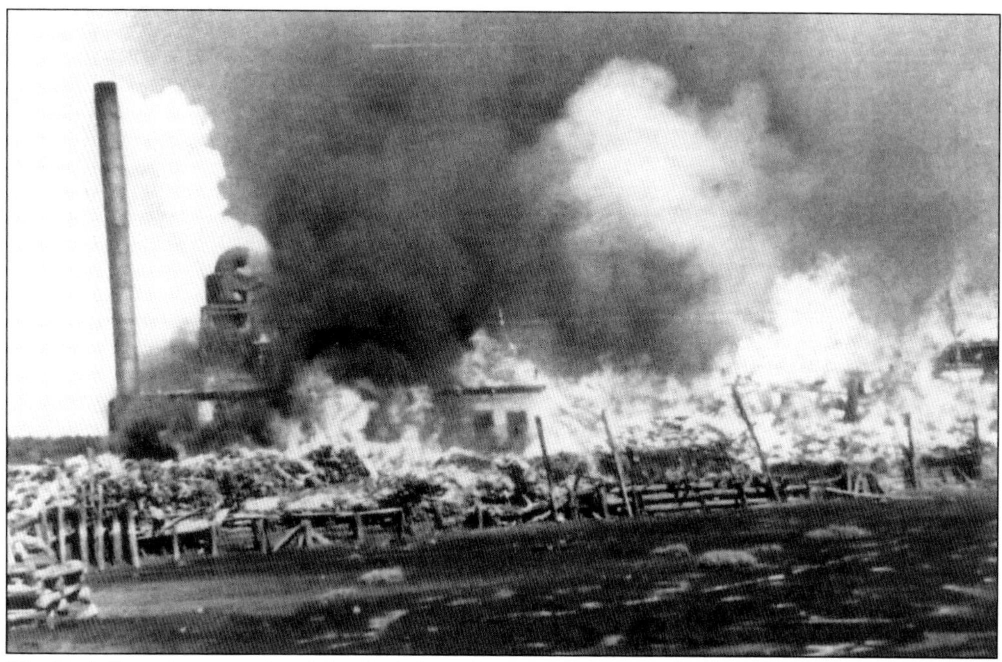

The Bath Box Company fire. The Bath Box Company was one of many lumber-based industries located on Trufant's Point, in the South End. The fire which consumed it in June 1946 was spectacular, fueled by plenty of dry wood.

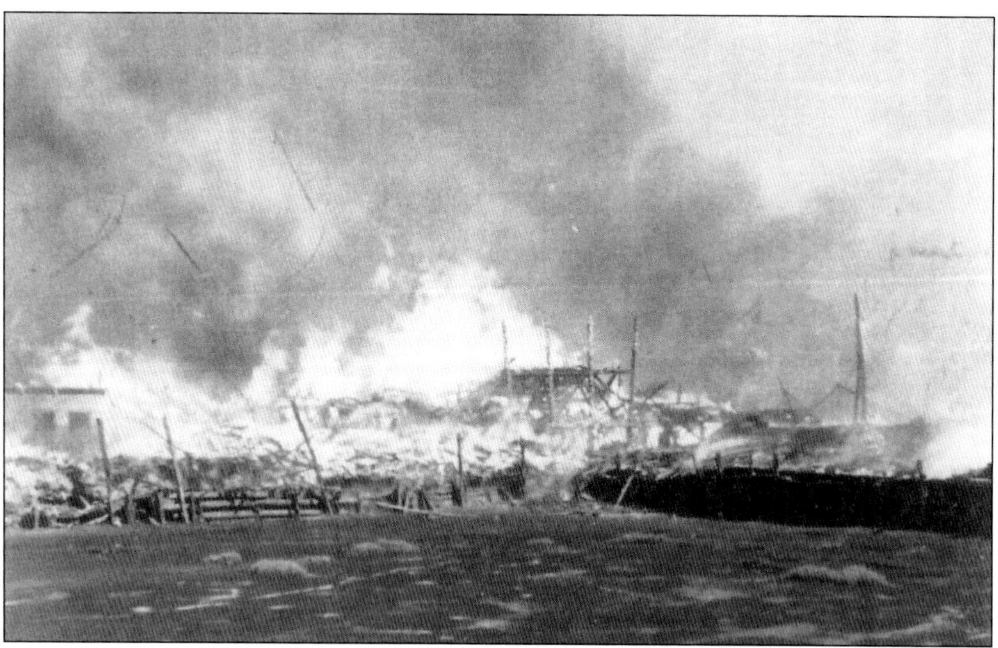

Another view of the fire. With nothing salvageable after the fire, the Bath Box Company moved operations to West Bath, but closed eight years afterward. (In 1958, that property also went up in flames.)

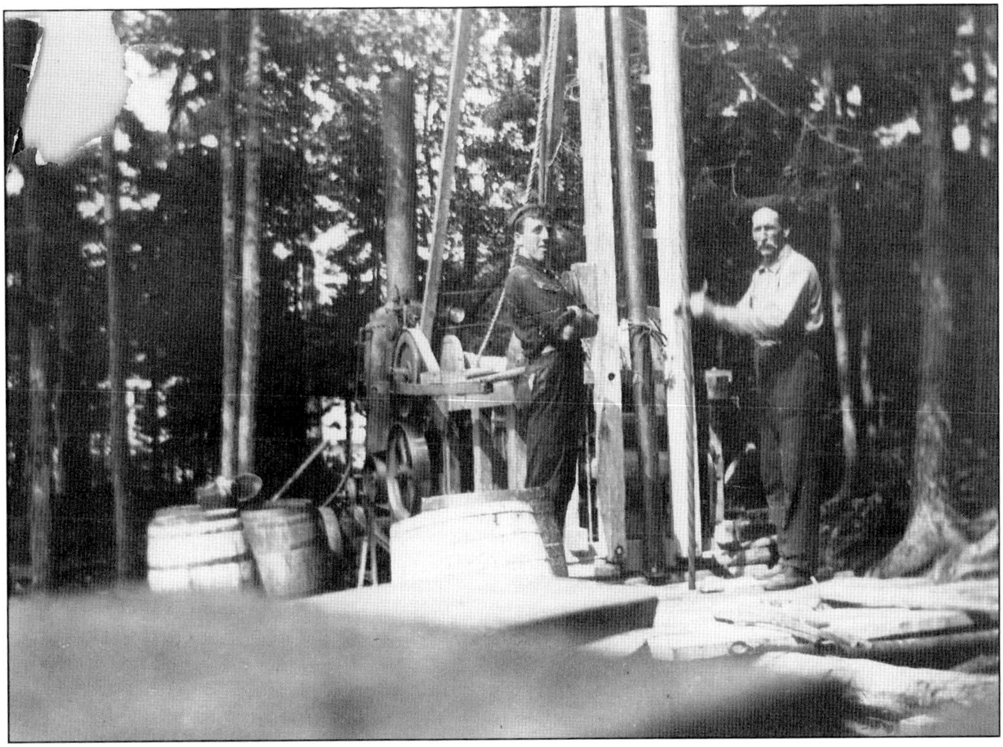

Well drillers in the 1910s. Rather than selecting one career for life, most individuals varied their work, sometimes carrying on more than one occupation at once. Edwin Trott, shown on the right, worked as a diver when the city was laying its water pipeline in the 1890s, painted the trim on vessels (see p. 57), and then had his own painting and wallpapering business. He and his son Will are shown here drilling a well, sometime before Will's death from influenza in 1918. (The influenza epidemic hit the city hard, causing more than sixty deaths in 1918–1919.)

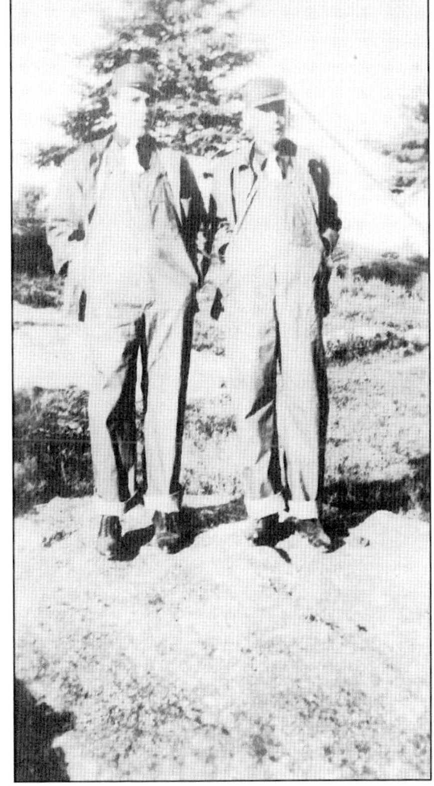

Part-time farmers. Edwin Trott also farmed part time, as did his son Raymond Trott and son-in-law Raymond Clark (both shown here). The younger men also worked in a shipyard.

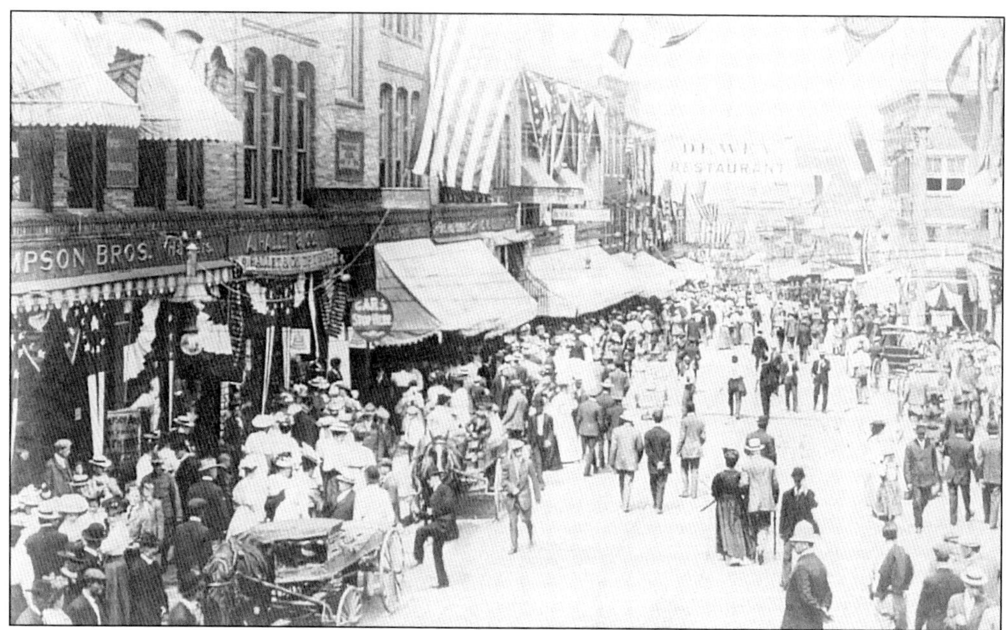

Celebrating shipbuilding, 1907. This crowd on Front Street was part of Bath's four-day "Tercentennial Celebration," organized to celebrate three hundred years of shipbuilding on the Kennebec. The date is in reference to the 1607 construction of the *Virginia*, downriver in Phippsburg, and provides an example of the many such fetes enjoyed in the city.

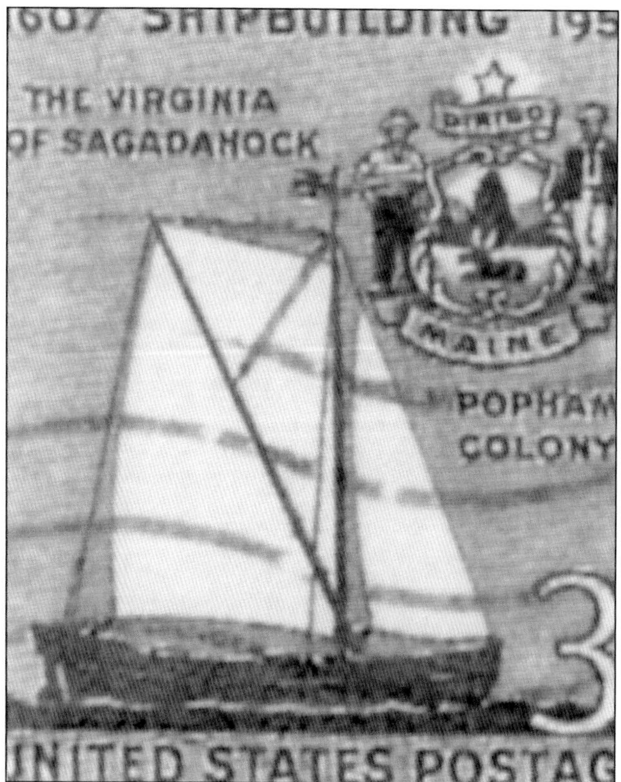

The area's first "ship," 1607. It was half a century later that the U.S. Post Office put the pinnace *Virginia* on a stamp. The price for first class postage will be nostalgic for those who remember the era.

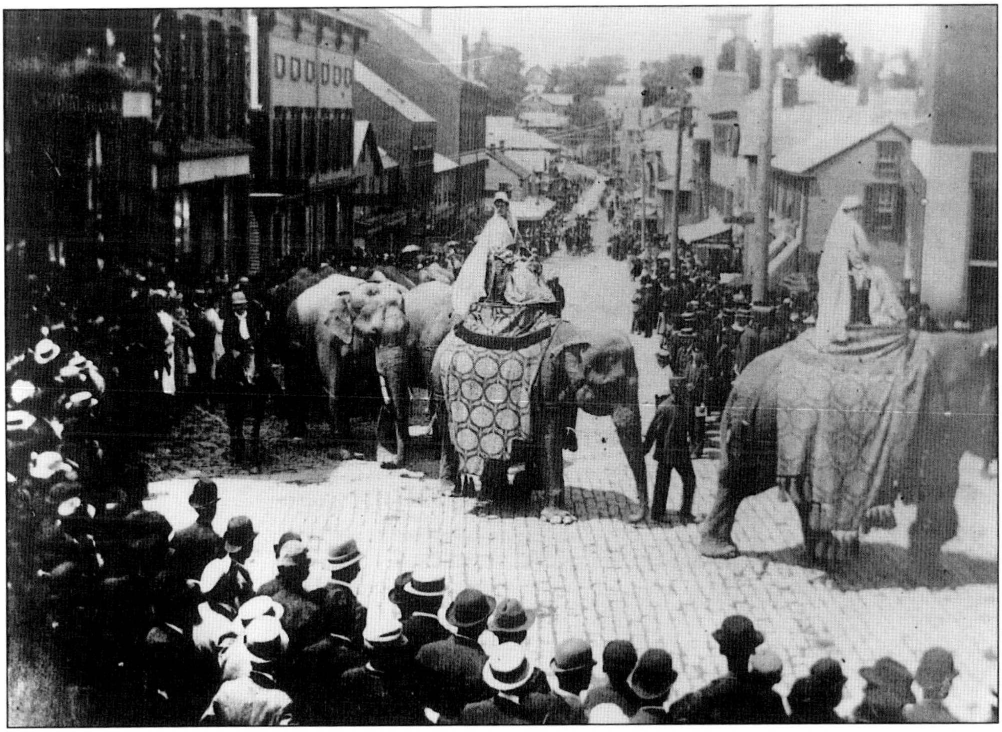

A circus parade in the 1890s. For years, a circus was a big event for the area, as the World of Mirth utilized a field on the western outskirts (later to become a shopping mall). Children from nearby slipped over to watch the tent go up, while children and adults living downtown had their appetites whetted by posters on almost every light pole, and perhaps by a parade of elephants up Center Street to Front Street. This early parade occurred after the street was paved, but before the fire of 1894.

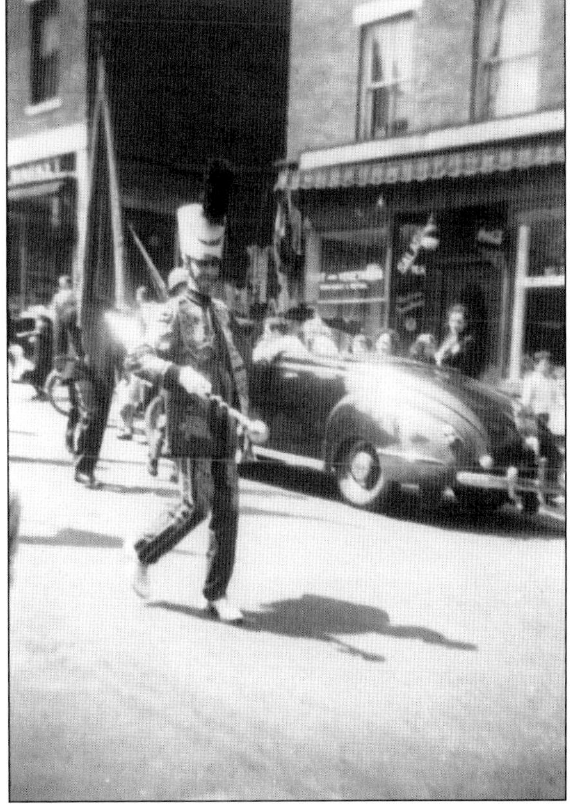

"Eddie" Emmons, the perennial drum major. Bath has enjoyed parades regularly, for special celebrations like the tercentennial and the bridge completion, as well as on the Fourth of July. For about four decades, through 1946, Edwin "Eddie" Emmons led local parades.

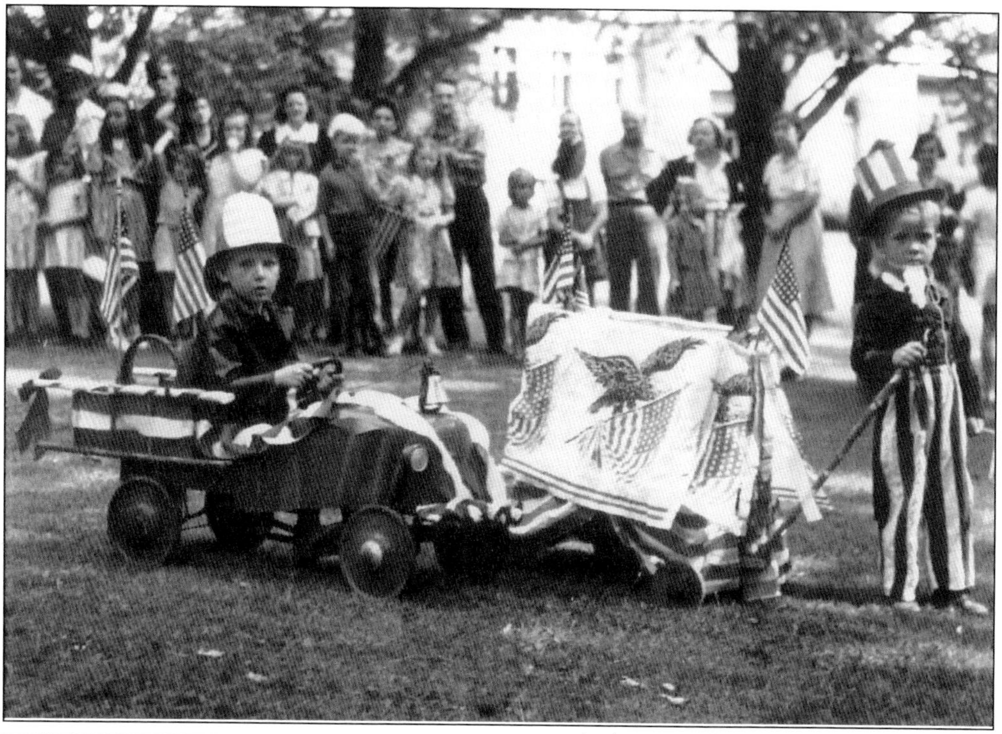

A playground parade, 1945. The patriotism of the World War II years is apparent in the figure of "Uncle Sam" and the many flags. The small pedal-driven fire engine had to have been of pre-war vintage, as the use of metal for toys was proscribed for the duration. Such a vehicle would have been the envy of other children.

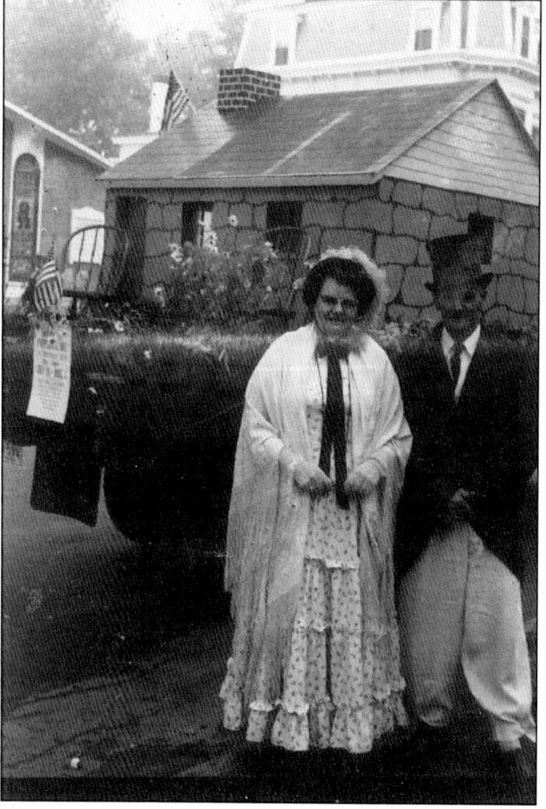

The prize-winning float. Floats were regularly prepared by a variety of organizations. The first prize winner on July 4, 1964, included individuals representing President and Mrs. Lincoln. Alice Munsey played Mary Lincoln, while her husband Lester was the float's driver.

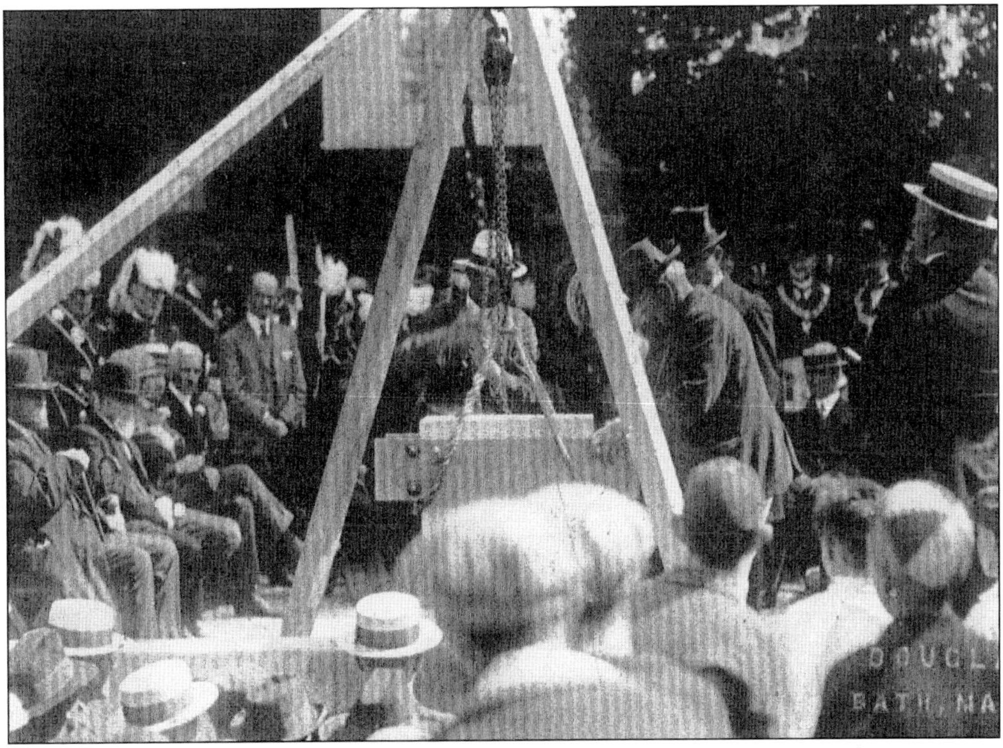

Laying a Masonic cornerstone, 1921. After purchasing the James Drummond mansion on Washington Street, Bath's Masonic Lodge enlarged it with an addition at the rear. N. Gratz Jackson presided at the cornerstone ceremony, and the completed temple was dedicated in March 1922.

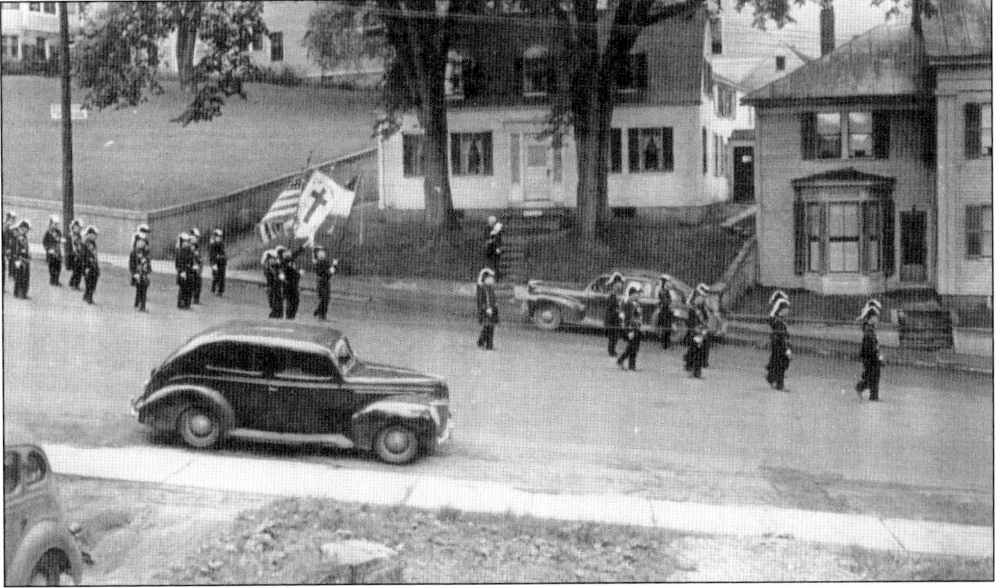

The Masons were another group that took part in parades. Here, in 1944, a commandery parade moves down the hill on Center Street, with N.G. Jackson reviewing from the steps of the small house next to the Hotel Sedgewick (to the left).

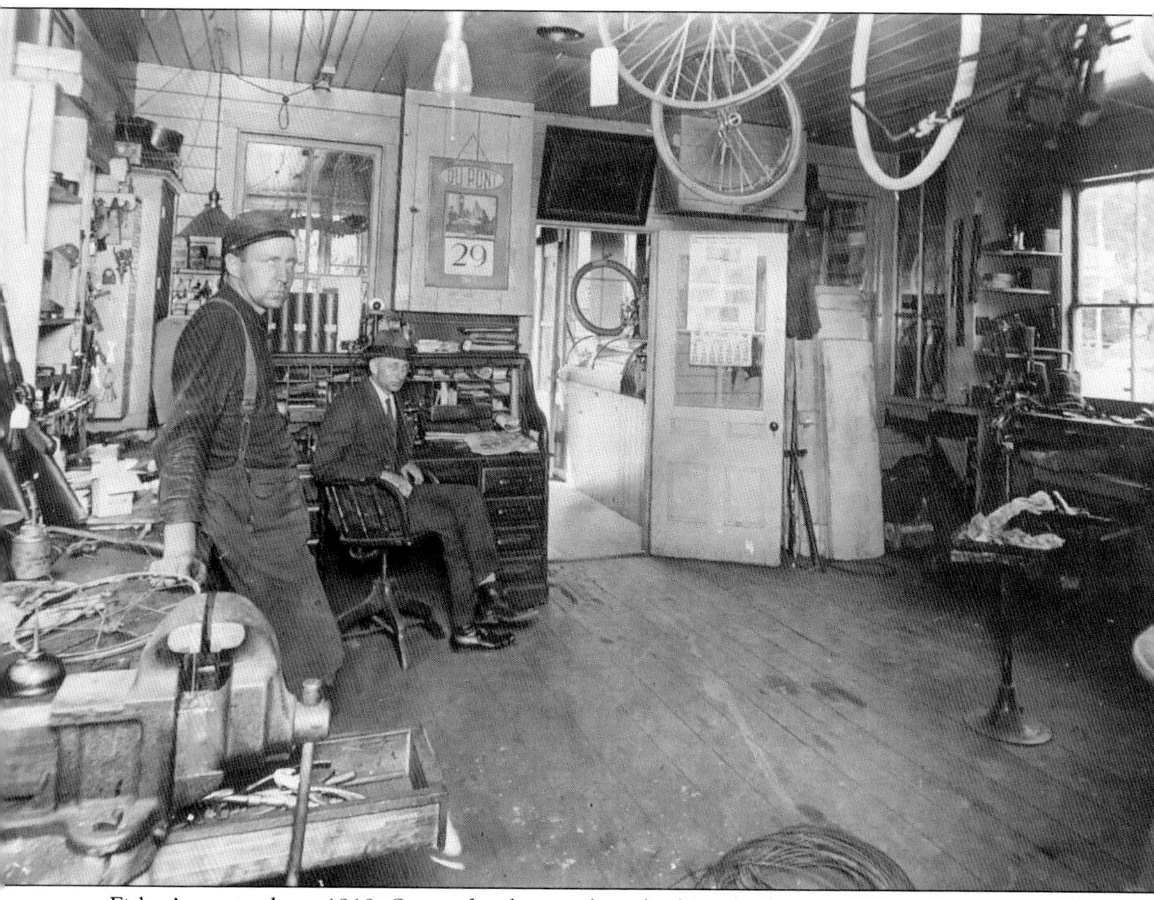

Fisher's sports shop, 1919. Soon after he purchased a bicycle shop on Water Street, near Elm Street, Alonzo G. Fisher had it photographed. That he repaired as well as sold bicycles and guns can be seen in this view of the shop portion of his establishment, with a calendar indicating the date to be July 1919. Fisher sits at his desk. The other man is unidentified, but appears to be an employee.

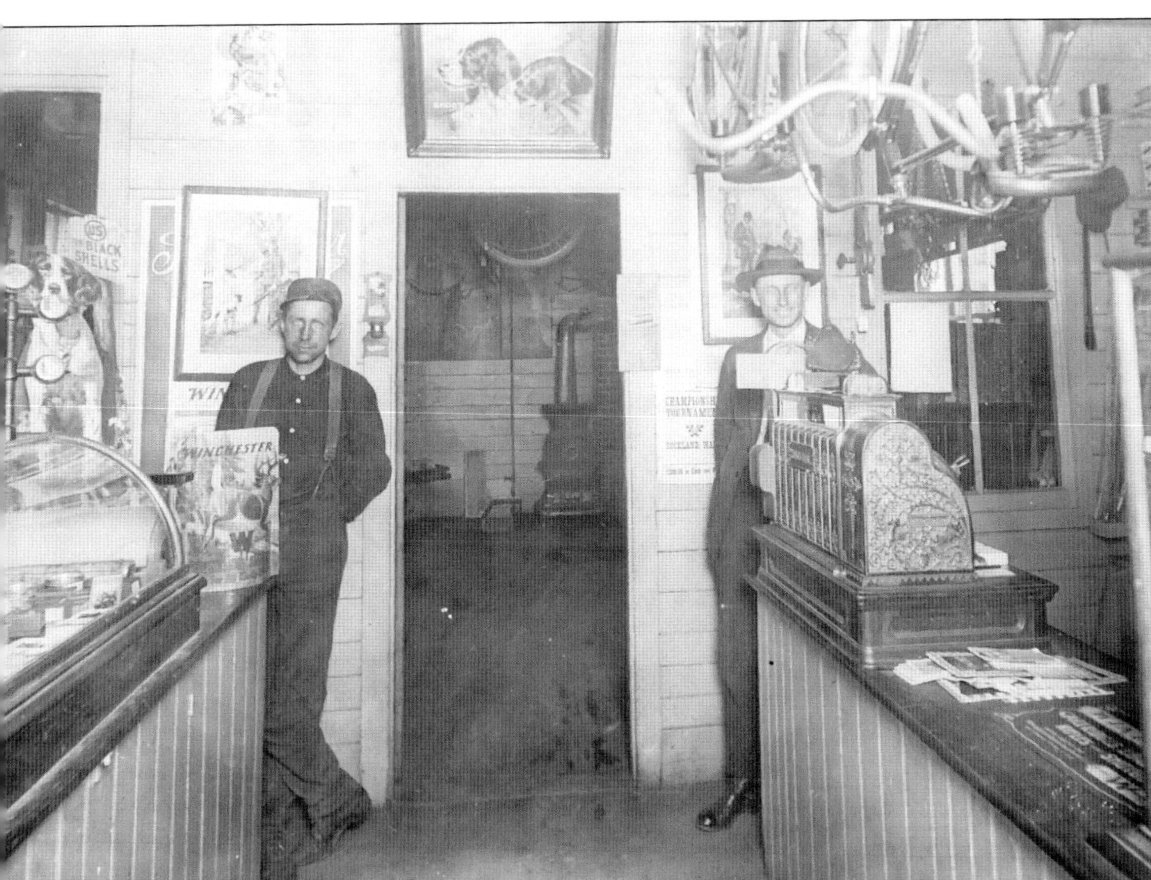

The front room of Fisher's sports shop. The front room of the building held display cases and shelves of ammunition, with bicycles hung overhead. The potbellied stove in the background would have heated both areas. Mr. Fisher stands on the right. He kept the shop for about a decade.

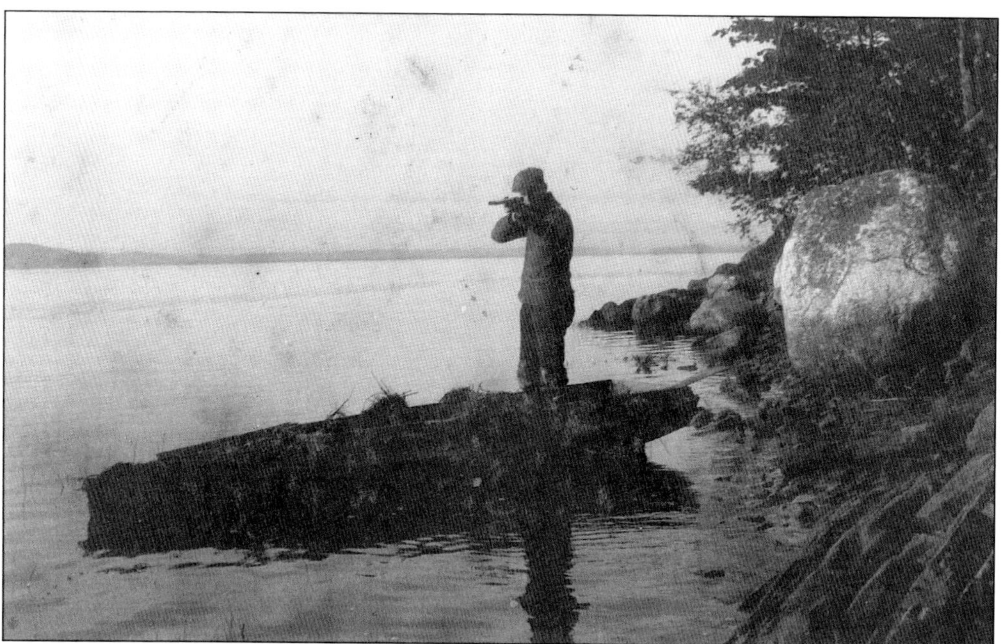

Duckhunting. Merrymeeting Bay, where the Androscoggin and Kennebec Rivers come together, is on the flight paths of migratory waterfowl and was thus a hunting area well before the first white settlers arrived in Maine. It is renowned as a good place to "gun for" ducks and geese. However, few serious hunters took their cameras along. Alonzo Fisher was probably posing for a photograph to use as a calendar-advertisement.

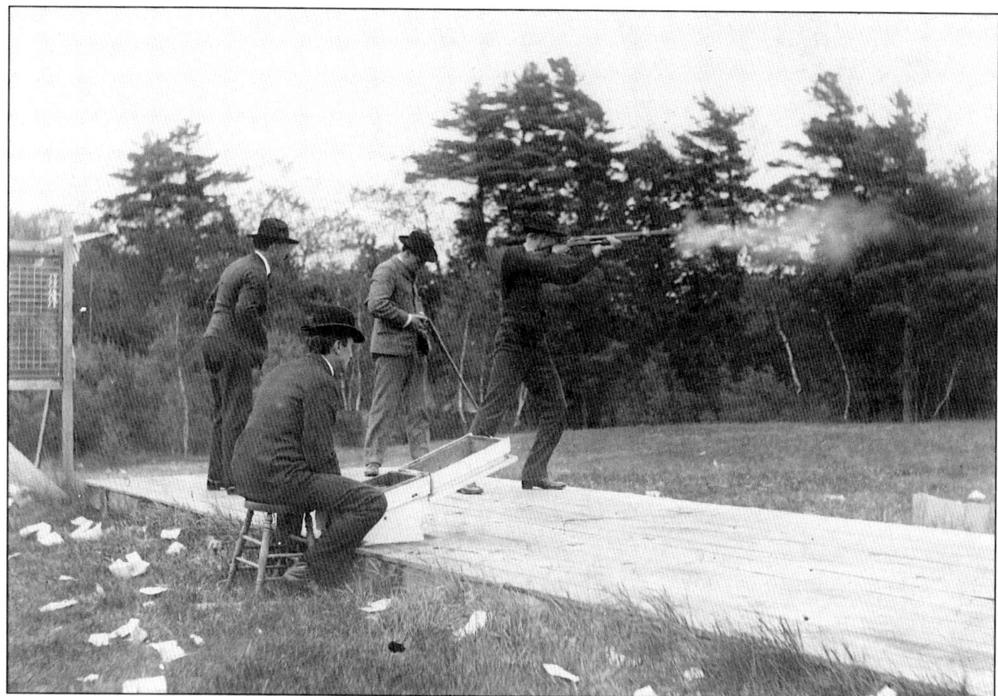

A skeet club. Out of season, men practiced with "clay pigeons"; this photograph depicts part of a North Bath skeet club in action.

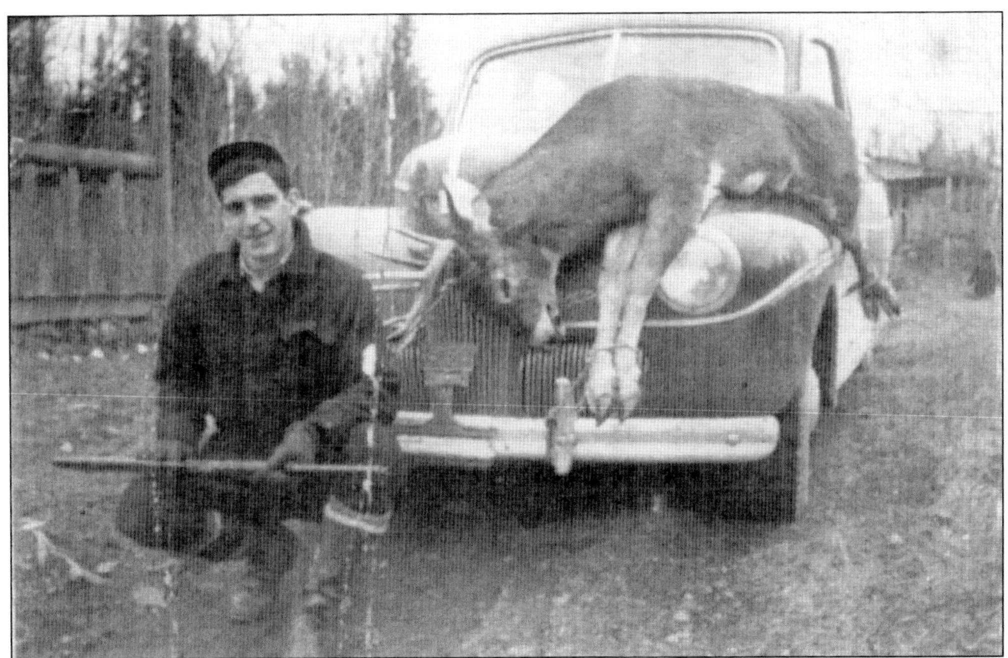

An impressive trophy, 1944. With wartime meat rationing in effect, a fat buck would have meant much more than a rack for the wall. John Hinds, of Engine House #2 on Washington Street, poses with the result of a hunt in the fall of 1944. Note how the upper half of his headlight is blocked out—a wartime requirement, to reduce light visible to planes overhead.

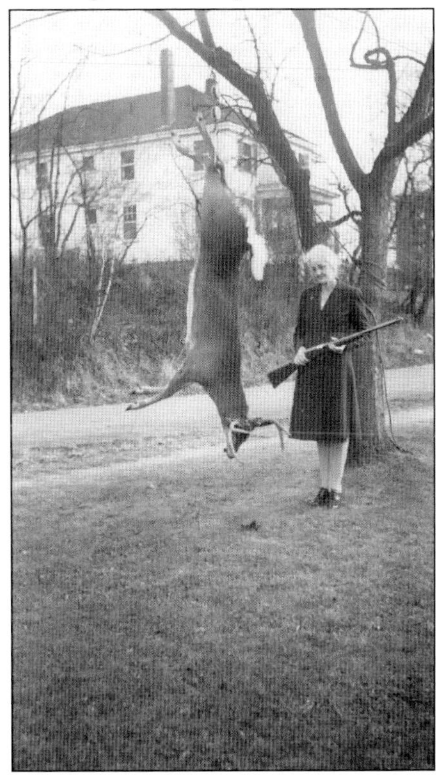

Photographs can be misleading. Blanche Fisher is holding her son's gun and posing by the deer *he* shot in 1947. The building behind her, on Winship Street, was a residence for nurses at the Bath Memorial Hospital.

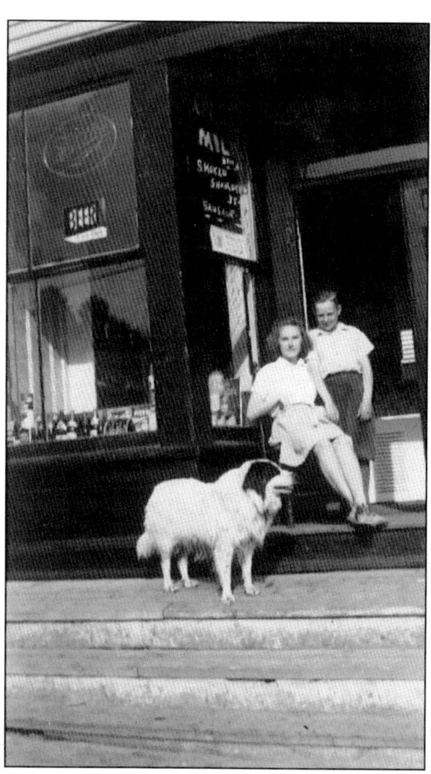

A store at Winnegance in the 1940s. Marian and Billy Wagner pose in front of the family store, set between the road and the river near the causeway at Winnegance. The Wagners' earlier store had been lost to a BIW expansion.

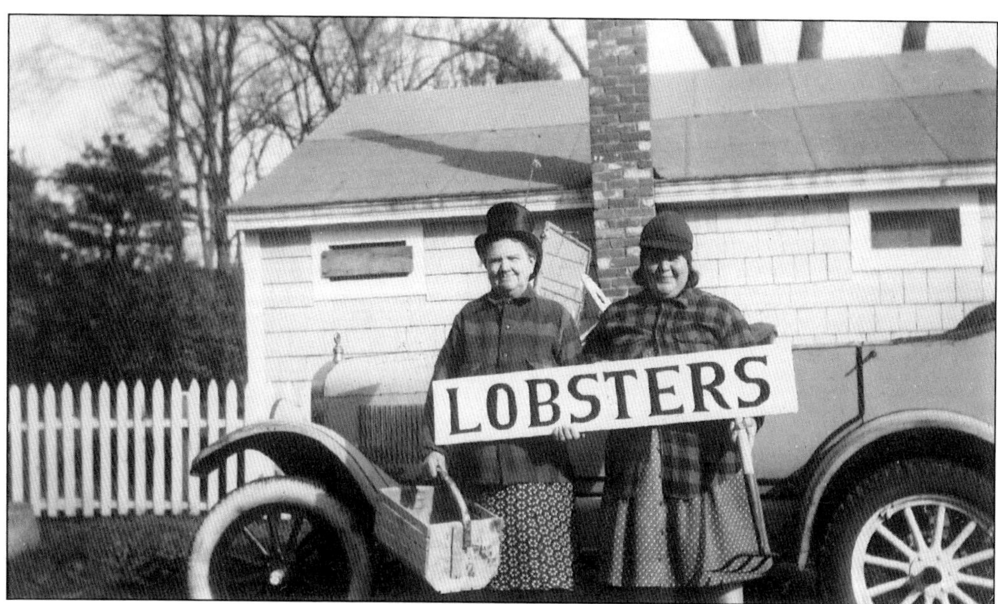

Clowning fishmongers, 1944. For years, Mabel Millet and family sold shellfish (note the clam hod and hoe, as well as the sign) from a small shop at Richardson Street and Western Avenue.

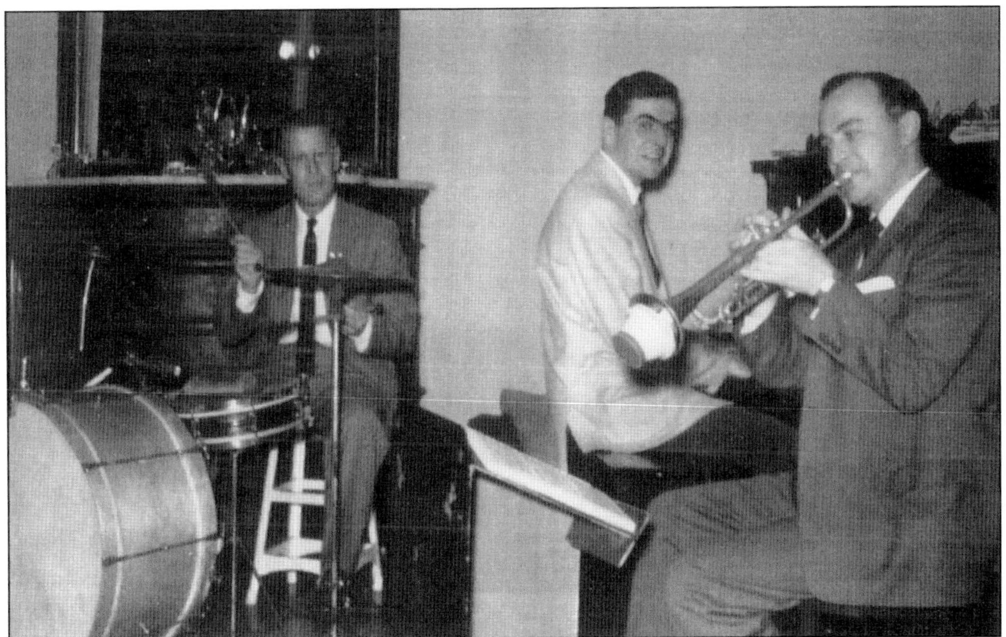

Music at the Phoenix. The Big Band era of the 1940s and '50s brought about the formation of orchestras and bands in many localities, and a night out might include dancing to a small group in one of the hotels. This trio of Vinnie Henderson (drums), Bob Rice (piano), and Hilton Libby (trumpet) were holding forth at Bath's popular Hotel Phoenix (razed in 1964, after a fire).

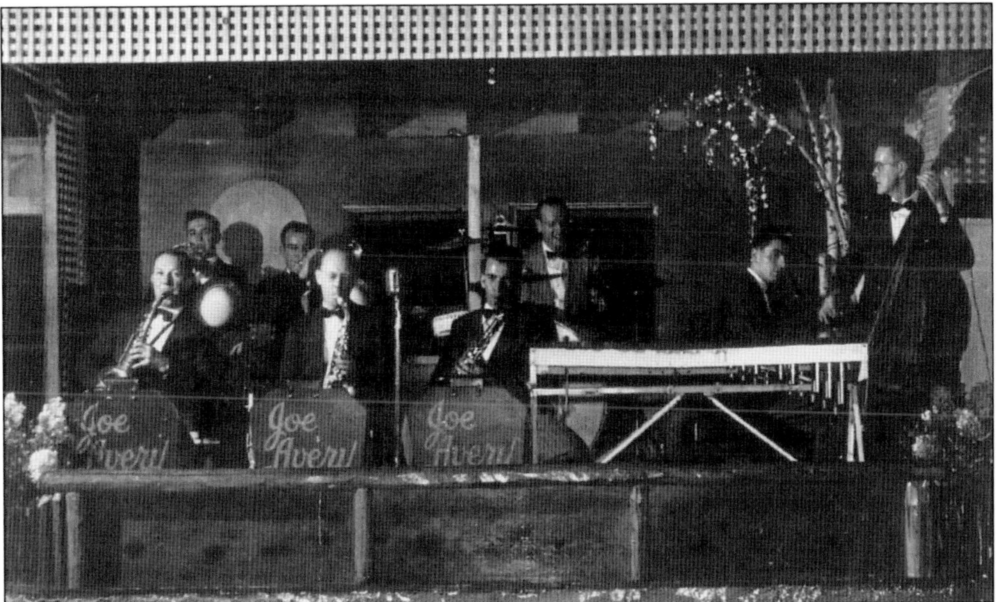

Joe Avery's Orchestra. Composed of local men, bands might be hired for proms and Mohiba dances, or to provide music at dance halls. This photograph was taken at Lakehurst Pavilion, in Damariscotta. From left to right are: (front row) Hollis Nelson, Cecil Roland, Chuck Page, Bob Rice, and Duane Bailey (with his bass viol); (back row) Hilton Libby, Johnny Wakefield, and Joe Avery.

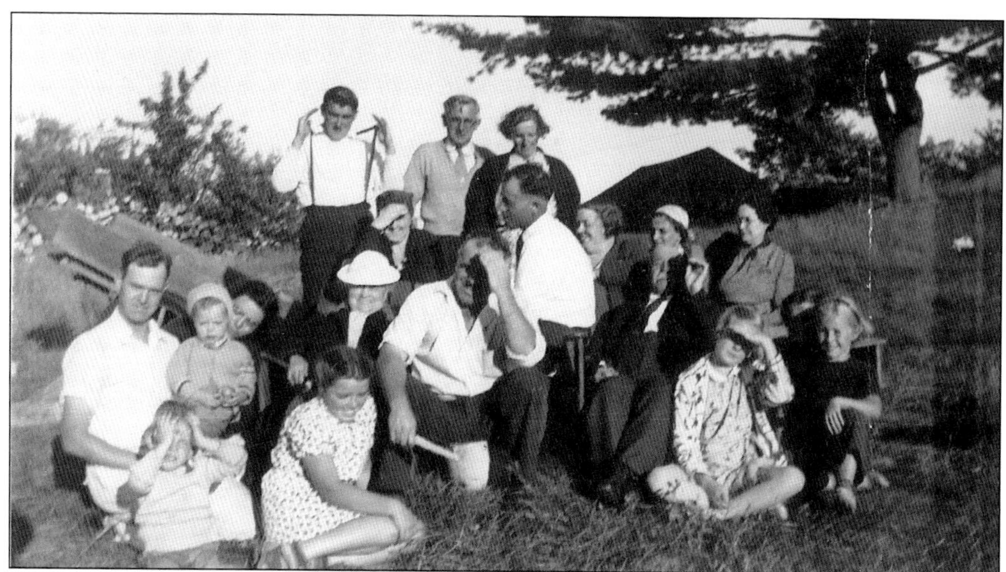

A family picnic. Quieter activities included gatherings of families like this one from the North End on the Fourth of July in 1940. From left to right are: (in the very front) Billy Fogg, Winona Clark, Gloria Leavitt, Kathleen Clark, and Gerry Fogg; (seated) Everett White (holding son Donald), Virginia White, Maud Clark, ? Walsh, Raymond Clark, John Clark, Bea Leavitt, Ruth Clark, Melville Clark, and Bunny Sturtevant; (standing) David Clark, Ed Leavitt, and Frances Clark.

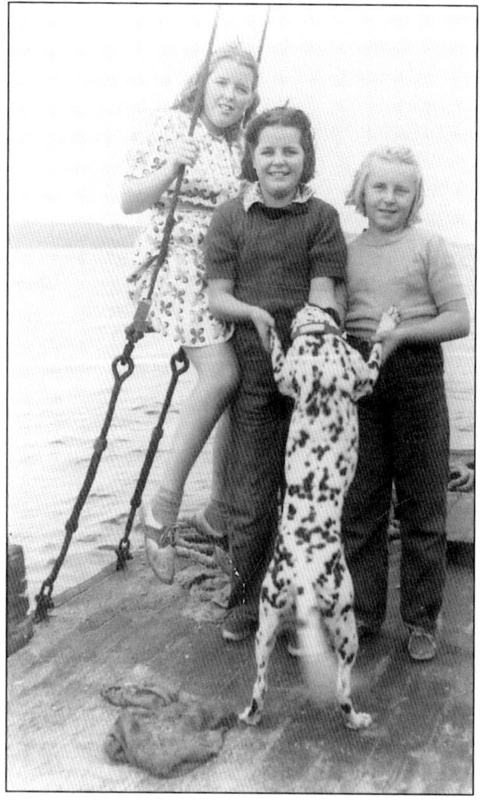

Playing on the scow. Children growing up in a seaport were accustomed to playing around boats. Noni Clark, Kay Clark, and Gerry Fogg (and "Peggy") pose on a scow which was regularly anchored near their homes if not employed on the river. When they went swimming, it served as a float from which to dive.

Nine

West Bath

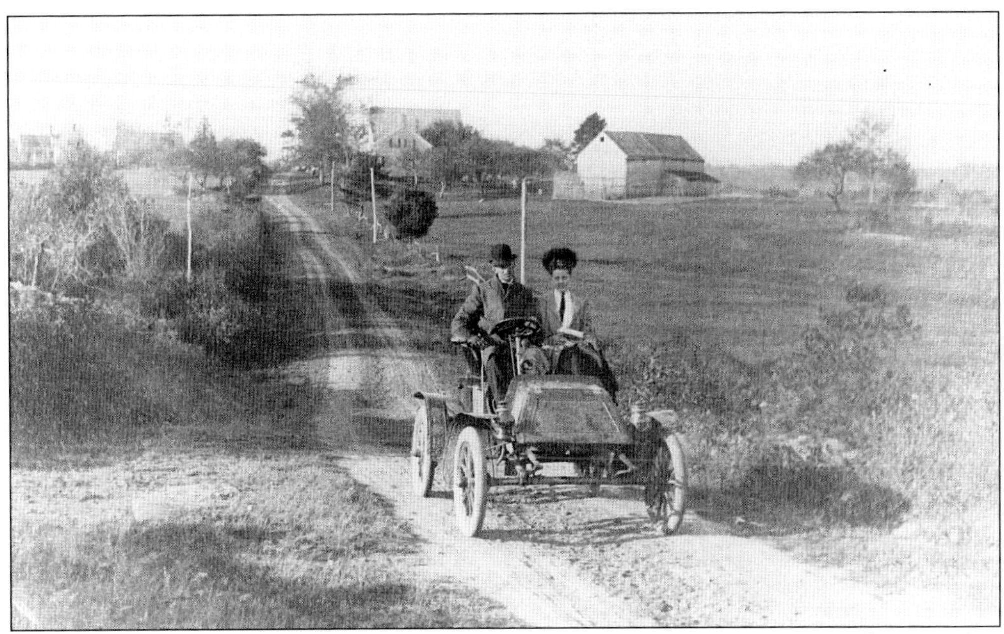

A rural scene, 1907. When first incorporated, the town of Bath stretched between the Kennebec and New Meadows Rivers. After the two sections were separated, West Bath remained largely farm-oriented: a storekeeper was the single businessman in town in 1880. These well-kept fields and farmhouses were on the Fosters Point Road. The rear-engine auto was made in Wisconsin; the driver, Alonzo Fisher, was giving Miss Blanche Williams a ride to school in Bath. The two married the following year.

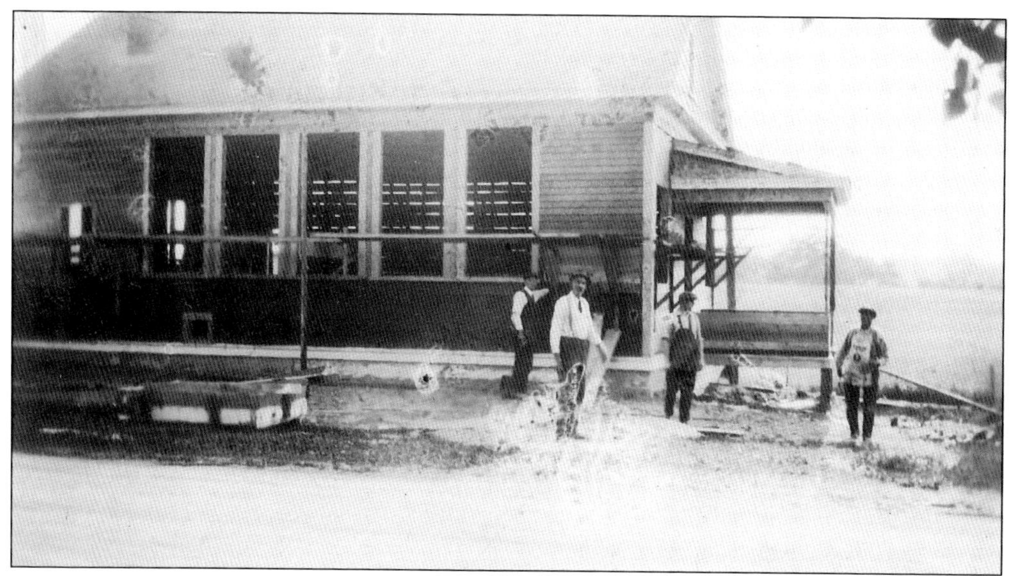

A schoolhouse under construction. The town maintained two schools in the twentieth century, each with a single room for all grades. The new Lowell School was built in 1923 and used until 1947.

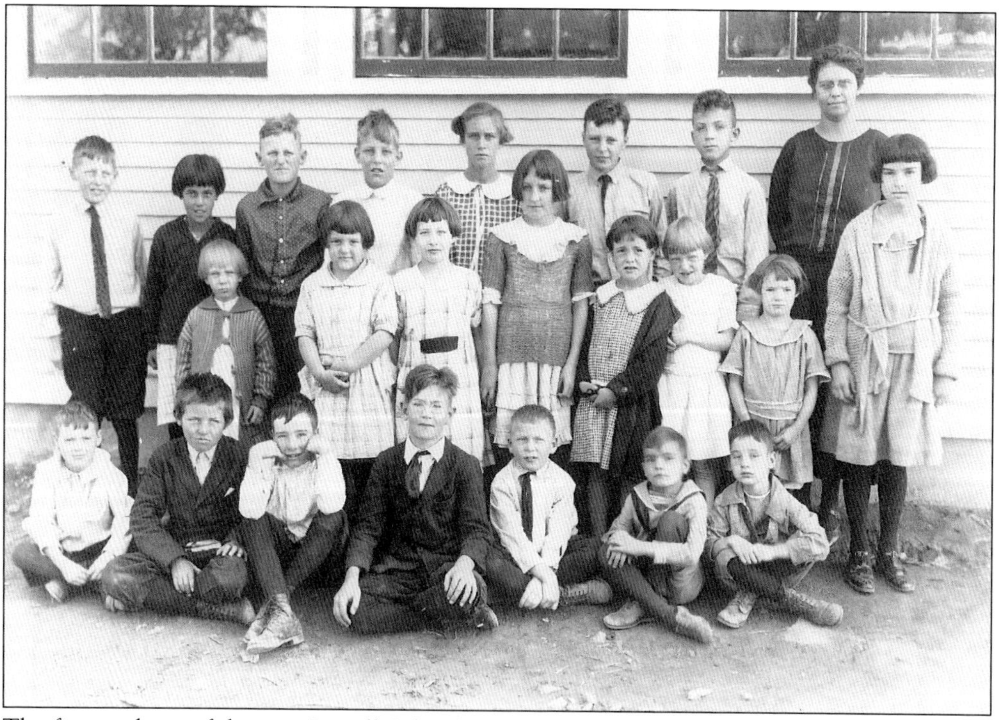

The first students of the new Lowell School, 1923. From left to right are: (front row) ? Brawn, Edward Larrabee, Stanley Brawn, Roger Holden, Erwin Whorff, Robert Fuller, and unknown; (middle row) Marian Rose, Emily Larrabee, Ellen ?, Anstress Larrabee, unknown, Marguerite Donnell, Edna Brawn, and Eleanor Brawn; (back row) David Whorff, Rachel ?, John Kenney, ? Curtis, Helen Curtis, Walter Larrabee, Hayden Rogers, and the teacher, Miss Philpott.

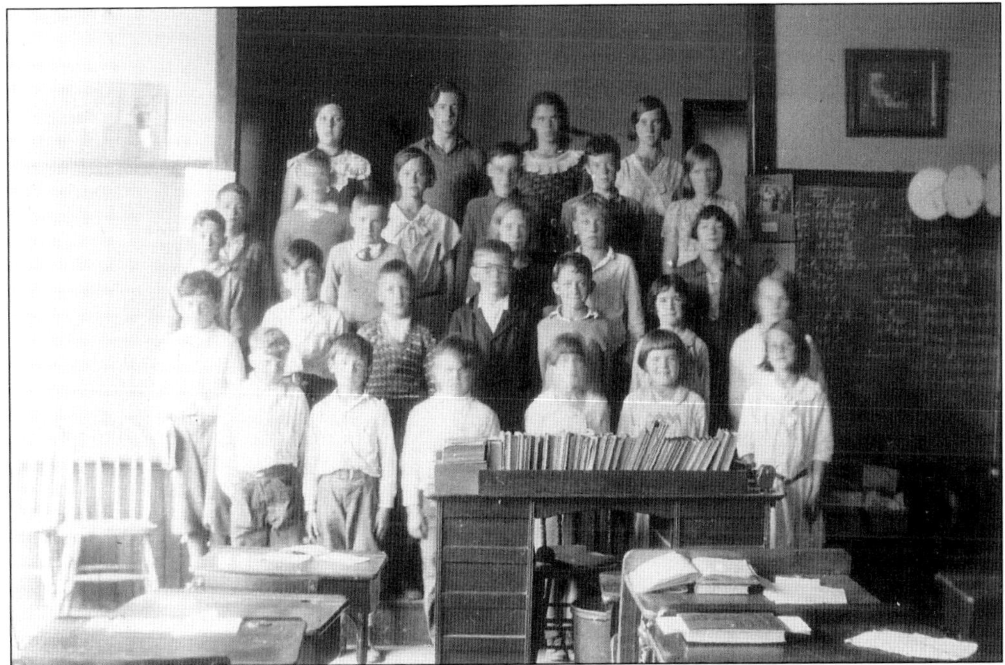

The school interior, 1931. Obviously planned with more than the "3 R's" in mind, the Lowell School contained a stage, shown here behind the students, who represent grades one through eight. The room was used for meetings of a men's club, a ladies' sewing circle, and the firemen.

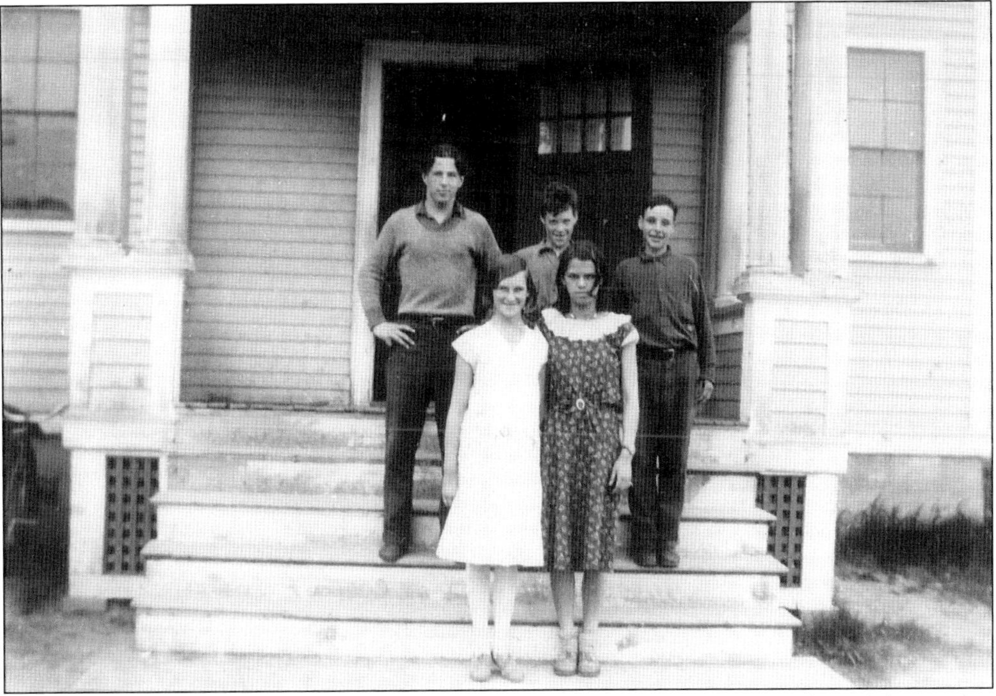

The eighth grade, 1931. Posed on the front steps of the same school are, from left to right: (front) Grace Waterman and Betty Rose; (back) Harlan Booker, Stanley Brawn, and Freddie Brawn.

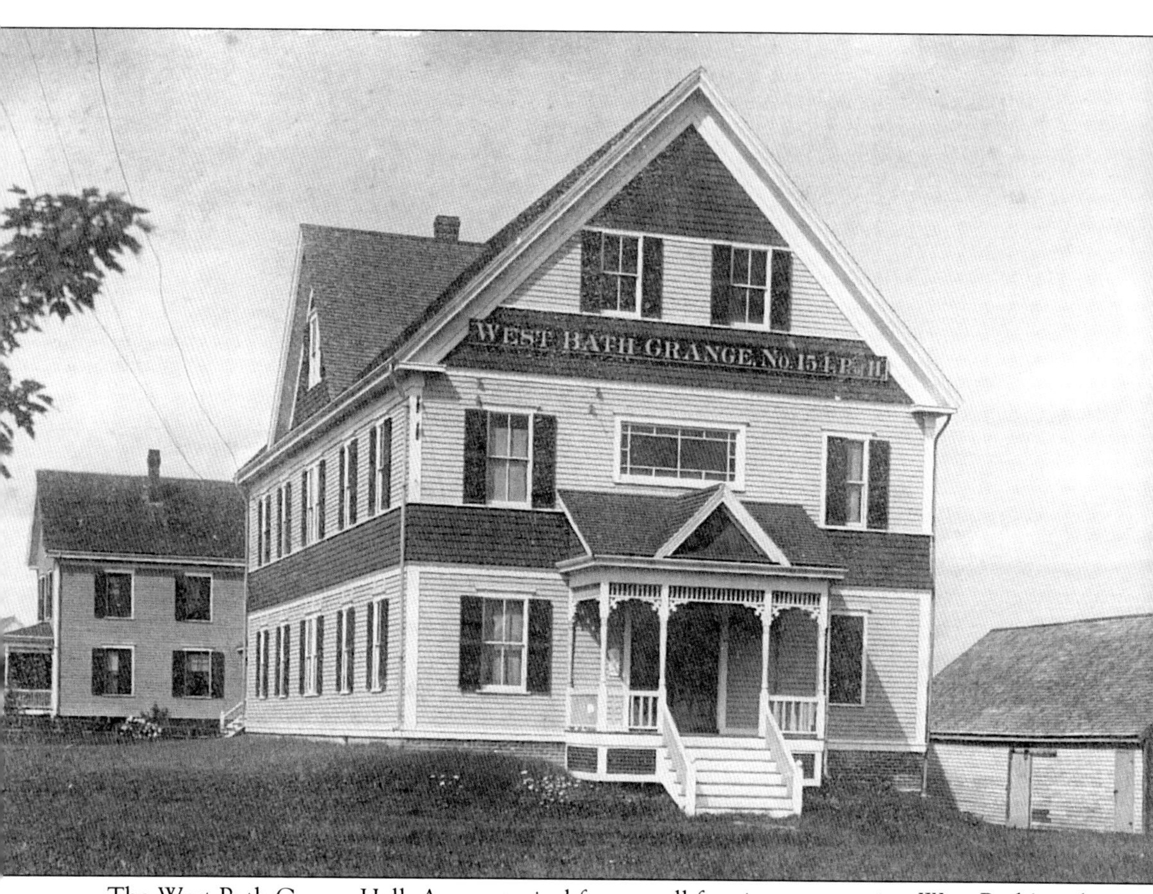

The West Bath Grange Hall. As was typical for a small farming community, West Bath's only major association was for many years the Grange. The West Bath Grange was founded in 1875; the Grange Hall dates to 1901.

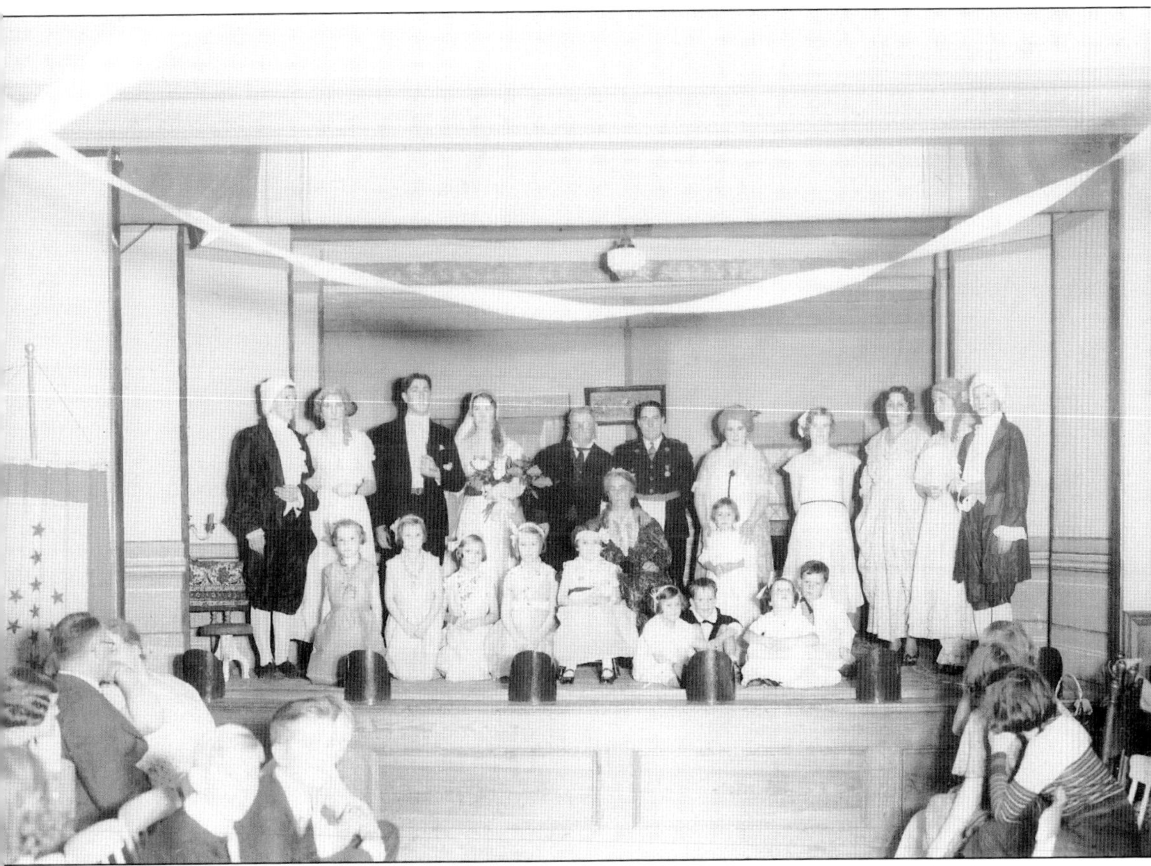

On stage in the 1930s. The Grange Hall provided accommodations for many types of gatherings other than meetings of the Patrons of Husbandry—from dances to suppers to theatrics. With the costumes representing varied eras, this must have been an historical pageant; but all that one small participant can remember is that her crepe paper dress was scratchy.

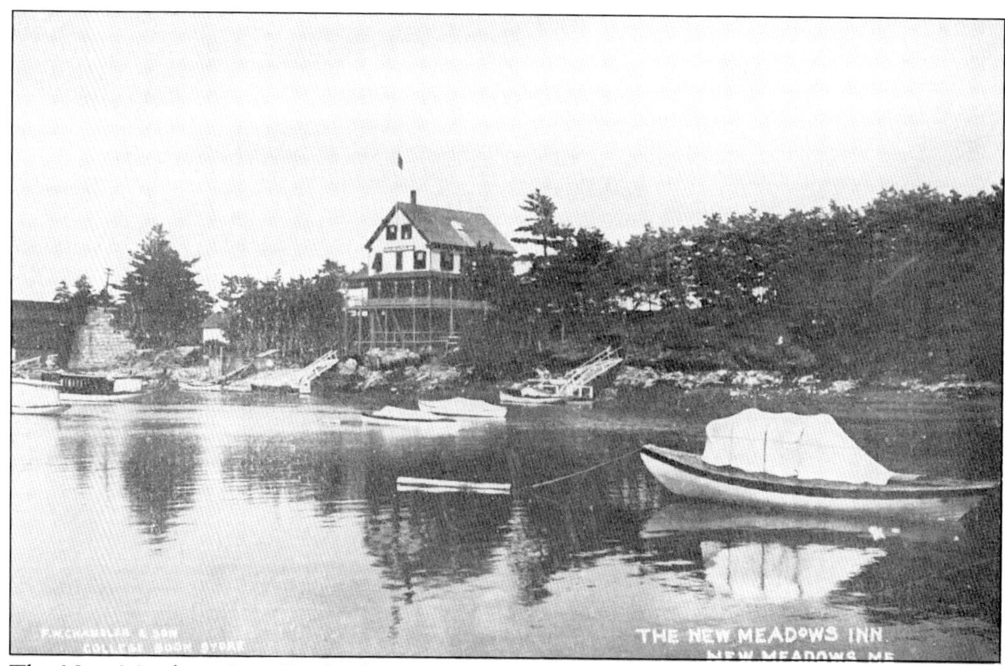

The New Meadows Inn. By the late nineteenth century, tourism had become important in Maine, and West Bath was much better suited to attract "rusticators" than was the nearby city. A few farms in the area took in summer boarders. Early in 1899 the area got a new attraction: the New Meadows Inn. At the time it was a year-round concern, although it would later be open only in the summer months.

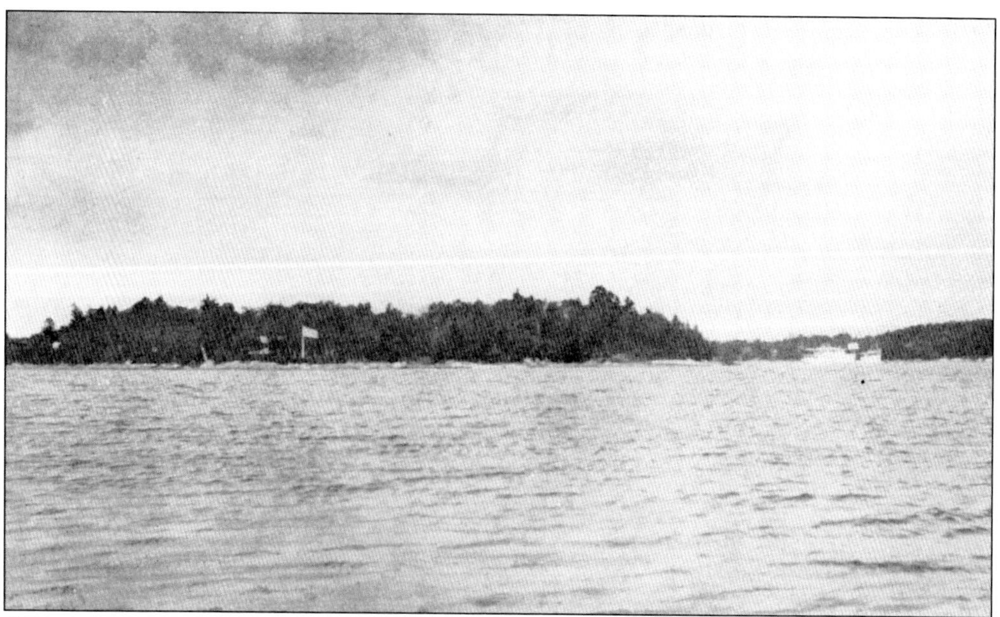

An excursion steamer in the 1910s. The inn received many visitors by water and became a destination for scenic cruises. One of the steamers is shown off Williams Island, in the southern end of town.

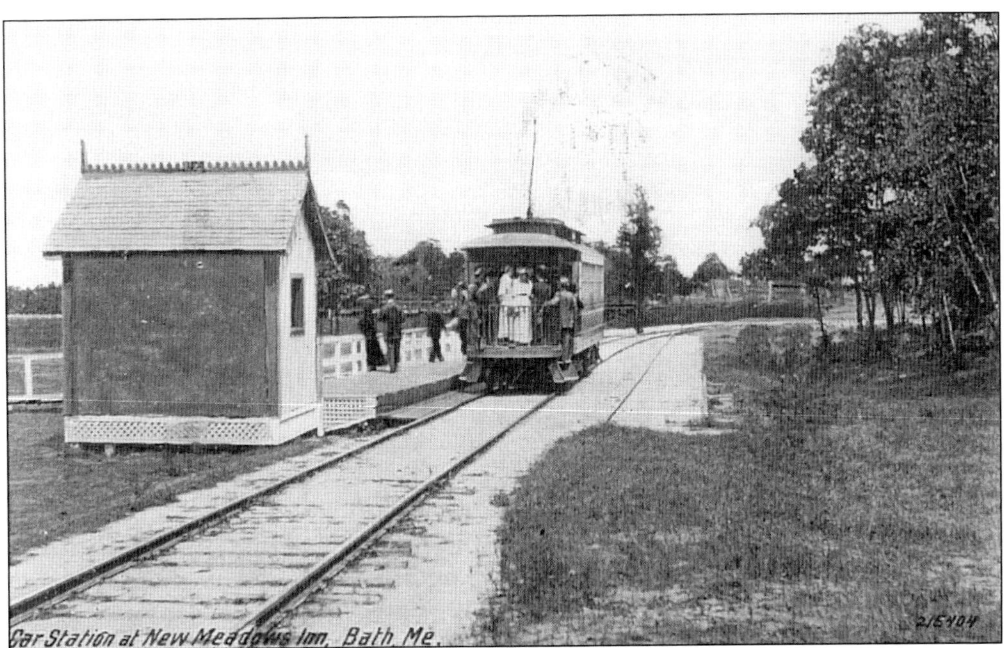

The trolley station. Other customers arrived by trolley: the streetcar line between Brunswick and Bath crossed the "river" nearby. The railroad also established a flag station there.

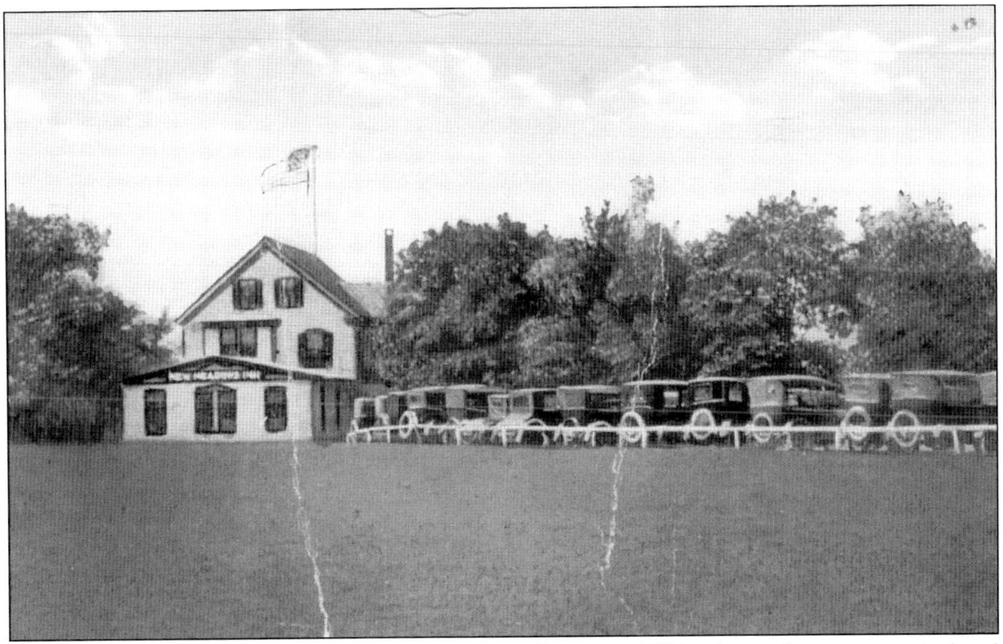
The New Meadow Inn parking lot in the 1920s. The new 1907 bridge and an increase in local automobile ownership helped business. New Meadows was a short drive from two urban areas, and it provided pleasant views as well as appealing shore dinners. Its popularity is indicated by the number of cars in the parking lot.

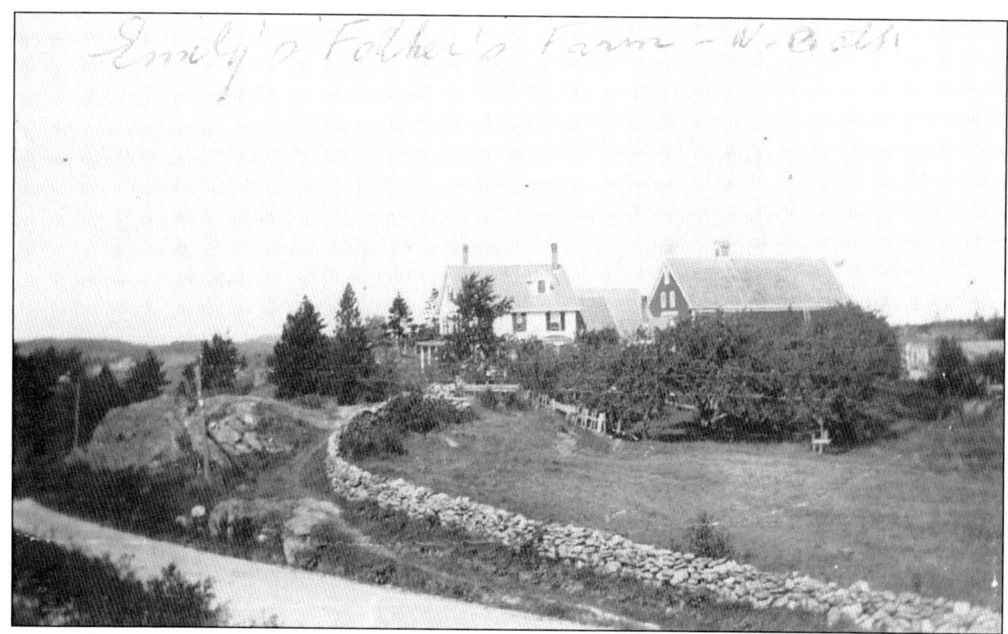

The White-Larrabee Farm. Joseph W. Larrabee lived in his grandfather's farmhouse until it burned in 1930. Later, he and his wife offered shore dinners on the property, called the Rocky Hill Inn.

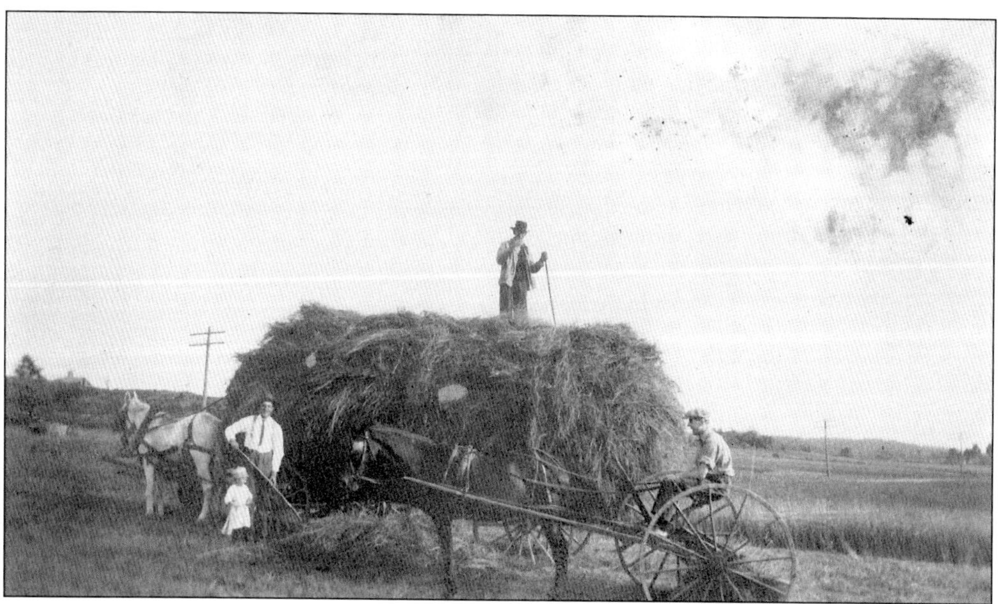

Haying in the 1920s. A horse-drawn rake cleans up the scatterings, and the load on the hayrack is nearly ready to be hauled to the barn. It all looks natural—except that the man who appears about to pitch another forkful on to the hayrack is wearing a white shirt and a necktie: not normal haying attire.

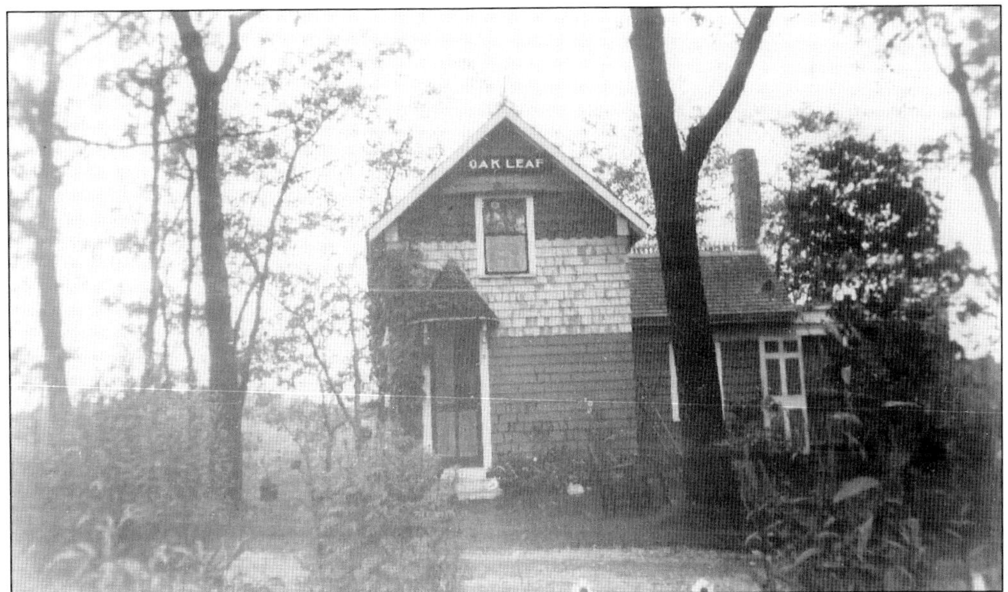

Oak Leaf cottage, 1940. When the building of the new road to Bath included a causeway instead of a bridge at New Meadows, a small lake was formed, and J.W. Larrabee used the land on its banks for rental cottages. This is the first of ten in "Larrabee Grove."

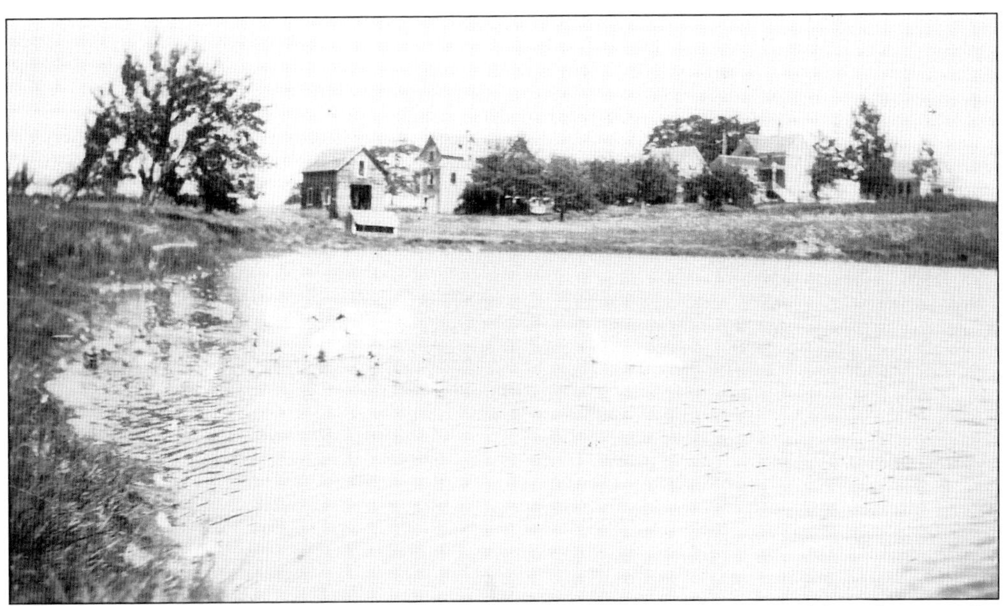

A duckpond. The road to the grove led between the farm pond and the neighbors' homes. The schoolhouse is on the right.

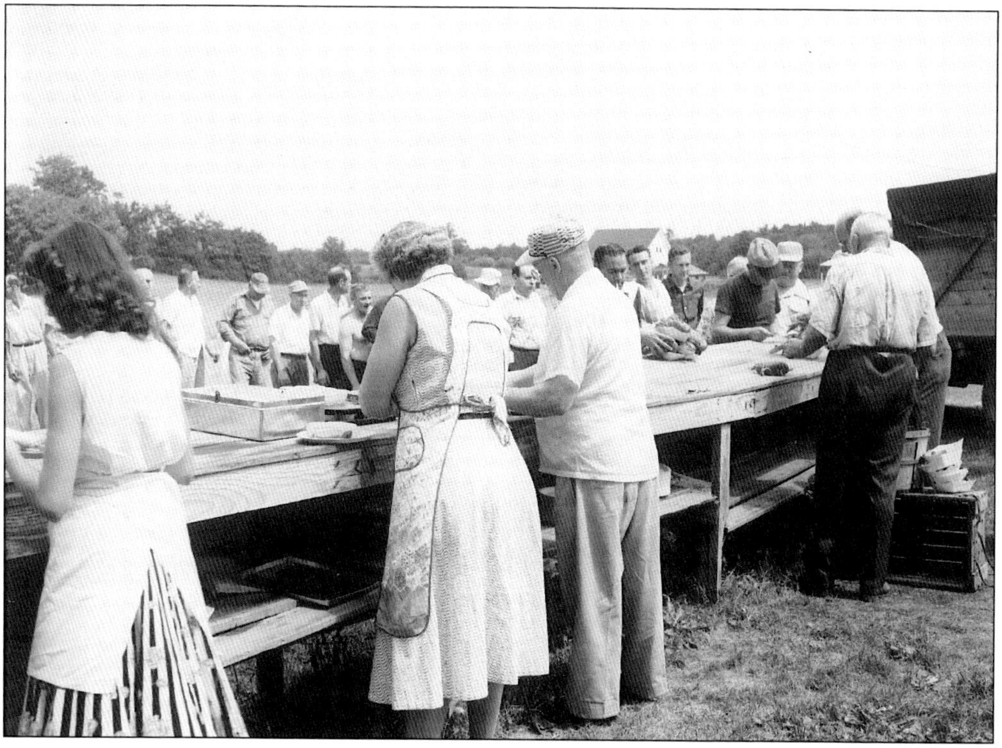

A clambake in the 1940s. The Larrabees also arranged clambakes. At an outing for Hyde Windlass workers, Joseph Larrabee and Wilbert Small are passing out lobsters (at the far right), while the former's daughter and son-in-law, Emily and "Red" McMann (at center), distribute corn and butter.

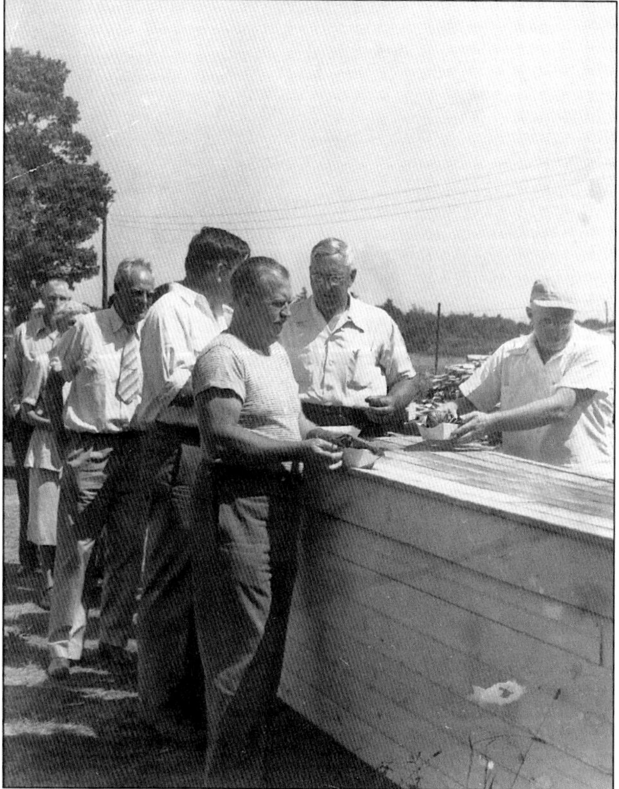

Another Larrabee clambake, 1940s. Guests at this affair were from the Maine state government. Joseph W. Larrabee, who himself served as a state representative and senator, is behind the counter on the left, with Edward "Red" McMann offering a lobster.

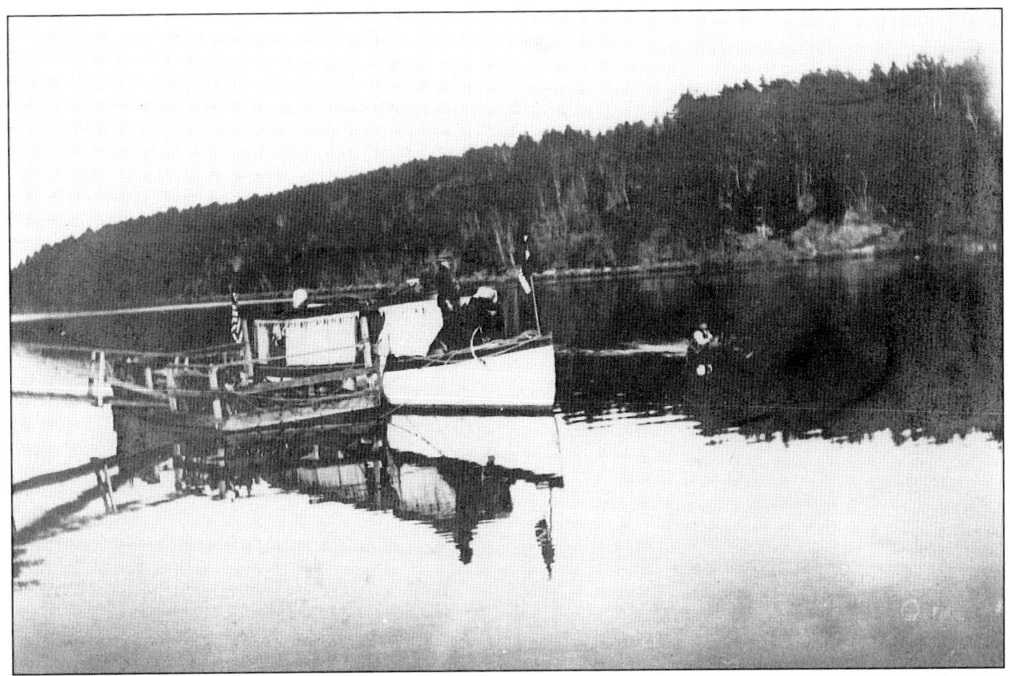

The dock at Fosters Point. Another summer concern was the store owned by Alonzo Fisher at Fosters Point in the 1920s, which found customers for ice creams and sundries among the boys and girls at summer camps nearby. Other customers arrived by water. Here a motor launch stops at his dock.

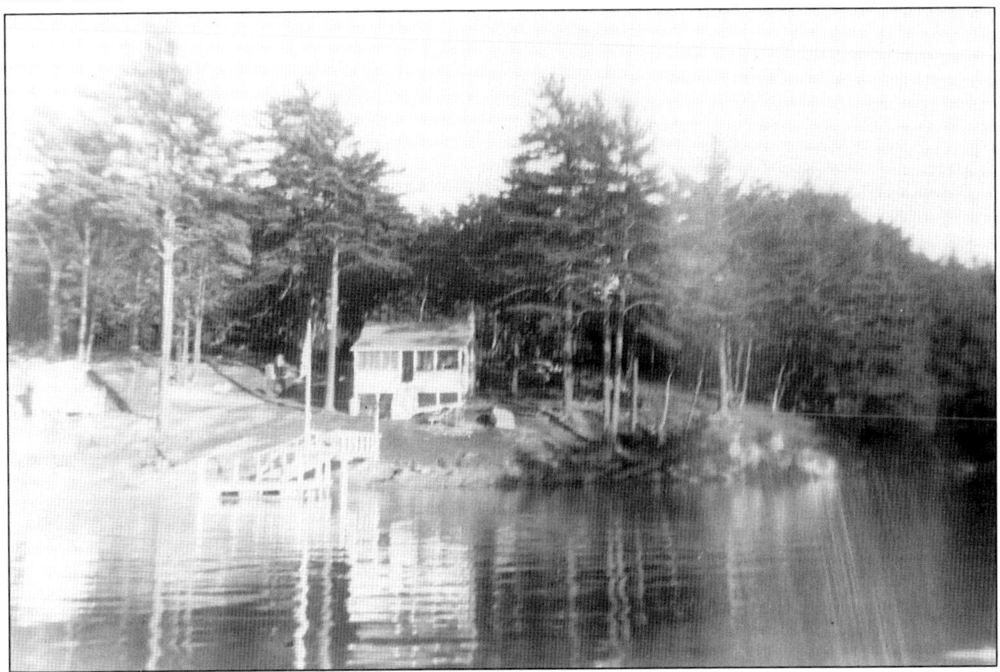

A summer cottage in the 1940s. Individual summer camps were erected along the banks of the New Meadows, and were typically small and with a large porch, like the one shown here. This cottage was built in the early 1940s by Leon Genthner.

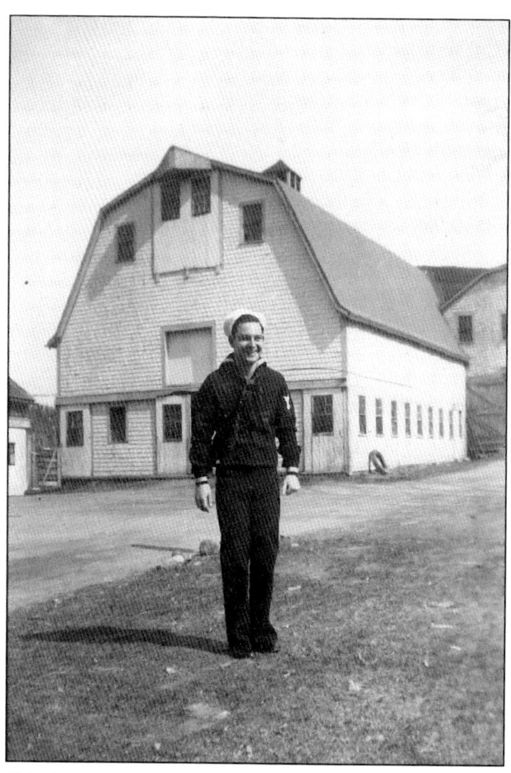

Rosedale Farm, 1941. The large barn, built in 1912, is evidence of the extensive dairy concern that once operated on Fosters Point Road. Richard Dobbins was home on leave and visiting an aunt when he posed for this snapshot: he was later one of the men lost with the sinking of the *Oklahoma*. In 1965, the farm was destroyed by fire. The site was then used for a new town hall.

A doll carriage parade in the 1950s. Like other areas, West Bath organized summer playground activities for its children in the 1950s; and the last day of "playground" brought special exercises, with families invited. The carriage in the center belonged to Paula McMann; the one on the right, to Nicolette Sylvester.

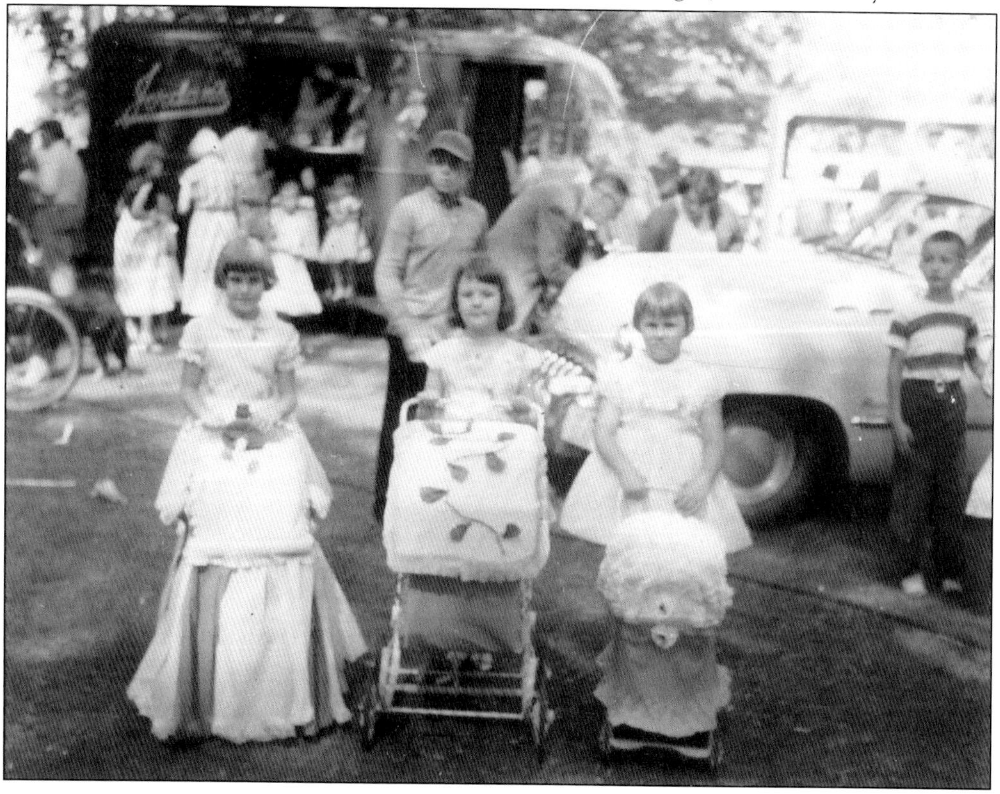